'This third volume in a creative series views I the lens of Shakespeare's *Tempest*. It is not j triumph, allowing contributors to explain the of FE in a rich, forceful and challenging way. show they have the collective, democratic powcɪ ɪɔ ɪɪaɪɪɔɪʊɪɪɪ ɪɪɪc ɔcɪ ɪʊɪ for the good and this volume will encourage many others to begin exercising that power.'

— Frank Coffield, Emeritus Professor, UCL Institute of Education

'*Caliban's Dance* is joyous, spirited, provocative, thoughtful and imaginative. Anyone interested in shaping the future of further education will find plenty to challenge and inspire their thinking.'

— Professor John Field , University of Stirling, Scotland

'This remarkable and original book brings the characters of Prospero, Miranda, Caliban, Sycorax, Ariel and others from Shakespeare's *Tempest* out of the shadows of allegory to illuminate a range of stakeholder perspectives on Further, Adult and Vocational Education. An impressive team of authors from the UK and Ireland explores issues ranging from the rise of neoliberalism in FE to imperialist and post-imperialist attitudes towards race, class and social justice in education; ESOL and citizenship; the relationship between practice and theory; relays of power and control in the implementation of education policy; issues in prison education; problems and possibilities in education leadership; and the role of practitioner research in improving educational practice.

The book imparts important insights into the dynamics of policy and practice and will find audiences among policy professionals, education leaders, teacher educators, teachers and their students across the sector.'

— Maggie Gregson, Professor of Vocational Education, University of Sunderland

'This trilogy offers a deeply thought-provoking set of perspectives that are "must reads" for policymakers, practitioners and academics. The analysis that this trilogy offers on the impact of policy on leadership, professional practice and wider perspectives on professional practice are exceptional in their accuracy and introspection. I would recommend the whole trilogy as part of the induction of all policymakers and leaders in FE in the UK.'

— **Ali Hadawi CBE, Principal and Chief Executive, Central Bedfordshire College**


'*Caliban's Dance* challenges all of FE to live by the words of the great Raymond Williams: "To be truly radical is to make hope possible rather than despair convincing." But it does more than challenge, it entices us to believe and provokes us to act.'

— **David Hughes, Chief Executive, Association of Colleges**


'Meaningful positive change for the people who need high-quality, emancipatory further education requires creative and courageous thinking by those with intimate understanding of FE. These authors, with their vast experience of the sector, combine creativity and courage in equal measure. Essential reading for all who seek to build the future of further education on the foundational values of social solidarity and social justice.'

— **Howard Stevenson, Professor of Educational Leadership and Policy Studies, University of Nottingham**


'The civic role of colleges in their communities has never been more important than now in providing moral and ethical leadership that enables colleges to play a meaningful and sustainable role in supporting individuals and facilitating economic recovery. The wide range of perspectives contribute to the leadership and policy debates at the heart of FE. The emancipatory conditions in which the mission of the sector could be advanced and transformed beyond today's confinements are thoughtfully and provocatively explored in this brilliantly optimistic but, sadly, final volume of the trilogy. They have saved the best for the last dance.'

— **Dr Sam Parrett OBE**

# Caliban's Dance

'Cast your dancing spell my way, I promise to go under it.'

(Bob Dylan)

Dedicated to each and every FE princess who, Caliban-like, and despite Machiavellian sectoral tempests, dances with joy and love over cynicism and hate.

Keep dancing ...

# Caliban's Dance

FE after The Tempest

Edited by Maire Daley, Kevin Orr and Joel Petrie

is an imprint of

First published in 2020 by the UCL Institute of Education Press, University College London, 20 Bedford Way, London WC1H 0AL

www.ucl-ioe-press.com

© Maire Daley, Kevin Orr and Joel Petrie 2020

British Library Cataloguing in Publication Data:
A catalogue record for this publication is available from the British Library

ISBNs
978-1-85856-924-6 (paperback)
978-1-85856-925-3 (PDF eBook)
978-1-85856-926-0 (ePub eBook)
978-1-85856-927-7 (Kindle eBook)

Every effort has been made to trace copyright holders and to obtain their permission for the use of copyright material. The publisher apologizes for any errors or omissions and would be grateful if notified of any corrections that should be incorporated in future reprints or editions of this book.

The opinions expressed in this publication are those of the authors and do not necessarily reflect the views of the UCL Institute of Education, University College London.

Typeset by Quadrant Infotech (India) Pvt Ltd
Printed by CPI Group (UK) Ltd, Croydon, CR0 4YY
Cover image: *The Tempest II*, by Johann Heinrich Ramberg

# Contents

# List of abbreviations

| | |
|---|---|
| AtoHE | access to Higher Education |
| AoC | Association of Colleges |
| CBHE | college based higher education |
| CEL | Centre for Excellence in Leadership |
| CEO | chief executive officer |
| CHE | college of higher education |
| CPD | continuing professional development |
| CSC | College Scholarship Centre |
| DfE | Department for Education |
| DYW | Developing the Young Workforce (Scotland) |
| EAL | English as an additional language |
| ESFA | Education and Skills Funding Agency |
| ESOL | English for speakers of other languages |
| FE | further education |
| FECs | further education colleges |
| FET | further education and training |
| GCSE | General Certificate of Secondary Education |
| HEIs | higher education institutions |
| ILEA | Inner London Education Authority |
| ITE | initial teacher education |
| KPIs | key performance indicators |
| LEA | local education authority |
| LGBT | lesbian, gay, bisexual and trans |
| NEET | not in education, employment or training |

| | |
|---|---|
| Nesta | National Endowment for Science, Technology and the Arts |
| MA | master of arts |
| MCA | Mayoral Combined Authority |
| Ofsted | Office for Standards in Education |
| QAA | Quality Assurance Agency |
| SFC | sixth form colleges |
| SMEs | small and medium-sized enterprises |
| SOLAS | An tSeirbhís Oideachais Leanúnaigh agus Scileanna [Further Education and Skills Service] (Irish) |
| SA | South Africa |
| STEM | science, technology, engineering and mathematics |
| UCU | University and College Union |
| WEA | Workers' Educational Association |

# List of illustrations and figures

# About the contributors

## Sarah Amsler

Sarah is an Associate Professor of Education at the University of Nottingham and member of the *Gesturing Towards Decolonial Futures* collective. She is learning to dance at the edges of the possible and otherwise, working with ontological pedagogies of possibility for systemic social change and problems of coloniality in educational practice.

## James Avis

James is professor of post-compulsory education, University of Derby and Emeritus Professor, University of Huddersfield. He does not take a particular position on dance, having once been an idiot dancer.

## Casey Beaumont

Casey has worked in HE for over 14 years in several academic and professional services roles, and currently manages the library's learning and teaching provision at Liverpool John Moores University. Despite her early training in the performing arts, she continues to resist any form of prescribed or timed movement, and prefers to go her own way.

## Pete Bennett

Pete worked for 19 years in a sixth form college that was closed following a merger with a larger FE college. The A level he ran for 19 years was done for by Gove's reforms. He has been a teacher educator for 14 years at Wolverhampton University, which is currently in the dance, but may only have five years left to cry in…

## Steve Brown

Steve spent much of his early career dancing around the world to a wide selection of tunes, before spending over 15 years cutting shapes as an ESOL lecturer and manager in the Scottish FE sector. He is now Director of Studies of the English Language Unit at University of the West of Scotland, where he tends to spend less time dancing and more time complaining about the music.

## Vicky Butterby

Vicky is a teacher and researcher with a passion for community learning. She completed her doctorate in 2019, using art and storytelling to explore loss in the lives of young people who offend. Currently working with Claire Collins Consultancy, Vicky supports a variety of FE-based projects, and facilitates PD North's Practitioner Research Professional Exchange. In her imagination, Vicky is an excellent dancer!

## Christine Calder

Christine started her career as a physical education teacher in secondary schools. After moving to work in the college sector as a Sport and Fitness lecturer she realized what truly inspirational and transformative places colleges are, for students and staff alike. She is currently the Academic Development Lead at Dundee and Angus College, and is partial to a bit of ceilidh dancing on occasion.

## Claire Collins

Claire has a research and teaching background in adult literacy and ESOL, specializing in socially excluded and marginalized students. She now leads projects in the FE sector. Claire has been known to move the wrong way in a line dance but, freestyle, she can make some shapes on the dance floor.

## Melanie Cooke

Melanie is a lecturer and researcher at King's College, London, a collaborator with English for Action and a trade unionist. Her most recent book is an edited collection (with Rob Peutrell) *Brokering Britain, Educating Citizens: exploring ESOL and citizenship*, published by Multilingual Matters. She vows that in retirement she will dance every day.

## Sarah-Jane Crowson

Sarah-Jane has worked in schools, FE and college HE. She currently works at Hereford College of Arts, a small, specialist creative arts college located in a county largely untouched by the Second Industrial Revolution. Sarah's creative practice is poetry. Her doctoral research looks at ideas of the critical radical rural. She has a healthy respect for Morris dancing and orchard-visiting wassail.

## Maire Daley

Maire taught in FE for more than 30 years prior to her retirement, latterly as a teacher educator. An active trade unionist she was a member of the National Executive Committee in NATFHE and UCU, chair of UCU's Education Committee, and a member of the Women's, LGBT and International Committees. Her 1980s NATFHE conference dance moves are legendary.

## Carol Azumah Dennis

Carol worked in FE for 20 or more years before completing her EdD, at which point she began working in HE. She now works for the Open University as a Senior Lecturer in Educational Leadership and Management. She has been known to occasionally dance backwards while wearing high heels.

## Steven Exley

Steven spent over a decade in education journalism, most recently as Further Education Editor at TES, before joining a social mobility charity and becoming a primary school governor. It's fair to say that he's gone native. Contrary to the spirit of lifelong learning, his dancing skills have, if anything, gone backwards.

## Fergal Finnegan

Fergal is an assistant professor in the Department of Adult and Community Education, Maynooth University. Before joining the university he was a community educator in Dublin. He has at times confused the pogo and the foxtrot. Now he just sways back and forth listening carefully to see if he can hear the sound – to borrow a phrase from Derek Walcott: 'like a rumour without echo, of History really beginning'.

## Jo Fletcher-Saxon

Jo began her career in post compulsory education in the late 1990s having previously worked as a nursery nurse. She has been a lecturer, course leader, department head and now teacher educator and senior leader. She is an advocate for practitioner research. She can most definitely dance, on and off the dance floor.

## Rania Hafez

Rania began her teaching career in FE, but for the past fifteen years has been a stowaway in HE. A teacher, writer, social commentator, she co-chairs the

London Learning and Skills Research Network, and was one of the first elected directors of the Institute for Learning. When not building Trojan horses, Rania can be found leading her postgraduate students in furious pedagogical dancing.

## Craig Hammond

Craig is a Senior Lecturer in the School of Education at Liverpool John Moores University (LJMU). Prior to moving to LJMU, Craig taught across further education and college based higher education for 18 years. He cannot dance, in any way, whatsoever.

## Gary Husband

Gary is a lecturer in professional education at the University of Stirling; however, this is what he does and not who he is. Gary is a father, husband, musician and writer who is searching for the big idea that will warrant a whole book of his own. Gary has been known to dance on occasion, but those around him are largely convinced he is dancing to a different tune.

## Sam Jones

Sam has taught in FE for 20 years and dances with practitioner-researchers across England and Wales. She is undertaking a part-time PhD at the University of Cambridge.

## Ewart Keep

Ewart holds a chair in Education, Training and Skills at Oxford University, and has been involved in and researched vocational education and training policy for 39 years. As a result, he is experiencing multilayer déjà vu, but is no longer surprised by anything! His dancing skills are weak.

## Gillian Klein

Gillian has danced – and written – her way through three careers since fleeing apartheid: 20 years as librarian and adviser in ILEA; exciting teaching at Warwick University, then full time in the publishing house she co-founded, because she loves her authors. She rejoices that her two children and four grandchildren were born here, but is horrified by politicians who love only themselves.

## Kate Lavender

Kate is a former HE lecturer in FE, and now works as a senior lecturer in lifelong learning at the University of Huddersfield. With a background in Sociology, she has always been fascinated by the social dynamics of dance.

## Lou Mycroft

Lou is a nomadic educator, writer, Thinking Environment facilitator and TEDx Doncaster speaker. One of the original Dancing Princesses, she opens up spaces to dance across FE, enabling practitioners to find new solutions in collaboration with others. Accompanied by her companion species the Bowerbird, she is currently researching posthuman approaches to rethinking community education.

## Jerry O'Neill

Jerry has been learning and working in adult education across the big islands off north-west Europe since the mid-1990s. He is interested in reflexive, creative and critical processes of educator inquiry and development. Although his body loves to sway, almost imperceptibly, to music he is useless at working out the dancer from the dance.

## Kevin Orr

Kevin is Professor of Work and Learning at the University of Huddersfield where he has been since 2006. Prior to that he taught in colleges around Greater Manchester for sixteen years. His research mainly focuses on Further Education and vocational education and training. He is an enthusiastic dancer.

## Damien Page

Damien is Professor of Education and Dean of the Carnegie School of Education at Leeds Beckett University. He cut his teaching teeth in inner-city FE, working on everything from Access courses to E2E (Entry to Employment). He will not dance, ever, even if you ask really nicely.

## Joel Petrie

Joel worked in post compulsory education as a lecturer, teacher educator, manager and trade unionist for longer than he cares to admit. He is currently completing an Educational Doctorate at Huddersfield University on leadership in FE. He cannot dance (but if Spiritualized plays he can be persuaded).

## Rob Peutrell

Rob is an ESOL lecturer and UCU activist in a further education college. He co-edited (with Melanie Cooke) *Brokering Britain, Educating Citizens: exploring ESOL and citizenship*, published by Multilingual Matters. Knowing the five basic foot positions in ballet has been of no value at all to Rob's FE career.

## Eddie Playfair

Eddie has worked in education for 37 years and was a college principal for 16 years until 2018. He is currently a senior policy manager at the Association of Colleges and writes here in a personal capacity. He loves music and has been known to dance.

## David Powell

David was introduced to FE in 1974 by his father, a Houghton Senior Lecturer in Graphic Design at Stafford College. Twelve years later, David started his own FE career as a part-time lecturer in Leisure and Tourism at the same college. A live music enthusiast, David is known to tap his feet at gigs.

## Cheryl Reynolds

Cheryl is a University Teaching Fellow at the University of Huddersfield. She studied A levels in FE after graduating from HE, loved it so much she stayed and taught there, sashayed into teaching HE in FE, before shimmying back to HE again. In short, has been doing the hokey cokey with FE since 1992.

## Howard Scott

Howard is a lecturer in post-compulsory education and researcher at the University of Wolverhampton. He previously worked as an English and Media lecturer in several FE colleges. He holds a doctorate from the University of Hull in Technology Enhanced Learning. Howard can often be found staring into the corner at discos, because he has two left feet and social anxiety.

## Lynne Sedgmore

Lynne spent 35 years dancing, facilitating, leading, rebelling, fighting, rejoicing and serving the success of students in Further Education. Her favourite dance move is the Northern Soul shuffle.

## Peter Shukie
Peter is an experimental educator, writer, artist, explorer of knowing and an advocate for promoting working class academics as a route toward a classless world. His only alignment with great doctrines of education is that, like Socrates, he is aware he knows nothing. In the past Peter danced his way to Blackburn from Wigan via London, in reterritorialized warehouses, the odd field, abandoned shops and transient clubs. He is an outstanding mover who continually impresses himself with his physical artistry.

## Paul Smith
Paul has worked in the FE sector since 2004. He has recently completed an MPhil focusing on the aspirations of young people without GCSEs. He is too busy collecting memorabilia and ephemera about FE and Adult Education to contemplate dancing.

## Curtis Tappenden
Curtis is a senior lecturer in FE at the University for the Creative Arts, Rochester, teaching on the Extended Diploma in Art and Design. He has worked as an illustrator and painter for the past 31 years, is an editorial artist for a national newspaper in London, has written 23 books on art and design practice, and is a performing poet. Curtis is a renowned circus artist with 39 drawings of life under the Big Top in the Victoria & Albert Museum, London. He is currently completing a PhD in education, exploring maverick educators in HE. A dancefloor enigma at soul all-nighters, back in the day he represented the UK as a dance skater.

## Julie Wilde
Julie has choreographed strategic and playful dances in post compulsory education and has freestyled and quick stepped through leadership and quality in FE. She is now a senior lecturer for teacher education at the University of Wolverhampton.

## Amy Woodrow
Amy is a learning and development coach at a large FE college in the South West, and also teaches on various hospitality programmes. Her interests lie within quality assurance and quality improvement, additionally working as an external verifier with two large awarding bodies. She goes tap dancing every Thursday after her young daughter inspired her to continue with her childhood passion.

## Rhian Wyn-Williams

Rhian began her teaching career 20 years ago in the secondary sector. After a PhD in history, she began work as a lecturer in HE, and taught Access and Teacher Education in FE. Having become increasingly interested in academic literacies, she is now an Academic Skills Tutor at Liverpool John Moores University where, when no one is looking, she dances with abandon.

# Acknowledgements

Joel Petrie wishes to thank his former colleagues of twenty-plus years in Liverpool Community College (as was, before it was hubristically rebranded as The City of Liverpool College and its community focus dimmed). This book, and the two that precede it, would not exist without the formative shared professional experience of working within this institution. He is also immeasurably grateful for the support of the following dancers and guardian angels who helped him to keep the faith during a very difficult year, after exiting FE: Laura Bejinaru, Jess Benson, Rowena Gander, the Reverend Tom Hiney, Rory Howard, Ina Lena, Councillor Clare McIntyre, Paul Murphy, Mick Smith, and Claudia, Demi and Sunny.

Joel also wishes to thank Salman Rushdie for kindly spending an evening with him discussing Grimm fairy tales, Machiavellian tactics, and Shakespearean island utopias. Finally, Joel here publicly celebrates working collectively and collaboratively on this St Vitus's dance with Maire Daley and Kevin Orr, who with both deep expertise and a willingness to try risky moves made working on the Dancing Princesses trilogy the most seminal experience of Joel's professional life.

The editors wish to recognize the invaluable guidance and consistent good humour over the publication of the Dancing Princesses trilogy of Gillian Klein, our publisher at Trentham, and of the support of the wider publishing team at UCL Press: Jonathan Dore, Sally Sigmund and Margie Coughlin, who have been a pleasure to work with. It is with some regret that we have submitted our final book to be published by them as a physical object in the world.

We are very grateful to maverick FE educator Curtis Tappenden, the de facto illustration editor of this book, and its prequel *The Principal: Power and Professionalism in FE*. It has been a privilege to work with his colleagues Sean Jeal, Gabi Mind and Rob Roach, and their exceptional Extended Diploma in Art and Design students from the University for the Creative Arts, Rochester. We are also grateful to Mia Sutherland, who generously sacrificed her place in the book, because we wanted to use her sophisticated interpretation of *The Tempest* to promote our book launch – *FE across the Mersey*. Finally, thanks to Tony O'Connell (aka Toc), whose illustration precedes Kevin Orr's conclusion.

The following illustrators enrich this text greatly: Tami Adesida, Charisma Andrews, Hadassah Asieba, Jess Baker, Daniel Bastable,

## Acknowledgements

Ella Benson, Winter Bourner, Erin Brett, Laks Butler-Kania, Holly Chandler, Livi Colley, Charlotte Costin, Phoebe Cripps, Cara Dyos, Gabriel Fassenfelt, Lawrence Fleming, Teo Forbes, Jake Forrest, Zoe Gardiner, Marcel Hara, James Harris, Sean Jeal, Olivia Kelly, Bronek Kutereba, Natene Larty, Adam Loizou, Tom Loughnane, Hayley Mills, Gabi Mind, Harvey Montford, Tony O'Connell, Charlie Ong, Aran Quinn, Emily Ransley, Eva Rati, Rob Roach, Oliver Snell, Jay Thomson-White, Curtis Tappenden, Eimantas Valiukenas, Kyana Veiga, Kaice Walker, Tia White, Erin Wilby, and Megan Willby.

> *A society must assume that it is stable, but the artist must know, and he must let us know, that there is nothing stable under heaven.*
> (James Baldwin)

*The dance has many functions. It has been a social icebreaker and a ritual cloudbreaker. It has been a mark of passion and a sign of hate. Stars have danced in young girls' eyes and death has danced with its unwilling family. Today, in the hollow of a wood, with the green light of the leaves playing about his face, stark naked, a grim-faced fat man called Virgil Jones was dancing for the life of his new friend.*

(Salman Rushdie)

Henry Fuseli, engraved by Peter Simon

overleaf: Tom Loughname

# Preface

*Ewart Keep*

 Metaphors are wonderful things, although this author has on more than one occasion been sternly reprimanded by journal referees for deploying such a frivolous device – the thinking seems to be that metaphors somehow undercut the serious, (possibly pseudo-) scientific nature of a proper research article. The referees were entirely incorrect, metaphors aid understanding and can engage the reader. The volume that follows bears testimony to this. It is the third in a series that has sought to deploy the overarching metaphor of dancing to reflect upon the past, present and future of further education, and this book sets the thinking within the context of Shakespeare's *The Tempest*.

What are the questions and issues that are covered? One strand in the overall message of many of the contributions can be summarized as arguing that FE (represented by the character Caliban) deserves a better future than its immediate past has offered it – it needs to be given its chance to dance. However, the desire for a time for revelry in turn poses a set of consequent questions about the dance – to what steps, to whose tune, with which partners, and, most importantly of all, who gets to choose? The danger, as ever, is that the answer to the last question is 'not Caliban'. In most formal dancing one partner leads and the other follows. The problem for FE in England is that in the recent past, insofar as it is ever invited to dance, it is usually expected to dance to a tune set by others, and follow the steps of a senior partner – generally national policymakers and funding agencies, but also parliamentarians, local government/combined authorities, employers, and of course other educational providers such as higher education institutions.

Thus, if FE is to engage in more enjoyable dancing (or pretty much anything else) then the dominance of, on one side, schools, and on the other, higher education institutions, is going to have to be challenged and a rebalancing of power relationships take place. The reality is that in a highly selective upper-secondary phase, in many areas of the country, school VI form is the goal for the majority of students and FE college is for the 'other people's children', aka the Caliban Kids. T-levels are meant to be going to change this, but it would be unwise for anyone to hold their breath on this one, as turning blue is not a good look.

When it comes to the other side of the 'rock and hard place' equation, in which FE finds itself trapped, the arrival of mass or universal higher education creates an even bigger bind. HE has annexed much of the dance floor and appears to be angling for yet further dominance. Universities, the HE lobby, and much of the associated academic research community that often seems to act more like cheerleaders than critical friends or dispassionate analysts, have all been incredibly successful in turning what was a minority route 30 years ago into a popular expectational trope ('going to uni') and also what some have gone so far as to claim is a fundamental human right ('going to uni'). They have also carefully defended a model of innovation policy and an industrial strategy that focuses on cutting-edge science and technological research, while ignoring or minimizing the role that can be played by colleges in many different forms of business support and innovation, particularly in relation to small and medium-sized enterprises (SME).

As the ubiquity of the university provision has grown, the dancing space of student numbers, funding and labour market opportunities that FE might occupy has dwindled. In 1979 just 11 per cent of the UK workforce possessed a degree or its equivalent, whereas the figure now has passed the 42 per cent mark. This is a fundamental transformation that carries with it profound consequences, about many of which policymakers are in deep denial. If FE colleges, in the main, are now Level 0 to 3 institutions (with the bulk of 16–19 and adult students at Level 2 or below, at lower-secondary level, or lower) then the labour market openings and outcomes available to its students will tend to be limited and its social prestige will accordingly be constrained. Elsewhere in Europe the equivalents of FE tend to operate at Level 3 and above, delivering large volumes of sub-degree, short-cycle tertiary education, and their status reflects this critical role in delivering technician and associate professional-level skills. In England, in recent times, the answer has been, at considerable expense, to try to fill Level 4 and 5 needs through Level 6 (bachelor's degree) provision, the majority of which is delivered in something called a university.

On numerous occasions in recent years the author has been involved in policy debates or roundtables where, when a bigger role and more resources for colleges have been mooted, powerful voices have struck up with a refrain that runs, 'if FE is to have more, this cannot ever, in any way, be at the expense of HE'. Responses to the Augar Review recommendations on sub-degree provision are a perfect example. Advocates of the dominance and seniority of HE's claims to resources have argued that this must not mean any diminution in HE student numbers or degree provision – new sub-degree courses have to be on top of, not instead of, current patterns of three-year, full honours, full-time bachelor's degree courses.

Some in HE bemoan that the issue is ever framed in terms of a zero-sum game, but the simple fact is that this is inevitable – even if money to fund provision were unlimited – which is highly unlikely whoever is in power – the number of potential students, particularly 18–24-year-olds is finite and currently dwindling. As one vice-chancellor put it when lamenting (not very hard) to the author the fact that their university was busy snatching students from local FE colleges, 'demographics trump policy'.

The other issue for FE that looms ever larger is a flawed and inadequate model of accountability (Keep, 2018). The post-92 incorporation settlement, whereby colleges became free agents operating in an atomized and increasingly marketized space is not looking as successful as once it did. The pages of *FE Week*, the effective equivalent of the *Daily Mail* for FE, are now littered with eye-grabbing headlines about principals' pay, principals' travel expenses, massive and unexpected holes appearing overnight in colleges' balance sheets, dodgy property deals, and endless exciting and creative forms of subcontracting of provision – sometimes to organizations that barely seem to exist. As a result of this, there ought to be many college senior-management and governance teams that fear the knock of the FE Commissioner or the Education and Skills Funding Agency (ESFA) on their door, but the worry has to be that in reality this fear is muted or absent and some colleges carry on playing fast and loose with the long-term future of their institution.

None of this is helped by structural underfunding of provision, but this arguably exists alongside a deeper malaise, noted in several contributions in this volume, that reflects a loss by some FE institutions of any deeply-held and widely-shared sense of purpose. What handbag exactly are they dancing around, why and for whose benefit? This problem is not just one for FE, it seems to be afflicting many secondary schools, who game the examinations system and off-roll students in pursuit of better league table rankings, and universities, some of which now appear to see their main role to be as a catalyst for local property developers to build yet more private halls of residence aimed at high-paying overseas students. Marketized, atomized, educational institutions in England have, to a considerable extent, lost their sense of direction and purpose, and this makes for a vacuum at the heart of institutional mission-setting and governance.

There are potentially a number of reasons for this state of affairs. First is the dismal impoverishment and partial abandonment within national policy of any acceptance that education has a role that extends beyond a purely utilitarian delivery of more units of certified human capital, in order to better meet the needs of the economy and to further social inclusion (in the labour market). This agenda, which has been the core staple of policy under successive governments formed by all the major political parties over the last 35 years, has two drawbacks.

The first is that it ignores all the other things, like civic values and wider notions of political and cultural citizenship, that FE (and other educational institutions) can help support, thereby impoverishing what education can do to help individuals and communities alike. Second, even judged in its own narrow terms, this approach to policy has failed. As noted above, we have undergone a skills revolution – the proportion of the workforce with no qualifications has shrunk from 42 per cent in 1979 to less than 8 per cent today – but the promised result of an economic miracle in the shape of a high-wage, high-skill, high-productivity economy has not been delivered. The workforce is better qualified than ever before, but in-work poverty has increased and so too has the underutilization of skills in the workplace. It turns out that a considerable portion of our 'skills problem' resides not within the skills supply system, but inside the firm and the workplace, where demand for skills is often lower than hoped-for and the ability of management to productively deploy enhanced levels of skill is patchy at best (Keep, Mayhew and Payne, 2006).

The other factor that has undermined ownership and governance practices has been the untethering of colleges from local government, which has occurred alongside a wider decline in the role and funding of local government and, in a broader sense, of local governance and accountability. The devolution agenda, still partial and haltingly embraced by Whitehall, raises the prospect that colleges may need to forge new relationships with government at the local level, rather than simply seek approbation from the Department for Education and its regulatory arms (ESFA, Ofsted, Office for Students). This does not necessarily mean de-incorporation, but it will surely entail new models of accountability between college and other significant stakeholders within the locality. Change is already underway on this front. The rise of the West Midlands FE Skills and Productivity Group, and the Greater Manchester Colleges Group represent useful attempts to construct a joined-up offer to the local Mayoral Combined Authority (MCA) around skills and wider policy agendas, like transport, social inclusion, inclusive growth, productivity and business support. In some places, colleges have realized that speaking with a single voice can help ensure that what they have to say gets heard.

All of this suggests that the time is ripe for some serious rethinking of what education is for and what role or set of roles FE ought to be playing. Such debates are already happening. The Four Nations College Alliance Commission on the College of the Future is one example, another is the recently published report by Audrey Cumberford and Paul Little (2020) on the future role of colleges in Scotland.

This book represents a third, and somewhat different approach to thinking about the past and working out what a better future might look like. Read, enjoy and tap your feet if you wish....

## References

Augar, P., Crewe, I., de Rojas, J., Peck, E., Robinson, B. and Wolf, A. (2019) *Independent Panel Report to the Review of Post-18 Education and Funding.* London: HMSO. Online. https://tinyurl.com/y3aj6xbo (accessed 6 May 2020).

Cumberford, A. and Little, P. (2020) *The Cumberford-Little Report. One Tertiary System: Agile, collaborative, inclusive*, Glasgow: City of Glasgow College. Online. http://hdl.voced.edu.au/10707/535975 (accessed 6 May 2020).

Keep, E. 2018. *Scripting the Future: Exploring potential strategic leadership responses to the marketization of English FE and vocational provision.* London: Further Education Trust for Leadership. Online. https://tinyurl.com/y36kt762 (accessed 6 May 2020).

Keep, E., Mayhew, K. and Payne, J. (2006) 'From Skills Revolution to Productivity Miracle: Not as easy as it sounds?' *Oxford Review of Economic Policy*, 22 (4), 539–59. Online. https://doi.org/10.1093/oxrep/grj032 (accessed 6 May 2020).

*Lord, let it rain on me*
*Now I know I'm goin' down*
*I've got a little knowledge, Lord*
*And I'm about ready now.*

(Spiritualized)

Curtis Tappenden

overleaf: Harvey Montford

# Introduction: Be not afeard, FE

## Maire Daley, Rania Hafez, Lou Mycroft, Kevin Orr, Damien Page, Joel Petrie and Rob Peutrell

## Our revels now are ended

> *Our revels now are ended. These our actors,*
> *As I foretold you, were all spirits and*
> *Are melted into air, into thin air:*
> *And, like the baseless fabric of this vision,*
> *The cloud-capp'd towers, the gorgeous palaces,*
> *The solemn temples, the great globe itself,*
> *Yea, all which it inherit, shall dissolve*
> *And, like this insubstantial pageant faded,*
> *Leave not a rack behind. We are such stuff*
> *As dreams are made on, and our little life*
> *Is rounded with a sleep.*
>
> (*The Tempest*, Act 4, Scene 1)

Written in a time of political, religious and intellectual conflict, *The Tempest* fuses love, magic, intrigue, the fantastic and power. It is a tale of Prospero, a magician usurped from his position as Duke of Milan, marooned with his daughter Miranda on an isle of mystical creatures. Yet fate (and the dark arts) delivers Prospero's betrayers into his grasp and – complicated by burgeoning romance, drunken dancing, and even more betrayal – the potential for revenge and reinstatement becomes realized. Yet while *The Tempest* is about the treachery and romantic endeavours of nobility, it is as much about the indigenous beings of the isle, of Caliban and Ariel, the colonized and recolonized, the powerless seeking freedom from the tortures of Prospero. And yet, perhaps more than any other Shakespeare play, it is about the imagining of life after the exeunt, of life after colonization.

It is about the blank page of Caliban, the possibility of freedom, a dimly envisioned utopia of what might be.

The Tempest was also the final play Shakespeare wrote (first produced circa 1611). Fitting, then, that those writers, illustrators and dancers who have pirouetted as Princesses until their shoes were worn, those nobles and peasants that have the scars of Machiavellian violence on their souls, would assemble, here, for the final spectacle of a book. Every teacher and every student that has been touched by Further Education (FE), and bled for it, shall have one last hurrah, and a final dance.

Ah, to dream. To dream of what could be, of what FE was always destined to be before the ravages of colonization and seduction and the intoxication of novelty. An isle beyond the ethereal spectacles and violent storms, an isle where ideals are not to be feared. What better way to conclude our trilogy?

## Deformed slave, misshapen knave, hag seed

For this, the final book in the trilogy, our central metaphor is Caliban. One interpretation of the play is that it operates as a manifesto for second chances, transformation, and, above all, learning – it is very FE. In *Further Education and the Twelve Dancing Princesses* (2015) we asked, 'Where is there space to dance in FE?' *The Principal: Power and Professionalism in FE* (2017) probed 'What impedes FE's dance?' In this book we speculate on 'What would FE look like with no restrictions?' An FE utopia? As a concept utopia has Latin and Greek roots, and suggests both 'good' place and 'no' place: it has been our intention in the three books to map existing territories while imagining new Arcadian FE possibilities, in the hope that others will be stimulated to travel in the spaces we explore. *The Tempest* has long inspired others: from Huxley's *Brave New World* (1932), to the 1956 American science fiction film *Forbidden Planet*, Salman Rushdie's *Grimus* (1975), and Neil Gaiman's 1996 metafiction *The Tempest* (from the *Sandman* DC comic series illustrated by Charles Vess). Prospero is key to *Super-Cannes* (2000) by J.G. Ballard, perhaps the most prescient dystopian seer of the past 30 years. In this novel we encounter the deeply disconcerting psychiatrist, Dr Wilder Penrose, described as an amiable Prospero, and 'the psychopomp who steered our darkest dreams towards the daylight' (Ballard, 2000: 3). We can only guess what Ballard would have made of the chaos wrought by the 2020 coronavirus crisis; his art made flesh. Most recently, Margaret Atwood riffed on *The Tempest* as a prison narrative in *Hag-Seed* (2016). The Calibans in these texts are outsiders, alien, liminal and hybrid – Caliban is perhaps the most mutable of Shakespeare's characters: he is black (or not), disabled (or not), a half-fish hag-seed, a man-monster, and a moon calf. FE too is a glorious fusion of further, adult, community, skills, land based, prison, ESOL and higher education learning. Our sector is the magical twin of Caliban, the forgotten bastard child of his mother, the witch Sycorax. And like Caliban, FE has the most enchanting poetry, and jigs to transformational tunes.

## How beauteous mankind is! O brave new world

We did not know where this journey would take us, or the steps of the dance, but we knew from the start who we were: educators who refuse to be cynical. Critical, yes, but in rejecting the Cinderella label we chose to dance together in joyful, activist militancy, rejecting the moribund negativity of comfort radicalism (Avis, 2017) in favour of an explicit ethics of affirmation. Our growing band of fellow travellers identified themselves not by role and rank, silo of discipline or organization but via the hashtag #DancingPrincesses. As Rosi Braidotti (2019) writes, we are not one-and-the-same, but we are all in this together.

Like all folklore's tendrils, tales of the #DancingPrincesses spread throughout the land: stubbornly and unexpectedly rhizomatic, resisting all attempts to be co-opted. We tapped into a different kind of power – not the 'potestas' of politics-as-usual but the 'potentia' of activism, finding spaces to shake up the gravitational pull of old thinking: in relationships, curricula, journalism, practices, workplaces.

In the early days when we set up the democratic network @tutorvoices, the pull towards structure and hierarchy was still strong. We learned instead to go where the potentia energy was, joyfully encountering new #DancingPrincesses and scattering our collective ideas, some of which took root in the projects and activist practices of today. We are six years on and the rhizome continues to thrive, way beyond our own horizons. Our cousins the #DancingMatildas of Australian vocational education, the #FEResearchMeet activists who have breathed new life into FE's evidence base, and #FESpeaks – the emerging voices of values-driven practitioners no longer willing to do what they have always done. We are speaking up, changing cultures, influencing policy, imagining our own destinies. We have pushed back the creaky old chairs of FE's thinking, rolled up the dusty carpet of outdated assumptions and, together, as one (but not one-and-the-same) we are dancing like no-one is watching.

# I am all the subjects that you have, which first was mine own king

Yet Caliban is no dancing Cinderella, and this is no fairy tale. We may be using metaphors, but the struggle is real and existential. Some princesses are still dancing, but others have grown weary, and many have forgotten the tune. The island's memory of a time before Prospero's reign grows dim; Caliban and the islanders barely dare dream of their liberation. Likewise, newcomers to FE know little of its glorious past. Weighed down by the burden of performativity, tutors and students alike labour under the stark inequalities that plague the sector, talk of parity long abandoned. Nonetheless our FE island is still a haven for many of society's dispossessed, offering an educational sanctuary to those failed time and again by society's persistent inequalities; FE's educators at once Caliban and Ariel, chained and brutalized, but also working their beautiful magic to guide students to safe shores.

Hence our vision for a future FE must be more than a dream. Even as we pen our utopian ideas, Prospero is still in charge, tempests continue to ravage FE, with no sign of abatement, and the future looks bleak. Caliban is heir to a kingdom, but first he must free himself from his bondage to reclaim it. FE is the beautiful island we dream of reconquering, but it cannot be regained simply via metaphor. Our FE is no utopia: it is a reality we must build together. Between the pages of this book we may be dreaming of what could be, in the hope our ephemeral thoughts can help to unshackle the visions of our FE comrades. But dreams are for those asleep. This is a wake-up call. We do not have the luxury of waiting for a tempest to sweep all before it, so we can rebuild anew. The time is now.

# I endowed thy purposes with words that made them known

This may be our final volume but it is not the final word. To follow the metaphor: there is no last dance, 'there is only the dance': the dance goes on.

We need ironic metaphors like the dancing princesses: irony, hope, a sense of tragedy, and a bit of realism are essential. Radicals without irony are usually overbearing. But equally, Princes love a prankster. Edgy associations with dancing princesses and Machiavellian ironists are a ploy for the powerfully self-promoting. So sometimes we need prophylactic irony, sometimes, darker irony, sometimes, irony that is militant. Maybe Caliban will be an ironic metaphor too far for our sector's Princes to ploy with?

We need more than episodic dancing. We need dance floors and dance halls that offer a bit of durability. Not top-down choreography, but spaces for developing collective moves. Our ironic acts of dancing – refusing non-participation, open democratic ways of thinking, irreverence, resisting the constraints of formal protocols – need connecting into more collective forms of dance. FE is a contested site. Power matters here. None of us are powerless – but sedimented, institutionalized power is hard to shift.

Sector teachers were proud of the successful UCU dispute in Nottingham (UCU, 2019), which tried to inject a dancing spirit into a Machiavellian moment of demotic revolt. The strike was joyful, bright, mobile, picketers marched, made noise, danced, sang ('We will strike 500 times and we will strike 500 more ...'), a Festival of Yearning was a riposte to the college's official Festival of Learning. When the college management announced free tea and coffee for teachers crossing picket lines activists countered with a Mad Hatter's Tea Party by the statue of Robin Hood. Is organized irony an oxymoron? Creating a space where branch members in sufficient numbers felt confident to dance took work – solid union resources (strike pay, officials' time), meetings, committees, branch-lists, phone rounds, and long-term relationships with local politicians.

So no last word. No final transformation. We need structures that can nurture creative discourse and action, and creative acts by many different Dancing Princesses, Machiavellis, and resistant Calibans, who can help these structures – unions, colleges, policy-making bodies – from getting stuck and ossified.

## Be wise hereafter and seek for grace

While still exploring the potential form and central metaphor of the final part of the trilogy, the editors went to an open-air production of *The Tempest.* We expected the drama and the push and pull of plot but in the magic of a summer evening there was a lightness and many more laughs than we expected – leaving we were all smiles. The focus clearing, we saw our challenge – as for FE – to hold tight to its true purpose, allow for lightness, offer a space for dreams ... and dance again.

The dance is rooted in trade unionism but is non-sectarian (and perhaps a little fairy dust is required in our industrial thinking – a single, united cradle-to-grave educational trade union is surely overdue). Our dance is deeply radical but not party political: FE is too important to be a political football, a smashed train set (Keep, 1999) or the plaything of Machiavellian or ignorant, hubristic ministers. The dancing princesses are our wonderful, magical students, dedicated business-support professionals, passionate teachers, committed trade unionists, ethical FE managers, progressive principals, allies in the wider sector's bodies, associations and press, and devotees in the whole post-compulsory sector in the UK and beyond this isle, their glass slippers discretely hidden under dusty academic gowns. We hope that our collective resistance to the deeply reductive treatment of FE by policymakers has been fertile (Daley, 2015), that our writing as resistance has inspired (Orr, 2015). The dancing princesses may have no royal power or prerogative, but if the FE sector is to be Grimm, let it be so on our own terms – as powerful, democratic, dancing professionals (Petrie, 2015).

At the conclusion of *The Tempest* Prospero recognizes the dangerous allure of unbridled power, and drowns his magical books 'deeper than did ever plummet sound' (5.1.57). We too now set aside our books, or rather entrust them to our FE readers and comrades. What follows in this collection, and characterized its prequels, is by no means a stereotypically academic book. It is playful, even scurrilous at times; it is richly illustrated by FE students, and the chapter and section authors present deeply personal, eclectic, compelling, and brave tales of our sector.

Be not afeard, FE. Dance with us. We are asking:

> *Be not afeard; the isle is full of noises,*
> *Sounds and sweet airs, that give delight and hurt not.*
> *Sometimes a thousand twangling instruments*
> *Will hum about mine ears, and sometime voices*
> *That, if I then had waked after long sleep,*
> *Will make me sleep again: and then, in dreaming,*
> *The clouds methought would open and show riches*
> *Ready to drop upon me that, when I waked,*
> *I cried to dream again.*
> (*The Tempest*, Act 3, Scene 2)

# References

Avis, J. (2017) 'Beyond cynicism, comfort radicalism and emancipatory practice: FE teachers'. In Daley, M., Orr, K. and Petrie, J. (eds) *The Principal: Power and professionalism in FE*. London: Trentham Books.

Ballard, J.G. (2000) *Super-Cannes*. London: Flamingo Press

Braidotti, R. (2019) *Posthuman Knowledge*. Cambridge: Polity Press.

Daley, M. (2015) Why teach? Not afraid to dance'. In Daley, M., Orr, K. and Petrie, J. (eds) *Further Education and the Twelve Dancing Princesses*. London: Trentham Books.

Keep, E. (1999) 'UK's VET Policy and the "Third Way": Following a high skills trajectory or running up a dead end street?' *Journal of Education and Work*, 12 (3), 323–46. Online. https://doi.org/10.1080/1363908990120307 (accessed 6 May 2020).

Orr, K. (2015) 'Coda: Writing as resistance'. In Daley, M., Orr, K. and Petrie, J. (eds) *Further Education and the Twelve Dancing Princesses*. London: Trentham Books.

Petrie, J. (2015) Introduction: How Grimm is FE?' In Daley, M., Orr, K. and Petrie, J. (eds) *Further Education and the Twelve Dancing Princesses*. London: Trentham Books.

UCU (2019) 'Long-running dispute at Nottingham College ends as college agrees deal on pay and workload'. 15 November. Online. www.ucu.org.uk/article/10431/Long-running-dispute-at-Nottingham-College-ends-as-college-agrees-deal-on-pay-and-workload (accessed 03 February 2020).

*We can only know what we can truly imagine. Finally what we see comes from ourselves.*

(Marge Piercy)

Detail of Caliban in *Scene from Shakespeare's The Tempest* – William Hogarth

overleaf: Cara Dyos

# Act 1: Introduction

*Gillian Klein*

Long, long ago and far away, was the cave where Sycorax bore Caliban. Long ago, one Neanderthal dipped a hand in dye, then pressed it against the wall of a cave. These red handprints are more than 64,000 years old. Humans have always wished to leave their mark on the world.

Alphabetical writing evolved sixty-or-so millennia later, preceded by some centuries of hieroglyphics. This consonantal system became the base for virtually all scripts used throughout the world from before the Christian era to today. Recording and communicating events and beliefs became imperative; men went blind inscribing manuscripts, women embroidering tapestries, all in the cause of immortality. Printing is, however, a recent invention. The oldest known printed text originated in China during the Tang Dynasty: the 'Diamond Sutra', a Buddhist book produced in around 868 CE. Not long afterwards, in 1476, William Caxton, an English merchant, diplomat and writer was, we're told, the first person to introduce a printing press into England.

Shakespeare, it is generally believed, was born in April 1564 in Stratford on Avon. He never published his plays, but luckily for posterity, two of his actors had the Folio versions of the plays printed after his death. We see something of the Caliban side of this successful Stratford businessman and London man of theatre in the verse he wrote for his grave, forbidding his bones to be exhumed to make room, as was the custom, for a new corpse:

> *Good friend for Jesus' sake forbear,*
> *To dig the dust enclosed here.*
> *Blest be the man that spares these stones,*
> *And curst be he that moves my bones.*

Of Shakespeare's many characters, Caliban is a favourite with audiences. He is both splendidly savage and endowed with an imaginative vocabulary. He tells Miranda: 'You taught me language / And my profit on't / is that I know how to curse' (1.2.368). His creator was a prolific wordsmith, credited with introducing thousands of words into the English language. As for me, it was my mother who gave me a love of words. She wrote popular stories for South African magazines – but she couldn't spell. By age 14 I was amending her stories so her heroines no longer 'padded bearfooted' (which on reflection seems like a loss). Never did publishing cross my mind; books were what I *read*. When I was barred from teacher training college because I married immediately after my degree, I settled for a PGC in Library and Information Science. That was in the early 1960s – but in South Africa the clocks were set back 50 years. And when I fled my beautiful homeland after the police massacred peaceful protesters at Sharpeville Township, I believed I'd left racism and social injustice behind. I soon learnt that this wasn't so. In the UK 'motherland' racial injustice just took different forms.

I was already checking my privilege while my subversive side set me on a rollercoaster of opportunities. The day my youngest child trotted happily into nursery school, I dried my tears and began work at a girls' grammar school, as one of the pioneer librarians to be placed in the secondary schools in ILEA – the Inner London Education Authority. All went smoothly, and then…

> Deputy Head of Girls' Grammar School (*grabbing sleeve of the hurrying young School Librarian*): You've been here for a year already, and we seem to be losing more books than ever!
>
> Librarian: But we're losing much better books now, aren't we?

Soon after I recounted this exchange to another of ILEA's 500 qualified school librarians, it reached the ears of stately Queen Liz I, aka the head of the service. The result: I became one of the ILEA's trainers of their librarians – Caliban was to give them dancing lessons. In 1974 I set up the library and information unit in the ILEA's own research centre, CUES. I read the books I bought for it, such as Franz Fanon's *Black Skins, White Masks* for the first time – such books were banned in South Africa (SA) and t'was indeed 'all new to me'.

So began my true education. That the SA authorities had banned *Black Beauty* no longer seemed funny, especially as they apparently deemed Noddy books and golliwogs acceptable for their children. Inspired by Dorothy Kuya, along with Judith Elkin, Children's Librarian at Birmingham, we at CUES published a slim booklet: *Assessing Children's Books in a Multi-ethnic Society*. It suggested ways to evaluate the printed word for schoolchildren, while roundly rejecting selection criteria that were too often used unquestioningly, especially: 'I read *Little Black Sambo* (or similar) when I was a child, and it didn't hurt **me**'.

The *Evening Standard* and *Daily Telegraph* seized on the booklet to send me up as a mobile left-wing Mary Whitehouse. ILEA's Press office persuaded me to go on TV's *Newsnight* – live – to put the record straight! Said Sue Lawley after grinding down terrified TV novice: 'Surely *Alice in Wonderland* is unfair to dormice and *Little Red Riding Hood* is unfair to wolves?' I replied that we didn't have many dormice or wolves in ILEA schools, before proclaiming that ILEA was *not* in the business of banning books and neither was I.

ILEA seconded me to the prestigious independent body, Schools Council, to undertake a project on what I renamed *Resources for Schools in Multicultural Society*. To four lists of publications, including one of novels for educators, I added a list of leading initiatives on this emerging topic of 'Multicultural Education' – and that was how I found Professor John Eggleston. Always at the leading edge of sociology of education, he'd set up a course at Keele University for teachers to learn about multicultural teaching for diverse society. He had already established a curriculum-changing journal reconceptualizing the school subject of 'Craft' as 'Design and Technology', which Barbara Wiggins, his retired PA at Keele, distributed from her home. John suggested I begin a journal that he'd fund for a year, that *had* to be called *Multicultural Teaching*. Other than the title, I'd have free reign. *MCT*, relaunched 20 years later as *Race Equality Teaching*, was a perfect vehicle for reviewing the 'multicultural' resources for schools that were slowly appearing, not all of them well thought out.

Back at ILEA in late 1982, after an eventful year as one of the first Research Fellows in Jagdish Gundara's Centre for Intercultural Education at London's Institute of Education, I was still also travelling to schools and conferences all over the UK with my four bags of books, containing a few examples of racist ones and a wide-ranging selection of inclusive materials, many of them just on the market. I was generally collected off a train by someone who'd been instructed to look for 'the bag lady'. In my travels, I found exciting teaching materials being developed in authorities outside London that would, I believed, have national relevance. It soon struck me that I could sell such books on the back of the journal – literally. And I knew where the gaps in resources for schools were. John Eggleston's printer and, amazingly, their brilliant designer, John Stipling, produced the books, as well as John's and my journals, all for Barbara to distribute from her front room in Trentham, Stoke-on-Trent!

So that's how I came to publish what I'd been preaching for a decade. The book list was mine. John developed new academic journals on various subjects, fattened up their subscription lists, then sold them off to

Taylor and Francis. Several are still going strong. We soon had to buy large premises, and we gave good jobs to five local people, under the competent management of Barbara Wiggins.

Fast-forward a few years ... The tanned, smart-suited director of a financially successful publishing house stood looking at the displays of our publications we'd each set out at an education conference, and remarked: 'Our books are market-driven; yours are editorially driven'. He sold his company a couple of years later, for £4 million. I've often thought about how right he was – from start to finish, Trentham Books has been about *content*.

The very first Trentham book was an A4 paperback called *Looking into Language* (1984), in which authors Audrey Gregory and Norah Woollard dared to suggest that children with no or little English did *not* have a language deficit – an argument that was carried forward over the years by scholars like Safder Alladina, Josie Levine, Maggie Gravelle, and Jim Cummins. In under a decade the entire discourse became about teaching EAL – English as an Additional Language – not ESL. The vocabulary was changing too – 'immigrants' became 'refugees' and then 'Muslims'.

It was predictable that Trentham would publish equally challenging books about Early Years Education, less so that Dorothy Heathcote and her admirers, of whom I was one, would choose Trentham as the platform for her exciting brand of Drama Education, through which students explored the world's dilemmas and their own. This unique list culminated in 2017 with David Davis's *Imagining the Real*.

Naturally, there were books on sustaining the planet, from Alan Peacock's *Eco-Literacy for Primary Schools* (2004) to *Education for Hope in Troubled Times* by David Hicks (2014). But much of the list focused on race and racism, on sexism and homophobia, and on human rights. And these concerns also infuse the titles that concern pedagogy, policy and curriculum. The authors of Trentham books about the stories and the educational needs of minoritized children were drawn from within their own groups. Some topics were harder to commission – it was five years before I found someone to write about the abysmal educational provision for Traveller children.

In 1989 Trentham published the first book in the UK on *Bullying in Schools*, followed by three more, and other publishers clambered aboard what quickly became a bandwagon. The discourse changed. Bullying was no longer a problem for victims or their families to deal with: it was the school's problem. The next year, *Daring to be a Teacher* appeared, the first of Robin Richardson's visions, grounded in practice, of what an educational

Utopia might be. He wrote or co-wrote nine more books for Trentham over 25 years, every one of them topical, illuminating and inspiring.

It may have been the fabulous, joyful *Catching Hell and Doing Well* (2015) about the Abasindi Woman's Cooperative, that signalled Trentham's hospitality to Black women academics who had something to say. Whatever the cause, we became, as Sheine Peart put it, 'the go-to publisher for British Black women academics'. Her books and the collections of Deborah Gabriel, of Jan Etienne and others, offer telling insights to all academics and managers, as does Suma Din's extensive research into what *Muslim Mothers* want from their children's schooling. When I retire to my island alone, I can do so in the knowledge that other academic publishers have taken up the dance, just as they did the topic of bullying, and will recognize the worrying subject of spiralling exclusions as marketable too.

Some months after John Eggleston died in December 2002, I spotted Alma Craft in a soft-play centre, staring at me over the heads of our grandchildren – two toddlers apiece. We'd co-edited *The Agenda for Multicultural Education* for Schools Council in 1986, before she spent 16 years working abroad. For Trentham's remaining independent years, she and I together selected which we should publish of the book proposals that flooded in. We never went campus calling, though we did take Trentham to conferences, where Alma did the selling while I listened to pitches.

When I sold my domain to IOE Press in 2013, because Barbara was gravely ill, I was grateful the imprint would survive and that I could run it with little restraint. The reward was to steer great new projects including the *Princesses* and the *Principal* through to production. When my owners killed the 33-year-old journal that had recorded the struggles for social and racial justice in education through the 1980s to 2017, they bulldozed the seedbed for the monographs Trentham produced.

There weren't that many FE titles in Trentham. Even Sheine's *Making Education Work: How Black men and boys navigate the Further Education sector* (2015) mainly contrasted the discrimination Black boys endured in schools with their positive response to receiving respectful treatment when – if – they reached college. So I don't know why the Tempestuous Trio brought their Dancing Princesses to me, and I didn't risk asking Joel in case they changed their minds. I just rejoiced silently. I hope this piece explains how an ill-fitting character on the edge of the educational establishment became the enthusiastic academic publisher of Caliban's songs. A sometime subversive who resisted the totemic, the conformist, the old ideas dressed in sparkling new words, is eager to take a little credit for bringing you, the reader, this FE-transforming trilogy of visionary books.

*It is a common fault of men not to reckon on storms in fair weather.*

(Niccolo Machiavelli)

Charlette Costin

opposite: Daniel Bastable

## Chapter 1

# Whither a politics of hope: Neoliberalism and revolutionary reformism?

*James Avis*

This chapter draws on Shakespeare's *The Tempest* to address three main political issues: the politics of hope, the moral high ground and finally the restitution of the status quo. Prospero in his engagement with Ariel seeks to shape a narrative that serves to secure his power and to construct Sycorax as his other. In this Chapter I construct a narrative that draws on submerged themes within the play to engage with contemporary debates and in the concluding section draw out the significance of the argument for Further Education (FE).

## The politics of hope

*The Tempest* can be read as an allegory of struggle, or perhaps of the politics of hope, one that is accented differently according to specific positions held by actors. For example, Prospero seeks to be restored to his dukedom. Caliban hopes to be rid of Prospero, the colonizer and global capitalist, thereby reversing the enclosure of the island (Federici, 2014; Loomba, 2005). Ariel wishes to be free and emancipated from slavery. Ferdinand seeks to gain the hand of Miranda, who by acceding to her father's wishes will become queen of Naples, thereby securing patriarchal relations (Blystone, 2012). For others the hope is to escape from the Island having first secured their future. These aspirations are marked by class, gender, and ethnicity and race but also by the pursuit of self-interest as well as the desire to acquire power and material advantage. This in turn serves as an allegory for struggle not only, between and within classes but also encompassing gender and ethnicity and race.

Following a rather bleak portrayal of working-class experiences in Teeside, Rob Macdonald (2019; and see MacDonald and Marsh, 2005;

Shildrick, MacDonald, Webster, Garthwaite, 2012) closed his professorial inaugural lecture by referring to a politics of hope. This he illustrated with a picture of a Corbyn rally in Newcastle. The photograph captured the youthful enthusiasm with which the then new leader of the Labour Party was met. Rob used this picture to illustrate a politics of hope that suggested that things could be different. This was a theme that ran throughout his lecture. He offered us a language of possibility and an aspiration for a better future. The Corbyn representation carries with it both a politics of hope but also, for some, of fear. Returning to *The Tempest*, in much of Prospero's rhetoric lies the 'spectre' of the other – Sycorax the witch. However, for Caliban and Sycorax, Prospero and his like are the other – settlers involved in the dispossession and expropriation of their land. That is to say: its enclosure in a process of what Marx would refer to as primitive accumulation.

Frequently papers written by those with leftist orientations that address the plight of further, general and higher vocational education and training or what might be described as post-secondary education (Aronowitz, 2000) as well as society, conclude by drawing out the radical possibilities that lie in the present and that presage the transformation of society – an imaginary vision of the future. Thus we may consider the limits and possibilities that arise in the current conjuncture or alternatively point towards a number of contradictions whose resolution requires fundamental societal change, albeit through practices of, or some notion of revolutionary reformism. In 1968 Gorz wrote:

> A struggle for non-reformist reforms – for anti-capitalist reforms – is one which does not base its validity and its right to exist on capitalist needs, criteria, and rationales. A non-reformist reform is determined not in terms of what can be, but what should be. (Gorz, 1968: 7–8)

This notion has been echoed in Nancy Fraser's more recent writing:

> When successful, non-reformist reforms change more than the specific institutional features they explicitly target. In addition, they alter the terrain upon which later struggles will be waged. By changing incentive structures and political opportunity structures, they expand the set of feasible options for future reform. Over time their cumulative effect could be to transform the underlying structures that generate injustice. (Fraser and Honneth, 2003: 79–80)

There are at least three dangers that flow from this form of intervention. First, to claim to speak the truth for the other – to be their voice while ensconced in the safety of the academy, may lead to another type of oppression. The second, leading on from the first, relates to a feeling of self-satisfaction and what the 'alt-right' refer to as virtue signalling. This is mirrored by a form of critique that is distanced from the materiality and harshness of politics and that is more rhetorical than 'real'. The third relates to the very real limits encountered by non-reformist reforms and their scope for domestication and co-optation.

## The moral high ground

Stephen Ball writes:

> Both those inside the policy discourse and those whose professional identities are established through antagonism towards the discourse benefit from the uncertainties and tragedies of reform. Critical researchers, apparently ensconced in the moral high ground, nonetheless make a livelihood trading in the artefacts of misery and broken dreams of practitioners. None of us remains untainted by the incentives and disciplines of the new moral economy. (Ball, 1997: 258)

Prospero conjures-up the storm that results in the shipwreck of Alonso and company on the island. This is their 'just deserts' for having connived in Prospero's downfall and exile. Prospero ensured that no one was physically harmed in the shipwreck, thus positioning himself to occupy the moral high ground. But what of the original inhabitants of the island, Caliban and his mother Sycorax? During its ascendancy the advocates of neoliberalism positioned free markets as both serving the interests of all members of society and as being the most appropriate way to manage economic and social relations. Neoliberals sought to present the free market as inevitable and without a realistic alternative. Pundits suggested that when neoliberalism encountered resistance this derived from the perverse interests of those opposing it – for example, professional capture by welfare specialists who sought to secure their narrow self-interest at the expense of wider society. Neoliberalism's moral force derived from such discourses and from its normalization of the status quo.

The structural relations of participants in the play are normalized and taken for granted. But as with any discourse, it raises the possibility of counter-discourses that could challenge the status quo. Caliban and his absent mother both challenge white supremacy and critique settler colonization, but in addition Sycorax in effect critiques patriarchal power that, paradoxically, Caliban supports. The crew of the shipwrecked vessel are largely absent in the play, thus represent the invisibility and marginalization of the working class, whose subordination is taken for granted. Sycorax is similarly invisible other than as a construct of Prospero's rhetoric. The figure of Caliban can be read in a number of ways – he could be perceived as a talisman of the universal aspirations of the working class for emancipation. This rests with an expansive notion of class that encompasses intersectionality in all its forms and that acknowledges those engaged in unwaged productive labour (Federici, 2014).

## An interregnum

*The Tempest* concludes by progressing towards some sort of resolution in which the conflicts and tension between participants remain in place, albeit submerged and largely unresolved. Prospero is restored to his dukedom, regaining his patrimonial power. Class, patriarchal and race relations remain as they were, albeit with a shuffling of positions. Perhaps this could stand as a metaphor for the adaptive capabilities of capital and its response to the current critique of neoliberalism, which in the current conjuncture may be reaching its limits. While neoliberalism may be replaced by a different variant of capitalism, the underpinning structural relations remain in place. To the extent that there is a transformation, this is located within the ruling class and can be conceived as a skirmish between the powerful. This process, using a Gramscian term, could be described as transformism in as much as there has been some change. However, this merely reflects the adaptive capabilities of the ruling class or capital, whereby the fundamental transformation of society is held in abeyance, leading to a hiatus (Fraser, 2019).

Earlier, Fraser's and Gorz's notion of non-reformist reform was discussed. This conceptualization carries with it a gradualist strategy that could be aligned to social democracy, though both writers would distance themselves from such an interpretation. Social democracy can be seen as capital's adjustment to the increasing power of the working class in western societies, a strategy of containment built upon concessions that left in place structural relations that secured the dominance of capital. In a similar vein, the transition from Fordism to Post-Fordism can be seen as a response to working-class struggle against Fordism. However, the shift to neoliberalism reflected a change in the balance of power between labour and capital in favour of the latter. Despite the visibility of the increasing failings of neoliberalism, its attendant capitalist relation seems to be relatively secure.

Arruza *et al.* suggest that the strategy of non-reformist reforms is no longer feasible and that there is an 'absence of any viable middle way' (2019: 3). Fraser and Jaeggi, reflecting on the adaptive capabilities of capital, point out:

> How 'tamed' capitalism can be and still be 'capitalism' is largely a semantic issue … at the same time, the excesses and threats posed by contemporary capitalism might give us pause over whether the idea of 'taming' capitalism is still adequate. (Fraser and Jaeggi, 2018: 5)

Whether capitalism can be tamed in the current conjuncture, one in which capital has gained ascendancy and where polarized politics and social relations are all-pervasive, is a moot point. Perhaps an anti-capitalist politics of the like practised by Extinction Rebellion would be more appropriate to break out of the interregnum. It is at this juncture that Frederici's reading of Caliban is significant as he 'represents not only the anti-colonial rebel… but is a symbol of the world proletariat' (Federici, 2014: 11).

## Further and vocational education and training

Prospero, prior to his exile, was passionate about learning. He was so preoccupied with the 'life of the mind' that he neglected the duties and social responsibilities of his Dukedom, leaving a space for his usurpation. Is there an analogy to be made with academics 'ensconced in the moral high ground' of the ivory tower – academics who are preoccupied with flights of intellectual fancy that serve to marginalize the theoretical and practical involvement of practitioners, 'trading in the artefacts of misery and broken dreams of practitioners' (Ball, 1997: 258)? Or is this merely a reflection of the struggle for positional advantage among those who share similar class positions and who themselves build careers on the suffering of others?

Caliban's fluency in the colonizer's language had been imposed upon him by Prospero. Could this be seen as 'civilizing the natives', as providing access to powerful knowledge, or was it an act of cultural genocide? How then could we, as advocates of FE, use this analogy to think about the curriculum in relation to its constructions of the student? Are we presenting our interests as those of the student? Critical race theorists have coined the term 'interest convergence', which comes close to describing such processes. But in this specific case are we attributing interests to the other, while at the same time appropriating these for our own edification? Vocational education and training is seen by many as preparing young people, as well as adults, for the world of work but also for participation in wider society. In the latter instance they are to become aware of the civic responsibilities of their particular occupation group, but are we merely reproducing the status quo? Yet at the same time we may view this education as contributing towards the development of a socially just society and as being but one of the ways to undercut and challenge the privileges of the elite. We may even see this as providing the possibility of some sort of mobility for oppressed groups in relation to class, race and gender. At the same time, we should be mindful of the falsities surrounding meritocratic claims.

In addition, schooling and education have a reproductive logic – are we, proponents of FE, merely contributing to the formation of the proletariat – those who sell their labour, as well as the unwaged who nevertheless create value? John Holloway suggests in his aptly-named text that: 'We are the crisis of capital', by which he has in mind the way that the proletariat – the working class – through its connivance with waged labour, serves to reproduce capitalism. He writes: 'we create each day the capitalist social relations we suffer', pointing out that this struggle against capital has to be mobilized collectively (Holloway, 2019: 230). However, while this struggle may be initiated by an individual the point is to develop spaces in which capitalist hegemony is challenged and where we break our complicity with capitalist relations. It is at this point that post-work and anti-work sentiments have a part to play as they can undermine capitalist wage relations.

## Conclusion: Caliban's dance

In this chapter I have used *The Tempest* as a springboard to engage with a number of contemporary debates. Mine is not a consistent reading of the play, indeed in some respects it breaks with traditional interpretations that emphasize colonization, patriarchy, neoliberalism and class. While it accepts these analyses it is not restricted to them. Shakespeare was of his time and his plays reflect the issues of the day. My reading of *The Tempest* is similarly socially situated, allowing me to engage with the politics of hope that break free from a narrow interpretation that associates it with the liberal left. This discussion led to reflections on the moral high ground and the manner in which academics and teachers are located. This section morphed into one that considered further and vocational education and training, which reflected on positionality, the curriculum, neoliberalism, social justice and their reproduction, and drew attention to a range of contradictions and tensions. Caliban's dance is messy, contradictory and stuttering and yet it may open-up glimpses of a different kind of society that is perhaps the best we can hope for, going beyond non-reformist reforms and anticipating the transcendence of capitalism.

# References

Aronowitz, S. (2001) *The Knowledge Factory: Dismantling the corporate university and creating true higher learning.* Boston: Beacon Press.

Arruzza, C., Bhattacharya, T. and Fraser, N. (2019) *Feminism for the 99%: A manifesto.* London: Verso.

Ball, S. (1997) 'Policy sociology and critical social research: A personal review of recent education policy and policy research'. *British Education Research Journal*, 23 (3), 257–74. Online. https://doi.org/10.1080/0141192970230302

Blystone, B. (2012) 'Extremes of gender and power: Sycorax's absence in Shakespeare's The Tempest'. *Selected Papers of the Ohio Valley Shakespeare Conference 5*, 73–83. Online. https://ideaexchange.uakron.edu/spovsc/vol5/iss2012/6/

Federici, S. (2014) *Caliban and the Witch.* New York: Autonomedia (2nd ed.).

Fraser, N. (2019) *The Old is Dying and the New Cannot be Born: From progressive neoliberalism to Trump and beyond.* London: Verso.

Fraser, N. and Honneth, A. (2004) *Redistribution or Recognition? A Political–Philosophical Exchange.* London: Verso.

Fraser, N. and Jaeggi, R. (2018) *Capitalism: A conversation in critical theory.* Cambridge: Polity Press.

Gorz, A. (1968) *Strategy for Labor: A radical proposal.* Boston: Beacon Press.

Holloway, J. (2019) *We Are the Crisis of Capital: A John Holloway Reader.* Oakland, CA: PM Press.

Loomba, A. (2005) *Colonialism/Postcolonialism.* London: Routledge (2nd ed.).

MacDonald, R. (2019) '"Not under conditions of their own choosing": Youth transitions, place and history'. Inaugural professorial lecture, University of Huddersfield, 28 March.

MacDonald, R. and Marsh, J. (2005) *Disconnected Youth? Growing up in Britain's poor neighbourhoods.* London: Palgrave Macmillan.

Shildrick, T., MacDonald, R., Webster, C. and Garthwaite, K. (2012) *Poverty and Insecurity: Life in low-pay, no-pay Britain.* Bristol: Policy Press.

*You don't need a weatherman to know which way the wind blows.*

(Bob Dylan)

Laks Butler-Kania

opposite: Phoebe Cripps

## Chapter 2

# Conjuring critical pedagogy

*Maire Daley*

Here we meet Caliban and Ariel after the tempest, they are left with an island, their freedom and a potential for magic. Their parts for Prospero have been played, while he had conjured his future they had imagined theirs. Ariel like a dancing princess had gathered steps for a new dance; with Caliban, she hoped for a good life for them and all comers.

Caliban: (*Sceptical*) Our experience of colonization and oppression gives you hope for a good future Ariel?

Ariel: It's where we start, where we go is up to us. Let's picture a different island where working people experienced extreme levels of poverty, high death rates, few or no workers' rights; housing is squalid and dangerous to health, education and training is limited and medical care sparse and primitive.

Caliban: Dystopias are easy to imagine, it's harder to conjure a peace than a tempest.

Ariel: In nineteenth-century Britain those conditions produced some great utopian ideals that brings us hope for our good life. Robert Owen set out his case for radical social reform in 'A New View of Society: Essays on the Principle of the Formation of the Human Character' (1813). It was a protest against the condition of the British poor and a call for educational, industrial and social reform. Owen argued that a person's character is formed by circumstances over which they have no control. His radical social experiment established New Lanark, a Scottish cotton mill, and around it he built a model utopian community. His ambition was to challenge ignorance through imaginative education, to use fair discipline and to offer regular work, good housing and health care. Its success demonstrated that a community could successfully tackle poverty, social disadvantage and ignorance. It led Owen to call for the reorganization of the whole of British society.

From a different standpoint, William Lever set out similar ideas for reform in 1888:

> It is my hope ... some day to build houses in which our work-people will be able to live and be comfortable. Semi-detached houses, with gardens back and front, in which they will be able to know more about the science of life than they can in a back slum, and in which they will learn that there is more enjoyment in life than mere going to and returning from work, and looking forward to Saturday night to draw their wages. (Hunter, 2019: 39)

Lever went on to set up the Port Sunlight soap factory, where workers benefited from shorter working hours, pensions and paid holidays. Alongside it he built one of the first garden villages, a community with over nine hundred houses, with a school, an apprentice training institute, library, hospital, church, pub, theatre, club houses, swimming pool, gymnasium and art gallery for the use of his workers. Life expectancy, literacy and general health of the workers and their families improved dramatically (Hunter, 2019).

A strong case is made for linking work, education, housing and health as contributors to the good life.

Caliban: Wonderful, utopias indeed. Owen and Lever were charismatic individuals with bold visions for a fairer future. Their experiments remain as beacons, but both were limited and didn't result in widespread change. They developed ideals of co-operation and mutual benefit by use of benevolent paternalism – paternalism, as we know Ariel, has its limitations.

Ariel: Fair points, but what is most interesting is their whole life approach. Maybe we should be even bolder and take time to dream.

In his dream of Nowhere, William Morris (1892) explores a whole society transformed. After a day of discussion about a socialist future, Morris wishes before he sleeps: 'If I could but see it!' (Morris, 1892: 3). His dream that night is vivid and takes him on an exploratory journey into the future. He finds a socialist society that, while it was tempestuous in its construction, is now settled and peaceful. He learns that no formal education is provided, the emphasis instead is placed on learning practical tasks. His guide informs him:

> You expected to see children thrust into schools when they had reached an age conventionally supposed to be the due age, whatever their varying faculties and dispositions might be, and

when there, with like disregard to facts to be subjected to a certain conventional course of 'learning'. My friend, can't you see that such a proceeding means ignoring the fact of **growth**, bodily and mental? No one could come out of such a mill uninjured, and those only would avoid being crushed by it who would have the spirit of rebellion strong in them ... In the nineteenth century, society was so miserably poor, owing to the systematized robbery on which it was founded, that real education was impossible for anybody. All that is past; we are no longer hurried, and the information lies ready to each one's hand when his own inclinations impel him to seek it. In this as in other matters we have become wealthy: we can afford to give ourselves time to grow. (Morris, 1892: 90)

Caliban: Ah 'when I waked, I cried to dream again' (3.2:136). A great vision, but there is a manipulation in dreams, they show us a future that slips between our fingers when we wake.

Ariel: It's a dream to provoke us to imagine. We know from our own experience that it is difficult to see clearly when caught in a tempest. Morris provides:

the challenge to the imagination to become immersed in the same open exploration. And in such an adventure two things happen: our habitual values the 'common sense' of bourgeois society are thrown into disarray. And we enter into Utopia's proper and newfound space: the education of desire ... to open a way to aspiration ... Morris's Utopianism, when it succeeds, liberates desire to an uninterrupted interrogation of our values and also to its own self-interrogation. (E.P. Thompson, quoted in Ellison, 2018)

Morris shows us a process, so that now when the tempest has subsided we can begin to create a vision of our future. 'And as the morning steals upon the night, melting the darkness, so their rising senses begin to chase the ignorant fumes that mantle their clearer reason'(5.1:66).

Let's leave dreams for a moment and go back to tempestuous times. Picture another island ruled by a corrupt leader whose interests are elsewhere and who uses the island as his own plaything. The leader is careless with the lives of the people and slowly removes from them any power they might have.

Caliban: We know this place!

Ariel: Now picture Cuba and a revolution: a successful overthrow of the state by the people who were thought to be powerless. Equally importantly, picture the time after the revolution when the biggest challenge was to make the change permanent. Echoing the call of a hero of the revolutionaries, José Martí – 'Being educated is the only way to be free' – education was identified as key in securing the new future. Education became part of the revolution, it was both *successful in its own right* (against every measure the education system in Cuba is successful and against similar types of societies it is significantly better (UNESCO, 2014)) but also in the embedding of the aims of the revolution into the everyday lives of Cubans.

Caliban: Hasta la victoria siempre! It's a great model, Viva! The success of education in Cuba is within their island transformed, education as an agent of freedom is a powerful idea; it worked because the newfound freedom sat within a socialist society.

By contrast, let's picture Britain again, but now in the twenty-first century. Students have access to free, full-time education to the age of eighteen, they are encouraged to participate and make the most of the opportunities offered to make a good life. However for some the concerns highlighted by Owen and Lever remain: there are 14 million people living in relative poverty, 4.5 million of them are children (Hood and Waters, 2017). Of those classified as being poor, 67 per cent are in work (Buttle UK, 2019). The Infant mortality rate in the most deprived areas is at 5.2 per 1,000 whereas in the least deprived areas it is 2.7 (ONS, 2017). There are 320,000 people classified as homeless and the average age of death of a homeless person is 44 years (Shelter, 2018). Education in Britain has not resulted in a good life for everyone; on its own education isn't delivering Marti's promise of freedom. Like our experience with Prospero, education is bound – Prospero's Machiavellian purpose was not to liberate us, but rather, by educating us he was able to secure his own aims.

(Ariel is dancing now; they are thinking on the same lines, she believes Caliban to be a little transformed.)

Ariel: Did Prospero really provide an education? We were his creatures, he filled us with his ideas and bound us to him; only now that he is gone are we able to dream. Like any education (vocational or academic) that does not offer possibilities for dreaming of freedom it was a conscious – or unconscious – act to maintain the status quo. Freire argued:

> The more education becomes empty of dreams to fight for, the
> more the emptiness left by those dreams becomes filled with
> technique, until the moment comes when education becomes
> reduced to that. Then education becomes pure training, it
> becomes pure transfer of content, it is almost like the training of
> animals, it is a mere exercise in adaptation to the world. (Freire,
> 2004: 84)

Leesa Wheelehan (2007) argues that competency-based training in vocational
education is one mechanism through which the working class is denied
access to powerful knowledge represented by the academic disciplines.
Robinson shows that young people following vocational pathways have
'lower educational and employment outcomes, and worse health outcomes
than their peers following academic routes' (Robinson, 2019: 7). Education
for work shouldn't only be about work, the curriculum needs to be rich to
ensure a transformation of aspiration and desire in the revaluing of work
and education. Wheelehan (2007) argues for the development of critical
realism in vocational education, a model that moves away from skills and
competency to build questioning and critical skills.

True education, whether vocational or academic, can offer the
possibility of dreams. Even in your example of Britain, Caliban, education
can inspire. I could show you examples of effective transformation of students
posted on every College of Further Education website or on UCU, WEA,
and Adult Learning websites. They demonstrate that profound change can
come about for individuals through critical education. There are conscious
teachers doing deliberate work to raise the critical learning of students.
There are mixed levels of success but in both academic and vocational
education lives are being transformed – there is some freedom in that.

Caliban: Is that enough Ariel? Further Education clearly offers some
individuals great experiences, but how does this link back to our utopian
desires where education, work and the good life are all connected?

Ariel: All those individuals come from somewhere and will go on somewhere
else and importantly they are gathered in a shared process that offers a
possibility of freedom. Think of bell hooks:

> The academy is not paradise. But learning is a place where
> paradise can be created. The classroom with all its limitations
> remains a location of possibility. In that field of possibility
> we have the opportunity to labour for freedom, to demand of
> ourselves and our comrades, an openness of mind and heart that

allows us to face reality even as we collectively imagine ways to move beyond boundaries, to transgress. This is education as the practice of freedom. (hooks, 2000: 207)

Caliban: I agree, education when it is a collective enterprise offers a potential for freedom and because Further Education is unique in its comprehensive format – with students entering at all levels to study a vast array of subjects – it has a Morris like potential to *liberate desire and aspiration* and so transform. Participation and achievement in education can result in a good life for an individual, but our desire for utopia inevitably pushes us to consider how this success might have a greater impact. We could join the lobby to get more working-class students into top universities or demand better paid apprenticeships, but so far that has not been enough to eradicate poverty, homelessness and unemployment.

Ariel: We have set ourselves a huge task, the complex relationship between the conditions of our utopian good life has focused us around the part education can play; its potential to awaken desire and aspiration and change individuals holds a possibility for broader change. Looking back, if we were to change our experience on the island it would require us to change Prospero: a different Prospero would have meant a different life. The transformation of individuals has the potential to transform society – where else will the change come from?

Abbs and Carey (1977) focused their ideas for a changed society on teacher education. They located an agency for change with teachers and conjured-up a utopian college where student teachers would be fully immersed in whole life learning. In it they would live and manage an ecological place and develop an educational aesthetic that would raise critical awareness. The focus would be on the transformation of themselves as well as their students. The process took time. With its echoes of the Bauhaus and Black Mountain College, it offered an alternative curriculum and pedagogy where students were expected to step outside their specialist areas and use practice to explore theory, thereby dismantling traditional subject-based paths of study. Their whole life approach, which required student teachers to be self-sufficient in their learning and conscious of their place in the community, has possibilities for our good life.

If our spell focuses on teacher education we could conjure brave new teachers and enable them to create the magic we need. It would be the teacher educators' challenge to support teachers in making the best impact on individuals within the classroom and the community at large.

Caliban: Change can come from the frustration of those who are most bound. They will conjure it!

Ariel: Here is the spell.

Teacher education will use a whole life education approach. Whether full or part time, initial programmes or professional development, teacher education will be properly funded, free and accessible. It will always be framed as education not training, deliberately broad and developmental, theoretical and practical and paced to allow for teacher transformation. It will model a collegiate space and support a broad community of learning and practice. The whole college: technicians, support staff, managers and administrators, together with students and the broader learning community will contribute by supporting teachers and input into the review of curriculum, methods and approaches.

It will dismantle the pedestal of academic learning, levelling it by the appreciation and valuing of all kinds of work and study. Within a college, the comprehensive learning environment will be put to use so that student teacher builders will also be weaving, cooks painting, mathematicians turning metal, and sociologists sewing costumes; they will all be dancing and reading *The Tempest*. The hierarchical separation between different educational institutions will be blurred and movement between them routine. Collaboration with trade unions, enlightened industry and business will be an essential part of the curriculum. The sharing of facilities like libraries, workshops and theatres, together with the skills of all staff with local communities, will help break down the separation between college, work and community.

Caliban: By looking outwards a broader responsibility will be inbuilt. Teachers will continue not only to offer their magic to individual students in the classroom but contribute to the content and focus of the curriculum, their colleges and the communities where their students live. A different kind of tempest but like lightening flashing and thunder rolling the world will be altered.

Ariel and Caliban: Let's cast the spell:

'Gentle breath of yours my sails must fill, or else my project fails
... Let your indulgence set me free' (5:11)

# References
Abbs, P. and Carey, G. (1977) *Proposal for a New College*. London: Heinemann Educational.

Buttle UK, 'Child poverty in the UK'. Online. www.buttleuk.org/news/child-poverty-in-uk-in-2019 (accessed 4 October 2019).

Ellison J. (2018) 'Dreaming of communism: News from Nowhere by William Morris'. Online: https://tinyurl.com/y8gfchcg (accessed 4 October 2019).

Freire, Paulo (2004) *Pedagogy of Indignation*. Boulder, CO: Paradigm.

Hood, A. and Waters, T. (2017) *Living Standards, Poverty and Inequality in the UK: 2017–18 to 2021–22*. London: Institute for Fiscal Studies. Online: www.ifs.org.uk/uploads/publications/comms/R136.pdf (accessed 4 October 2019).

hooks, b. (2000) *Where we Stand: Class matters*. London: Routledge

Hunter, G. (2019) *Leverhulme: The life of William Hesketh Lever*. Wirral: Gavin Hunter

Morris, W. (1892) *News from Nowhere*. Facsimile edition, 2017. New York: Thames and Hudson.

ONS (2017) 'Child and infant mortality in England and Wales: 2017'. Online. https://tinyurl.com/y6hbkoad (accessed 4 October 2019).

Owen, R. (1813) 'A New View of Society: Essays on the Principle of the Formation of the Human Character'. In Owen, R. (1991) *A New View of Society and other writings*. Harmondsworth: Penguin Classics.

Robinson, D. (2019) *Further education pathways. Securing a successful and healthy life after education*. London: Education Policy Institute. Online. https://epi.org.uk/publications-and-research/further-education-pathways/ (accessed 6 May 2020).

Shelter (2018) '320,000 people in Britain are now homeless, as numbers keep rising'. Online: https://tinyurl.com/yatjr8jg (accessed 4 October 2019)

UNESCO (2014) 'Cuba rates the highest EFA Development Index in Latin America and the Caribbean'. Online: https://tinyurl.com/y7349h9f (accessed 6 May 2020).

Wheelahan, L. (2007) 'How competency-based training locks the working class out of powerful knowledge: A modified Bernsteinian analysis'. *British Journal of Sociology of Education*, 28 (5), 637–51. Online. https://doi.org/10.1080/01425690701505540

*Commander John J. Adams: 'Nice climate you have here. High oxygen content.'*
*Robby the Robot: 'I seldom use it myself, sir. It promotes rust.'*

(The Forbidden Planet)

Rob Roach

overleaf: Tami Adesida

*Chapter 3*

# 'They are all enchantment, those who once behold 'em / Are made their slaves forever'

*Christine Calder and Gary Husband*

As The *Tempest* opens, we are aboard a ship that is inexorably being drawn ashore in an enchantment-driven rising storm. The futility of the crew's battle with the sea to save the integrity of the vessel offers a rich metaphor to usefully explore further education. We take the storm as our specific focus for this chapter.

Try reading this through an FE lens: the leadership of a vessel in stormy waters, aligned with the mystery of an impending disaster, itself caused by a distant and poorly understood power. The scene is saturated with allegorical potential as an analytical tool with which to explore FE. Using this metaphorical lens we can investigate power, structure, relationships and constructions of policy. In this chapter we ask: who steers the ship? Who is left to navigate the sea of policy, predicting currents and responding to the unpredictable storms?

Every ship has a master. We consider such questions as: who are the masters? Where are decisions made and by which authority; by whom and in what conditions? Is it really the master steering the ship, or as we see in *The Tempest*'s opening scene, does the practical boatswain have his hand firmly on the tiller? This offers a potential way to dissect layers of leadership and management in both a broader visionary and conceptual interpretation, and also through the daily experience of educators leading learning. Before delving into the sources of enchantment, we must seek to find the boatswains of FE and explore the realities of how those in positions of power are navigating the churning seas of policy.

In following the thread of enchantment in *The Tempest*, we try to expand the beginnings of this emerging metaphor and explore the possibility that policy itself is the enchantment in modern further education. Enchantment sounds like fairy dust but it can also be dark sorcery. Like the incantations of Potteresque children's stories, policy often presents as an enacting wish with no explanation of how the conjuring trick is to be performed. Like magic, policy can often seem to necessitate that we pluck from thin air that which is desired or required – with no obvious resources and without paying heed to the laws of physics. Rizvi and Lingard (2009) use a working definition of policy as being the authoritative allocation of value that is published from a position of power and the assumption of compliance and agreement. This description invites a discussion around the imposition of policy.

We argue that through repetition and through the forced authoritative allocation of value, policy performs by sleight of hand the trick of fixing both the boundaries and horizons of education at all levels. As impenetrable as the enchantment on the wind in *The Tempest*, so too is policy, in its opaque and overlapping construction in FE – as evidenced by the repeated rounds of reviews of further adult education in England between 2013 and 2019. We are faced with not one incantation but many, a weave of policy that is interlinked, overlapped, entwined, tangled and – just like the waves created by the enchantment in *The Tempest* – surely erodes the shore upon which it crashes. For evidence of this see the UK Parliament's own damning review of the 2017 apprenticeship levy policy (House of Commons Committee of Public Accounts, 2019) – a perfect illustration of policy damaging a sector it was purporting to support. Where order should exist there is often chaos, and where transparency would aid the implementation, opacity frequently stymies efforts and thwarts the very outcomes the policy itself was created to produce.

Given the significant complexities of policy and the propensity for constantly changing priorities and destinations, how do we imagine a future where skilled boatswains can avoid both the tempest and the rocks, while offering critical guidance to masters? We are interested in exploring the reform of leadership in FE and how we imagine it being shaped without the need for enchantment or, indeed, a storm. A vision where the sector empowers the boatswains to not only steer the ship away from harm but also – and importantly – decide upon the desired course, delivering passengers and crew safely. So, who are the boatswains of FE and how are they situated within the structures of leadership and command?

The command structures within a large seafaring vessel run on an historically militaristic pattern of hierarchy leadership and a reliance upon titular power. The idea of management within such situations is highly contextual and the influences on leadership of environmental factors cannot be underestimated. It is not too great a stretch of the imagination to see parallels between the leadership and command structures traditionally prevailing at sea and those within large organizations such as colleges. We can equate college principals with the master or captain who occupies a senior position. This gives us a contextual comparison and allows us to imagine middle leaders as boatswains. Boatswains sit below the commissioned ranks of senior leadership and executive, with a derived power base and distributed responsibility to leadership. This is an invidious position, that Gleeson and Shain define as an 'ideological buffer' between senior managers and lecturers, one through which market reform is filtered in the FE workplace (1999).

Before we venture into leadership as a discrete territory, let us pause to consider that leadership is not relished or desired by all managers. Gleeson and Knights (2008) point out that some managers see the responsibility of leadership alongside management as moving away from the business of curriculum. They could be described as reluctant leaders. With senior roles often focusing on performance management by inspection, results and subsequent funding, there are undeniable complications when leadership of education becomes an additional responsibility. In many cases, the burden of leadership requires the individual to revisit their reasons for accepting promotion and perhaps question their identity as a leader.

Our seafaring metaphor might collapse under examination when we consider the giving and receiving of orders. The boatswain enacts orders from above but his expertise is crucial. Being able to interpret the sea, look at the waves, the storm, the coast and the weather to determine the best course of action, advise on how to proceed and in turn be listened to, is the boatswain's role. The autonomy to enact such decisions places the boatswain at the tiller of the ship with their knowledge and experience guiding the vessel. Such autonomy is often lacking in FE, as middle managers (the boatswains) are seldom trusted to lead; they are expected to simply enact and implement orders from above. As Ball (2003) highlights, lecturers and middle leaders have become gripped by what he terms 'value schizophrenia': fearing the consequences of non-compliance, they acquiesce with regulation and performative measures, enacting orders that are contrary to their own beliefs and values as educators. As Mather *et al.* (2012) rather bleakly point out, superficial compliance is often the best survival strategy. The boatswain in *The Tempest* is in control at the helm. Regardless of the futility of his attempts, he is afforded the trust and autonomy to at least try. He is the vessel's best and only hope. An alternative future for leadership in FE could be sought by examining the relationship between the master and his boatswain, in particular the trust placed in their experience and their ability to read the weather and the sea.

Persisting with the maritime metaphor offers an opportunity to indulge in a brief but interesting sojourn into what we might learn about the importance of colleges as organizations and their multiple purposes within society. In 1775, restrictions implemented by both the British Crown and the new American governments effectively banned all non-military shipping and direct trade between the British Empire and the 13 rebellious colonies of the Americas. This of course had the desired effect and rapidly reduced availability of both arms and supplies, which inevitably undermined the fighting capabilities of both sides.

Furthermore, restrictions were placed upon other activities that relied on international movement: exploration, engagement with the arts and sciences, technological advancement. This had a noticeable and significant economic impact. People could not move and consequently, with communication reliant on shipping, the movement of ideas also ceased. Effectively, viewing shipping as only a means to transport goods and soldiers had such a detrimental impact on the economies of both warring factions that even before the war ended, both parties agreed to lift restrictions on all non-military shipping. Incredibly, the two nations not only traded and collaborated with each other while still at war, but also afforded protections to vessels at sea and agreed not to purposely put them under attack.

If we focus on the ship, and compare this to a modern FE college, we can begin to see the metaphoric parallels. As shipping in 1775 was not merely about transporting goods, education is not – despite the claims of policymakers and infrastructure organizations – just about training for jobs and careers. If this historical event teaches us anything that might help to construct our metaphorical FE ship, it must be not to view colleges or the whole FE sector as a single means of production. FE does more than transport students towards work. FE establishments support creativity, exploration, innovation and even a Platonic route to fulfilment. Employment may be the intended destination, but there are opportunities for so many more positive outcomes.

The parallels between FE and the ship navigating Shakespeare's tempest are now drawn, but how do they help us imagine a different future for leadership? What impact might these imaginations have on FE?

Primarily, the relationship between the master and the boatswain teaches us about trust. The master entrusted the steering of the ship to the boatswain, recognizing the experience and expertise that he brought to his responsibilities. The title of boatswain acknowledges years of learning leading to expertise. Comparing the boatswain to those holding middle leadership roles in FE offers two perspectives. Those who are promoted to middle leadership positions may feel underprepared because they lack the training and support needed to undertake the role. While trying to balance their values as educators with the organization's focus on results and performance, middle managers often experience difficulty in reconciling their values as educators with management responsibilities. There follows a perfect storm, where individuals are appointed to roles that are poorly supported and where the demands of extensive accountability structures prevent them from practising autonomously – unlike the boatswain. The lesson to be learned is that colleges should be seeking to promote the most able and experienced individual into a role that is well supported and where that individual is trusted to lead, and not just manage. This, however, hinges on levels of trust that are lacking in performative cultures.

To conclude, when we consider the role of FE in society, the importance of its provision and the diversity of the communities it supports, we must always recognize that FE provides far more than a route to work. FE has many capable and experienced boatswains. Foregrounding their experience – and trusting them to steer and lead – could be seen as sensible sea craft.

## References

Ball, S. (2003) 'The teacher's soul and the terrors of performativity.' *Journal of Education Policy*, 18 (2), 215–28. Online. https://doi.org/10.1080/0268093022000043065 (accessed 6 May 2020).

Gleeson, D. and Knights, D. (2008) 'Reluctant leaders: An analysis of middle managers' perceptions of leadership in further education in England'. *Leadership*, 4 (1), 49–72. Online. https://doi.org/10.1177/1742715007085769 (accessed 6 May 2020).

Gleeson, D. and Shain. F. (1999) 'Managing ambiguity: Between markets and managerialism – a case study of "middle" managers in further education'. *Sociological Review* 47 (3), 461–90. Online. https://doi.org/10.1111/1467-954X.00181 (accessed 6 May 2020).

House of Commons Committee of Public Accounts (2019) *The Apprenticeships Programme: Progress Review*, 15 May. Online. https://tinyurl.com/y9gaeq2j (accessed 6 May 2020).

Mather, K., Worrall, L. and Mather, G. (2012) 'Engineering compliance and worker resistance in UK further education: The creation of the Stepford lecturer'. *Employee Relations* 34 (5), 534–54. Online. https://doi.org/10.1108/01425451211248541 (accessed 6 May 2020).

Rizvi, F. and Lingard, B. (2009) *Globalizing Education Policy*. London: Routledge.

*The fishermen know that the sea is dangerous and the storm terrible, but they have never found these dangers sufficient reason for remaining ashore.*

(Vincent Van Gogh)

Holly Chandler

overleaf: Charisma Andrews

## Chapter 4

# 'You cram these words into mine ears!' The experiences of HE in FE students

### Kate Lavender and Cheryl Reynolds

Students studying for Higher Education qualifications experience Further Education differently than other FE students. In this chapter, we present accounts that illustrate how HE in FE liberates learners, even while it circumscribes them, making them likely to be immeasurably grateful for the opportunities it presents, as they are seething with frustration at the demands and constraints it places upon them. In this, they are like both Ariel and Caliban in their relationship to Prospero in *The Tempest*. Prospero sets his subjects free from prior limitations, even while he tethers them to his tiny kingdom and commands their every action. Shakespeare's masterful portrayal of this conflicted predicament gives us a rich and engaging way to gain fresh insights into the ambiguous, complex, contradictory relationships of HE students within FE settings.

This chapter explores those relationships, using the voices of HE in FE students Matt, Nathan, John, Clare, Carolyn and Donna (Lavender, 2016) 'abstract': The expansion of higher education (HE. Matt (22) is a joiner, studying for a Higher National Diploma in Business. Nathan (26) is an electrician, studying for a Higher National Certificate in Construction Management. John (51), an ex-banker turned mental health support worker is undertaking a Foundation Degree in Health and Social Care. Clare (48), a stay-at-home wife and mother before the untimely death of her husband is undertaking a Foundation Degree in 3D Design. Carolyn (45) is a teaching assistant on a Foundation Degree in Early Years and Donna (38) runs her own cleaning business, while studying a Foundation Degree in Acting Performance.

# Ariel

In an early scene in *The Tempest*, Ariel challenges Prospero to grant her the freedom she has been promised. In this short exchange, we learn a number of important things: that before Prospero arrived, Ariel was gripped close in a pine tree, imprisoned there by the sorceress, Sycorax; that Prospero freed Ariel; that in recompense she promised to serve him for a term of years, at the end of which she would be set free; that Ariel grows impatient of her freedom and reminds Prospero of his promise of a year's abatement of her sentence. Prospero balks at the request. This is a tense exchange, in which we see the battle between a controlling force and a subservient but gifted minion, eager for release. The dynamic will be familiar to many a tutor of HE in FE, which often attracts students of much potential and promise, with curious minds and a zest for learning.

**John:** *I was always in the academic sets. So, you know, at school I did enough to get by without really excelling. Which I probably could have done, but I guess since I've been working, and started learning again, I do push myself to try and be the best I can be. So, my aim on this course is to get a distinction, if I didn't get that you know, I'd be pleased with a pass, but I suppose I'll be disappointed in myself if I don't achieve what I'm capable of. So yeh, a lot of it is driven by my need or desire to get a degree.*

To hold such students in thrall while they gain their rite of passage to other forms of HE or employment stretches FE's potential to its limits. This is one of the joys of teaching HE in FE, which requires teachers to develop expertise, insights and practice. It is also one of the sector's greatest challenges, not least when the qualifications delivered are limited in content, in progression opportunities or in how effectively FE is able to resource them.

There are other important parallels here between Ariel's predicament and that of HE in FE students. Just as Prospero liberates Ariel from the torment of Sycorax's prison, FE can play a vital role in freeing people from the grinding poverty of dead-end, no-pay, low-pay cycles of employment. Just as this freedom comes at the cost to Ariel of a period of servitude, students of FE must serve their term and fulfil FE's requirements before they can be free to move on. Like Ariel, some of these students would rather be elsewhere, describing the atmosphere and ethos of FE as restrictive or a poor fit for their own circumstances and preferences. Their levels of maturity and attitudes to study may appear to be out of step with younger FE students, with whom they often have to share social and study spaces.

**Matt:** *When I was coming to a college rather than a university, I think one of the main things for me was 'oh, there's going to be loads of kids around' sort of thing, and it's all gonna be sort of catered to that, that sort of way. I mean obviously we do have the HE department up here that separates us from the rest ... But I think, yeh I know, from talking to friends and things, that they say 'oh, you're going to College' rather than university. It seems to be, not looked down on as such, but it doesn't seem to be taken as that sort of higher level ... Personally, I like the idea of the whole scholarly research sort of thing ... I kind of feel like if that is how I should be doing it there (in a university), then that is how I should be doing it here (in a college).*

Some students are, however, constrained to work through a HE entry qualification at a FE institution before they can progress to further qualifications.

**Donna:** *You know – a BA looks better on your CV than a diploma or whatever, (laughs) do you know what I mean?*

In identifying a distinction, HE in FE students cite and reinforce the dominant ideology that positions HE as superior to FE, even when they appreciate and enjoy the particular benefits FE confers. This contains something of the conflicted positioning of Ariel towards Prospero, obediently grateful yet with a restive ambition to leave. The ambition and drive of such students means that they possess the compelling quality that resides in Ariel's struggle to acquiesce to a powerful but flawed master and in her desire and potential to apply her considerable abilities in a wider sphere of action, beyond the island. The analogy serves to remind HE in FE practitioners of their duty to stretch these students to the limits of their ability and help them carve a path to contexts where they will be able to develop and exercise their abilities to the full. Letting go of these 'tricksy spirits' can often be bittersweet: 'Why, that's my dainty Ariel! I shall miss thee: But yet thou shalt have freedom: so, so, so' (5.I:94–5).

## Caliban

Others hold more circumscribed aspirations, which can be just as challenging, though in different ways. Caliban is born on the island, which he sees as his sphere and his inheritance. With no desire to leave, the extent of his ambition is to regain dominion of the place, to take a wife and to people the island with his own children. In this, he is like the students who see HE in FE as a means to a material end, a way to acquire the skills and knowledge that they will need to get a good job, to earn a decent living, to raise a family in a secure home. The policy rhetoric around HE in FE echoes this vocational instrumentalism, which assumes students come to FE to learn a profession or a trade and which renders them economically valuable units for the new, global economy, while simultaneously tying students into place by developing the skills needed by local industry and getting them into local employment.

**Nathan:** *Cause you need the paperwork to get a job and money, experience doesn't really count. You need experience, but you need the qualification as well to get your foot in the door.*

This perspective, however, oversimplifies the aspirations of many higher-level vocational students. Just as Caliban seethes with indignation at the menial tasks he is compelled to undertake, many HE in FE students question the conditions under which they labour and bridle at the constraints FE places upon them. Trainee teachers in FE are a prime example. Invariably, teacher education includes critical pedagogy, theories of learning and sociological theory more generally. This is arguably the 'powerful knowledge' posited by Michael Young (2013), providing scope to question how things are and how they ought to be and giving us the means to think 'the not-yet thought' (Bernstein, 2000: 30). Trainee teachers often experience this as 'troublesome knowledge' (Meyer and Land, 2003: 1) and they vociferously question its relevance to their daily lives and to the prosaic struggles in which they have to engage as part of their classroom practice. Like Caliban, they curse it:

> You taught me language, and my profit on 't
> Is, I know how to curse. The red plague rid you
> For learning me your language! (1.2:366–8)

and echo Alonso's cry of frustration:

> You cram these words into mine ears against
> The stomach of my sense. (2.1:102–3)

This is a rational complaint when theory is being served up for theory's sake, or when students are asked to swallow an idea that does not appear to bear any relation to their own practical wisdom or common sense.

**Matt:** *(Reflective practice) It's a dull part of it! I'm having to do a lot more, I think when we was talking about that last time, I was talking about the personal and professional development unit, which was about reflection in that sense, whereas now I've got to a point where I'm having to reflect on my actual work, which I can see is why it's important, … actually no*

*I can't! it's important because it gets my grade up so it's important in that sense, erm ... but I don't particularly find it that useful to reflect on my assignments.*

Moreover, Caliban's complaint speaks to the way in which language shapes, as well as expresses, thought. We can only express something if we have the words. The contested but constrained meanings of words shape what we are able to communicate and hence, who we are able to be. In lamenting the loss of his own language, Caliban laments the loss of a way of speaking and, therefore, of seeing and being, which belonged to him before Prospero began to shape him into somebody else. Yet, we frequently witness ways in which the new ideas and language to which we expose trainee teachers brings about a sea-change in their lives as teachers. It can give them a new way to reach their own students, or to understand the vagaries of their social world. This knowledge allows the questioning of practice and enables the challenge of social inequality that is apparent in educational settings. The salutary lesson here for HE in FE practitioners is well summed up by Freire when he suggested that a democratic and tolerant teacher must:

> first make clear to the kids or the adults that their way of speaking is *as beautiful* as our way of speaking. Second, that they have the right to speak like this. Third, nevertheless, they need to learn the so-called dominant syntax. (LiteracyDotOrg, 1996)

**Nathan:** *It's much more theory-based I suppose, 'cause all my other training has been – you learn something and then you go and do it straight away. Whereas this is more of the theory side of it, like I've got to research things and write about it, as opposed to actually going and building a house and stuff.*

**Donna:** *I can sort of like argue the point with somebody in a proper manner, you know if someone disagrees with whatever and I can say 'well you know, it's x, y and z and this is why I feel like it's x, y and z'. It's sort of like given me that extra boost, whereas I would have just at one time said, 'oh right, if that's how you feel then that's fine'.*

## Shipwrecked voyagers

Everybody on Prospero's island except Caliban and Ariel is shipwrecked there and this too resonates with HE in FE. As we noted above, policymakers are fond of oversimplifying the reasons why people end up in FE and tend to present these reasons as logical, pragmatic choices made in order to fulfil vocational and economic imperatives. The reality is that people end up studying HE in FE for all sorts of complex financial, familial and social reasons. Their trajectories are as likely to entail a difficult voyage through the school system as they are to arise from some catastrophic life event that leaves them stranded in a place where going to university seems a world away. For those we call our *shipwrecked voyagers*, this is emphatically *not* the disaster or the lesser choice that our Ariels may perceive it to be. Studying HE within the intimate, supportive and nurturing world of FE can be exactly what students need to overcome the tempests of the past and to see themselves as students worthy of the time and care invested in them by FE – and ultimately as scholars and graduates.

Be not afeard. The isle is full of noises,

Sounds, and sweet airs that give delight and hurt not. (3.2:129–30)

**Clare:** *I did not think I would be able to achieve what I have actually achieved. Obviously having the dyslexia as well, erm ... that's played a massive part. It's given me the confidence now to actually believe in myself, that maybe I could go on to uni, maybe carry on. Well I've got the thirst for learning now, you know? It's a bit of a bug, yeh I think.*

Similarly, Carolyn spoke about how her FE tutors made her feel valued as an expert in her own field. She said she'd have found the prospect of going to university with 'professors and researchers' daunting, but the College's familiarity made it easy for her to access HE. Nathan, too, felt that the small class sizes in FE were a strength of the College's approach to HE. Based on his friends' and family's experiences of HE, he pictured university HE as typically delivered in lecture theatre to hundreds of students at a time. Consequently, Nathan valued the one-to-one time he was able to spend with his tutors and the interaction that small class sizes facilitated.

## Epilogue

Fiction provides a powerful vehicle for exploring the human condition, experiencing different lives, places and perspectives, and reflecting on choices, ethics and relationships. (Jarvis and Gouthro, 2019: 1)

Debates around the role of FE in society often reduce its complexities to a finite or even binary set of categories for describing learners' motivations and outcomes. By contrast, the analysis we have presented here exploits fiction as a way to explore the human condition anew. Using *The Tempest* as a way of re-examining data and characterizing conflicting voices can help us to revisit how we understand the complexity of characters' positions and dispositions within a complex setting. We argue that it allows the expression of a more nuanced, artful and respectful interpretation of the roles of various actors: a play and not a script, an expressive dance and not merely a sequence of steps.

> Literary communication encompasses a wide range of tropes, including allegory, metaphor and metonymy. What these have in common is that they stretch the meaning of words beyond the literal, and develop language's polysemic properties, so that meaning becomes plastic, expensive and negotiable. (Jarvis and Gouthro 2019: 11)

We offer the powerfully imagined world of *The Tempest* as a way to think again about HE in FE, in all of its richness and intricacy: Ariel, the gifted and impatient minion, full of potential and eager for release; Caliban, the pragmatic but often incurably restive inhabitant, who at times loves and at others deeply resents his master; and the shipwrecked voyagers, who find themselves stranded in FE but then find joy in learning there that leads to a kind of liberation and a new sense of themselves as scholars. We hope others may recognize in these voices their own Ariels, Calibans and shipwrecked voyagers from among their students, and that framing their experiences in these ways helps to reveal these students' complex motivations and outcomes, prefiguring ways to better serve their aims and aspirations.

## References

Bernstein, B. (2000) *Pedagogy, Symbolic Control, and Identity: Theory, research, critique.* Lanham, MD: Rowman and Littlefield.

Jarvis, C. and Gouthro, P. (eds) (2019) *Professional Education with Fiction Media: Imagination for engagement and empathy in learning.* London: Palgrave. Online. https://doi.org/10.1007/978-3-030-17693-8 (accessed 17 February 2020).

Lavender, K. (2016) 'Mature Students, Resistance, and Higher Vocational Education: A multiple case study' (unpublished PhD dissertation). University of Huddersfield. Online. http://eprints.hud.ac.uk/id/eprint/29158/ (accessed 17 February 2020).

LiteracyDotOrg (1996) 'Paulo Freire: An incredible conversation' [Video]. Online. www.youtube.com/watch?v=aFWjnkFypFA (accessed 17 February 2020).

Meyer, J. and Land, R. (2003) *Threshold concepts and troublesome knowledge: Linkages to ways of thinking and practising within the disciplines.* Online. www.dkit.ie/ga/system/files/Threshold_Concepts__and_Troublesome_Knowledge_by_Professor_Ray_Land.pdf (accessed 17 February 2020).

Young, M. (2013) 'Powerful knowledge: An analytically useful concept or just a "sexy sounding term"? A response to John Beck's "Powerful knowledge, esoteric knowledge, curriculum knowledge"'. *Cambridge Journal of Education*, 43 (2), 195–98. Online. https://doi.org/10.1080/0305764X.2013.776356 (accessed 17 February 2020).

*But I don't want comfort. I want God, I want poetry. I want real danger, I want freedom, I want goodness. I want sin.*

(Aldous Huxley)

Adam Loizou

opposite: Hadassah Asieba

*Chapter 5*

# 'Poor worm, thou art infected!': Seduction and colonization in Further Education

*Damien Page*

## Introduction

An island enveloped in artful storms, a product of detritus, pilgrims and marauders washed up on an inhospitable shore, Further Education stands, simultaneously occupied and alive yet relentlessly manufactured as barren and devoid of noble life. A land of artifice and artefact, a landscape of devils and saviours, FE has been colonized and recolonized, fashioned and refashioned. This chapter focuses on the very processes of seduction, the tyranny of novelty and the sorcery of leadership that has tamed a hostile land, that has employed language and love and passion and guile to seduce both savages and the outcasts into their own colonization.

## With rotten lungs

How many beleaguered souls have found themselves tossed on industrial seas and, plucked from the raging waves of unfulfilled existence, been flotsam'd upon colleges with no drowning marks upon them? How many wide-chopp'd rascals cast from the hell of indentur'd servitude, racked with old cramps, washed up on the littered shores of FE? How many have found a refuge within teaching, within a potential paradise of learning, teaching, community? How many souls found promis'd salvation in the solemn temples of professional practice, the cloud capp'd tow'rs of changing lives, the solemn temples of crafted pedagogy? Yet how many didst find the visions of FE melted into air, into thin air, that the promises and potential dissolved, an insubstantial pageant fading into base corporatization and colonized dreams of what was? How many now canst remember the time before they came to their cell? How distant in the dark backward abysm of time the nostalgia of the mythical silver book and trust and autonomy and collegiality? Fie, tis but an apparition. For these shores of devils and saviours are colonized lands, with nary a free soul. At once the magic of visioning, the conjuration of wondrous sights of what could be; at another, the arts of seduction and love; thrice, the lure of intoxication. For the island may breathe upon the jetsam'd most sweetly but it is with rotten lungs intended to make vassals of all.

## Hell is empty

Tomes to fill a multitude of caverns have been writ on the tempestuous force of managerialist aggression within FE. Battered, enleatherned pages filled with tales of destruction, of brutalist principals raising storms to impoverish professionalism, to crush the collectivist ideals of freckled whelps, to grind unions (aside) not honor'd with a human shape and capable of all ill (thunder and lightning) into the dust. Force remains potent within FE, a necessary art to free Caliban from the Sycorax of the past, to free those disproportion'd in manners and shape from pedagogic bedevilment, the torment of past practice that didst make students howl, howls that did penetrate the breasts of an ever-angry inspectorate. Hell is empty and all the devils are within colleges. Little wonder, then, that principals will create direful spectacles to pound those found base and brutal.

Yet let us remember that tempests are not the first acts of colonization. The first acts are not dreadful thunderclaps or Jove's lightning, nor are they cramps, side-stitches or pinches as thick as honeycomb; nay, (enter cherubic spirits bearing a banquet) the first act is love. When Prospero first arrived did he not strok'st and make much of Caliban? Did he not proffer water with berries and teach him how to name the sun and the moon, did he not give him tongue where before was but monstrous barking? Did he not, after all, acknowledge this thing of darkness his? And Caliban, in return, didst love his new master and render his knowledge of the topography of the land, of fresh springs and barrenness. As with Prospero, colonizers do not arrive on the island in a blaze of brimstone scattering a pox. Rather, they arrive, their bold head 'bove the contentious waves, with good arms making lusty strokes, with love. They do not rain down brimstone as an inaugural act. Instead, they adorn with garlands of hope. Not cankers but new visions. Not a plague but empowerment. Not autocracy but distributed leadership. Not power but consent. The promises of FE are varied and trip lightly from the tongue of colonizers who arrive with a most majestic vision to charm even the most foul conspiracy. And they do not always arrive in the guise of a sorcerer portending dire deeds. Sometimes, they come as a Fernando, so goodly that good things will strive to dwell't, a spectacle not dire but wondrous. With a consultative art, natives are seduced, a saviour to free them from the torment of the tyranny of past failures and distant 'membered strife.

## Infecting the worm

Each new secretary of state dropp'd from heaven in the garb of FE promises to bring real change and stay the dark forces of universities (that foul conspiracy that doth suck the very marrow from education coffers), and bring colleges into a new, gleaming land of plenty. And promises are attended by policy shifts to clarify FE (poor wretch that be ignorant of what thou art) to free the sector from torment as would lay upon the damn'd. Colonization, then, arrives in beatific shape, and – rather than raging – seduces, infecting the worm to not seek gratification of its needs but instead to inspire an ever-increasing intensity of desire. For what is the Tempest but a play of desire? Miranda and Ferdinand desire each other; Caliban and Ariel desire freedom; Prospero desires reinstatement; Antonio desires absolute power.

Desire then, is the ultimate colonizer of FE, sprite-like eluding detection, weaving between the wails of subjugation at the tempests of managerialist excess, the savagery of cuts and the sores of new contracts. Desire drives employees towards not just riches and security but inclusion, the entering and remaining within a commodified isle. For Bauman:

> the test they need to pass in order to be admitted to the social prizes they covet demands them to recast themselves as commodities: that is, as products capable of catching the attention and attracting demand and customers. (Bauman, 2007: 6)

Like Caliban, teachers within FE must continually recreate themselves to become the mirr'r of that which is covet'd, to engage in the endless toil of attaining the perfection of employable, seduced by the promise of (and desire for) gratification.

But to conjure a Caliban, desire needs to be frustrated, it must needs remain elusive and unfulfill'd, to seduce the devils into a perpetual promulgation towards the hope of quenching unspeakable organizational desire. Promises must necessarily be broken, visions – most auspicious stars – must be wrought from baseless fabric to seduce the natives into corporate colonization, not through force but through desire. For what is professionalism but the desire for fulfilment? Tis a garb practitioners enrobe, as Prospero doth put on his magic garment for conjuration and Gonzalo doth marvel at his garments new dyed, as fresh as when first put on in Afric. And it is the very gown that frustrates desire, that createth all else an abhorrence to thine eye, that conjures the fearful art of a Diderot effect, that foul source of corporate commodification.

## A gown

(*Patience with your narrator*) Denis Diderot, writing over a hundred years after Shakespeare's death, did scribe an essay entitled: *Regrets in Parting with My Old Dressing Gown*. Beginning in his elegant, immaculately appointed study, Diderot cannot help but spy ought but grimness, so distant it now stands from the jumbled, threadbare – yet happy – room it once was. This direful transmogrification, Diderot ruefully recalls, was conjured by the gift of a dressing gown, an imperious garment that caused him immediately to discard his previous gown, a 'ragged, humble, comfortable old wrapper'. Yet hark, now that his new garb shone in the dingy room, his desk didst of a sudden appear broke and dishevell'd and so a new one was purchased. With the new pair of gown and desk, the tapestries – previously cherished in their dustiness – now chided as threadbare, so were at once replaced in loathness.

Similarly all the other old, worn items – the books, the chairs, the engravings – all antique and rott'n, all gone, cast out from his cell. For the dressing gown had dread power and 'forced everything to conform with its own elegant tone'. Where once was harmony and accord, now was discord and disharmony, as the old rankl'd with the new. While the dusty, broken-down contents were scruffy – a good dullness – by being consistently so, there was, at least, a unity. The refurbishment rendered no comfort; where once was dishevelled completeness, 'all is now discordant. No more coordination, no more unity, no more beauty.' And thus didst he curse that dressing gown that engender'd the ravages of luxury. 'I was once the absolute master of my old robe. I have become the slave of the new one.' All lost! With the introduction – nay, the colonization – of the imperious purple robe, that unity was destroyed by a tempest of novelty that created a dissatisfaction and perpetual replacement in an effort to once again achieve harmony.

Alas, poor Diderot, whose plight doth provide the perfect metaphor for the consumerist society (McCracken, 1990). As consumers we seek a Diderot Unity, (star lights appear) the perfect 'product constellation' of complementary goods. The Diderot Effect (wretch'd garment) describes the tempest of introducing a new, disruptive item, that shatters the constellation, rendering all else unsatisfactory. This is the frustration of desire that pulls us ever more certainly towards a consumptive spiral of purchasing more and more goods to a futile attempt to achieve harmony. But enough: whither FE?

## Prospero's embrace

Are not the teachers o' th' isle desirous of professional constellation? That complement of theory, practice, experience, innovation, that wouldst ensure security, meaning and fulfilment. And is that constellation (a constellation right apt) not knowable? Is the pathway not seen (if thorny)? Yet, the *fulfilment* of that desire would similarly *end* the desire and potentially plunge colleges into the depths of mediocrity, a hell of its own making. Instead, the constellation is disrupted with new, brave utensils. A new vision. A new policy. A new measure. A new Ofsted framework. A new teaching and learning strategy. A new technology (damn'd engine). Each shift, each interloper, each Prospero, each Fernando, each Antonio shatters the whole, destroys the unity, an infinite loss. Each is a new magic gown, adorned, casting vile shade on that which was once there. All is new! And the prior practices and skills and experiences – artisanaly crafted – are rendered antique, threadbare. The new vision (trumpets sound, enter spirits, dancing) engrimes the one that teachers crafted to obsolescence. The new measure of outcomes robs the meaning from meaningfulness.

And so, rather than the force of autocratic tempests enveloping teachers, they are, instead, seduced into the Sisyphean task of perma-creation, of continual commodification and re-commodification, to chase the base spectacle of 'employable', of 'secure', of 'professional'. Desires are frustrated by the new, the old rendered worthless and cast out, things we do not love to look on. Where once was the torment of Sycorax, now is the emancipatory embrace of Prospero. Where once was the tortoise Caliban, now is the beauty of Fernando, a thing divine. Practice is simulacremated. Without the raising of a sword, the disruption of the FE constellation seduces with love, honey'd words to gild the lily, to make frustrated desires sweeter to the tongue. The endless travail, to ever strive for perfection in the reflection of the new – itself oft replaced – seduces the haunted souls to commodify and re-commodify, to continually toil in servility to that which is proffered but never offered.

All is turmoil, all is force, all is autocracy, go the howls. A plague upon the howling! So much attention is paid to the tempest of FE that too little is saved for seduction, the chief means of corporate colonization with colleges. This is not Prospero visiting whelps upon Caliban to achieve obedience;

this is the cherubim words and strokes that made Caliban dissatisfied with what he knew, that fired his desire to become worthy by showing his new master the qualities o' th' isle that he might remain favoured and secure. Not overwhelm'd was Caliban, not beaten, not pox'd; instead seduced, co-opted into his own colonization, first by the love of Prospero, then made tame by the unearthly liquor poured down his throat by Stephano. In the colonization of FE, seduction is far more potent than force.

## Epilogue

Yet what of Caliban once the invaders have left? What does the colonized do without the perpetual frustration their desires? Does the removal of constellation-smiting leave Caliban dancing up to th' chin in the foul lake of professional autonomy that o'stinks his feet? Does he thrash in the foul lake of mediocrity? Perhaps. Or perhaps a new desire emerges. Perhaps the misshapen knave is left to imagine his own visions of an isle made in his own image, one that emerges from the riches under his feet, an isle free from flotsam and jetsam and apparitions that melt into air. Perhaps once the Prosperos and Fernandos and Stephanos and Antonios are guided by some heavenly power out of this fearful country, then, perchance, might Caliban craft a new practice, rooted, substantial, emergent, and meaningful, and make this place Paradise. Ah, perhaps.

*[Exeunt]*

## References

Bauman, Z. (2007) *Consuming life*. Cambridge: Polity Press.

Diderot, D. (1769) 'Regrets for my old dressing gown'. Online www.marxists.org/reference/archive/diderot/1769/regrets.htm (accessed 17 February 2020).

McCracken, G.D. (1990) *Culture and consumption: New approaches to the symbolic character of consumer goods and activities*. Bloomington: Indiana University Press.

*Someday I'll wish upon a star*
*And wake up where the clouds*
*Are far behind me.*
*Where troubles melt like lemon drops*
*Away above the chimney tops,*
*That's where you'll find me.*

(The Wizard of Oz)

Jess Baker

overleaf: Gabriel Fassenfelt

## Chapter 6

# A brave new education

*Eddie Playfair*

## Our storm

*The Tempest* suggests many metaphors for our current condition: the raging storm, utopian hope, dystopian reality, exploitation, the promise of a better life.

We live in tempestuous times with catastrophic climate change, an unsustainable economic system, gross inequalities and the proliferation of injustices. Our social fabric and shared values are everywhere under threat, violent conflict is endemic, and our very survival is in question. In such a storm, resignation and despair can seem like the only possible response. But we cannot afford to give up hope. We may reject many aspects of our world as it is, but if we turn our backs on it, we deny what it could be. More than ever, we need utopian thinking and utopian method.

Sociologist Ruth Levitas describes utopia as 'The expression of the desire for a better way of being or living … braided through human culture [and] better understood as a method than a goal' (Levitas, 2013: xii). For Levitas, the utopian method is an imaginary reconstitution of society that starts with prefigurative practices where different ways of being or doing things are tried out.

As educators, we need to try to describe and understand what it is we face and to engage in creating the conditions for improvement at every level where we have influence. Philosopher Hannah Arendt defined education as 'the point at which we decide whether we love the world enough to assume responsibility for it' (Arendt, 1961: 193). We urgently need to make that decision and assume that responsibility.

Our colleges are navigating tempests that threaten to wreck everything that's best about them. They struggle to stay afloat and chart a course towards a better place. The young people who depend on them also face many obstacles as they steer through the choppy waters of early adulthood.

Often tempests accompany our students to college, tempests that may limit their ability to achieve their goals. Growing up in a fractured society is bad for their health and can threaten their safety. Amid these storms, young people need safe places, life-affirming communities from which to explore and extend the boundaries of their knowledge, where they can build social bonds, learn to resist resignation and, with others, exercise some control over their world. Like the Tempest's 'enchanted isle', college can be a place to be charmed and challenged by what is not yet fully understood, part of the world but also apart from the world.

The education England offers 16–19-year-olds is uniquely narrow and under-resourced. It has no agreed common content or sense of overarching purpose beyond delivering the bare requirements for progression to employment or higher education. Funding is so squeezed that colleges struggle to ensure even the minimum level of provision and have little margin to provide the personal and social development, broadening and enhancement opportunities that more privileged students take for granted. Instead, our students are expected to compete in a zero-sum game of adding value and achieving upward social-mobility based on minimal investment.

## Exploration, decolonization, liberation, transformation

Education entails exploration of new territory. To engage with education is to go in search of what we don't yet know and can't yet do, to understand our potential and our limitations and to discover the liberating power of new ideas and new ways of thinking and doing, individually and collectively. Young people today can feel as though they're running up a down escalator, faster and faster, just to keep-up in the rush towards an uncertain destination. They are expected to show ever more aspiration and commitment, greater skills, more character and grit, and to gain better qualifications merely to stay on the escalator. The system rewards those who succeed first time around; second chances aren't easy to access, and for many there's no safety net. When students falter on the journey, they risk sliding towards precarity and insecurity.

In their journey towards the not-yet-known, students bring who they are and what they already know. They all need to add awareness that there's so much more, and the openness to reach for that so-much-more. What students do at college should be liberating and transformative, nourishing their thirst for understanding and meaning, rather than offering them nothing more than credentials for progression and work. College should give students, as part of their lifelong learning journey, opportunities to engage with knowledge, experience and culture in a wider, more challenging way than was offered at school.

*The Tempest* can yield new perspectives with every reading and it has been reworked as an anti-colonial narrative by a number of writers. Postcolonial readings of *The Tempest* highlight how Prospero's assumption of control and the master-slave power relations he creates on the island colonize the minds of its inhabitants and corrupt and undermine their humanity.

In Kenyan writer Ngũgĩ wa Thiong'o's novel *A Grain of Wheat* (1967), the British district officer is working on a book to be called 'Prospero in Africa'. He starts with a vision of empire as an enlightened multicultural community of equals but is transformed into a torturer by the brutal colonial system he works within. Barbadian poet Kamau Brathwaite's poem '*Caliban*' speaks of the search for a post-colonial identity. The novel *Water with Berries,* by George Lamming, also from Barbados, explores the violent legacy of slavery and colonialism (1971), and in *The Pleasures of Exile*, Lamming returns repeatedly to the themes of *The Tempest* from the perspective of a descendant of both Caliban and Prospero (Lamming, 1960).

Aimé Césaire, the Martiniquan poet, essayist and politician, dedicated his life to exposing the ideology of colonialism and the de-civilizing effects of its associated racism and violence on both oppressor and oppressed. In his retelling of *The Tempest* as '*A Tempest*' (*Une Tempête*), Caliban and Ariel are colonial subjects challenging Prospero's dominance, his lies and sense of entitlement and superiority, and his claim to universal values (Césaire, 2002; French original 1969). Of universals, Césaire wrote: 'I have a different idea of a universal ... rich with all that is particular, rich with all the particulars there are, the deepening of each particular, the co-existence of them all' (Césaire, 1957: 14).

So the play's meanings are constantly being rediscovered and redefined, just as the act of learning requires us to rediscover and redefine what we know. Our students aren't empty vessels; they bring their particular histories and hopes with them and every encounter with others, and what they know should expand rather than narrow their horizons. Education should not set out to reproduce the current social order but help us question and challenge our view of our society and of ourselves. Colleges should be places where we try out new ways of thinking, more critical perspectives, open ourselves to new truths, unravel the strangeness we find around us, and tell richer stories.

So how should education promote the best human values? A genuinely liberating education needs to be based on equality and universal human rights and challenge inequality and oppression. We need to recognize, for example, that definitions of democracy, law, respect and tolerance – sometimes described as British values – are contingent and evolving and are neither permanent nor uniquely British. If we are to decolonize our education, we need to critically examine all claims to universalism and include more of those particulars that are so often left out. We can then build a shared, democratic and inclusive universalism where people can live and work together as equals.

## Another college is possible

Another college is possible, and it should be founded on an agreed public purpose and shared values. While college cannot aspire to be utopia it can be a place where we imagine and discuss utopia, making new connections and expanding our reach and our ambition for ourselves and our world. Starting with the knowns we bring with us, the utopian imagination can help us to dismantle what is given and construct something better. This is the sort of approach described by US educationalists David Tyack and Larry Cuban as 'tinkering towards utopia':

> Utopian thinking can be dismissed as pie-in-the-sky or valued as visionary; tinkering can be condemned as mere incrementalism or praised as a common-sense remedy for everyday problems ... We favour attempts to bring about such improvements by working from the inside out, especially by enlisting the support and skills of teachers as key actors in reform. (Tyack and Cuban, 1995: 1,10)

Rather than merely defending what we have, we need to imagine better colleges where communities can come together to work out, and try out, their own solutions. A place where students, teachers and others can meet and speak and work on terms of equality, democracy and mutual respect. As well as learning about the best that has been thought and said, our students need to acquire the skills to make their own judgements and join the human conversation as equals.

How should we conceive the curriculum for our better college? It should have today's and tomorrow's challenges at its heart, starting from the pressing needs of our students and communities. It should be rooted in an understanding of the past as well as the present, and should equip young people with the analytical and practical tools they will need in the future. It should offer students more time to engage with human culture in greater depth and breadth. It should give them the opportunity to create a masterpiece, their best contribution so far, and to engage with others in the work of citizenship, community care and peace building.

Is this 'such stuff as dreams are made on'? Absolutely. Is it impossible? Absolutely not.

Many of the elements of this better college exist within today's colleges, in the moments when learning comes to life and things suddenly make sense, or when students start to apply what they've learnt unprompted, to shape their own activity and pursue new avenues independently, or when they initiate and engage in reading, research, social action, or campaigning for a purpose of their own choosing.

We need to nurture these opportunities and start building the college of the future around them, even if our current tools and resources are inadequate. The Spanish poet Antonio Machado says: 'there is no path, the path is made by walking' (Machado, 1912). It is up to us to decide which direction to go in and to make our path the best we can.

## The brave new world

We need to be brave enough to loosen our attachment to some of our certainties and ways of doing things, to question and be questioned and to face our own fears in order to be able to hope, dream, experiment and act. But all our bravery, questioning and imagination will be an 'insubstantial pageant' destined to 'melt into air' unless it has some tangible impact on the way we live and shape our world. We need to follow reflection with action, however limited.

Oscar Wilde wrote that 'progress is the realisation of utopias' and 'a map of the world that does not include utopia is not worth even glancing at' (Wilde, 2013: 34). So, what practical tinkering can we engage in to help place our colleges in the same atlas as utopia, if not in utopia itself? On a large scale, political, systemic and institutional reform are certainly necessary. But change can also start on a small scale at the margins and move to the centre. What starts as prefigurative practice can end up at the heart of a college's work.

Here are a few questions that any member of a college community could ask, as a starting point for developing what is on offer in their college:

- How do we introduce our students to a wider range of cultural experiences so as to develop their cultural literacy and critical skills, through reading and discussion groups for example?
- How do we develop a democratic, deliberative approach to educating about major global and local concerns, with students evaluating

evidence, engaging in dialogue, learning to disagree and resolve conflict?

- How do we promote student engagement and representation practices and structures and develop the leadership and advocacy skills to make them effective?
- How do we create a coherent, engaging political literacy programme that teaches students about power, rights and values?
- How do we support and value the production of student masterpieces, through research, performance, creative or community activity?

Students' experience of college should help them reassess their values and the meaning of their lives. They should emerge both wiser and less convinced of their wisdom, aware of both their power and their responsibilities. As well as preparing them for progression and work, we need to see them as citizens, creators and carers, skilled in the democratic habits of participation, representation, leadership and change-making. Colleges can be where these habits are learned and practised. Because they reach into every community and meet such a broad range of educational needs, colleges are uniquely placed to help us to navigate the tempests we encounter, challenge the tyranny of 'no alternatives', engage with the not-yet-known, and become the 'gorgeous palaces' and 'solemn temples' that will help to shape the brave new world we know is possible.

# References

Arendt, H. (1961) *Between Past and Future: Six exercises in political thought.* London: Faber and Faber.

Césaire, A. (1957) *Letter to Maurice Thorez.* Paris: Présence Africaine.

Césaire, A. (2002) *A Tempest.* Trans. Miller, R. New York: TCG Editions.

Lamming G. (1960) *The Pleasures of Exile.* London: Pluto Classics.

Lamming G. (1971) *Water with Berries.* London: Longman Caribbean.

Levitas, R. (2013) *Utopia as Method: The imaginary reconstitution of Society.* London: Palgrave Macmillan.

Machado, A. (1912) 'Campos de Castilla', 'Proverbs' and 'Songs 29', trans. Craige, B.J. In *Selected poems of Antonio Machado* (1979). Baton Rouge: Louisiana State University Press.

Thiong'o, N.W. [as James Ngugi] (1967) *A Grain of Wheat.* London: Heinemann.

Tyack D. and Cuban L. (1995) *Tinkering Toward Utopia: A century of public school reform.* Cambridge, MA: Harvard University Press.

Wilde, O. (2013; original publication 1891) De Profundis and Other Prison Writings. Harmondsworth: Penguin.

*It is only in sorrow bad weather masters us; in joy we face the storm and defy it.*

(Emilia Barr)

*Caliban* – John Hamilton Mortimer

opposite: Aimee-Jay Thompson-White

# Act 2: Introduction

*Lynne Sedgmore*

This section explores how we might achieve FE utopias. A utopia is an imagined community or society that affords its citizens highly desirable or nearly perfect qualities. Utopia focuses on equality in all aspects of the community's civic, political, educational, economic, social and personal domains. How, why and in what form the utopia is achieved varies depending on the nature of the ideology underpinning it. Simon (2016) provides a comprehensive summary:

> Utopianism ... is a means of holding in our mind's eye the possibility of a world free of oppression and domination and charting an ever-closer course towards its shore. Less a blueprint than a direction, Utopia is an ideal against which we can compare our own society – a fiction that can help us understand where we fall short and where we can go from here.

Looking through the lens of Shakespeare's play *The Tempest,* the authors in this section think freely, radically, magically and inspirationally – yet they also flavour their proposed utopias with pragmatism and evidence-based realism to invite and engage the reader. They imagine a better world through utopias in FE and offer radical alternatives.

Amsler explores resisting and moving beyond established norms and 'capitalist profit-seeking' in this time of both metaphorical and meteorological tempests. She offers new ways in FE to re-enchant learning futures with unimaginable (magical) possibilities through the embodied practices of recent resistance movements.

Hafez calls for the forging of a new 'language and practice of pedagogical leadership' so we can dance to a new tune. She calls for decolonizing and imagining a future FE, liberated from the shackles of those who inhabit it. She looks afresh at the nature of governance.

Crowson, Fletcher-Saxon, Jones and Woodrow consider four potential futures for practitioner research across distinct areas of the FE sector. They synthesize these four perspectives to reimagine a research utopia with new rhythms to dance to through drawing upon dialogic methods. Together they dance, weaving new movements and concepts into inspiring reimagined futures.

Cooke and Peutrell promote participatory inclusive notions of citizenship with ESOL teachers (English for Speakers of Other languages) as mediators of citizenship in everyday action, as well as being resisters of dominant discourses. They suggest new possibilities and key principles to underpin participatory, inclusive citizenship education in ESOL.

Bennet, Scott and Wilde establish the need for a brave new world beyond the instrumentalist confines of the vocational curriculum and explicitly question the responsibility we assume teachers have for the subjectivity of their students, both the wild and the free.

Shukie explores how different educational purpose can be co-created within a pedagogical space in which learners create their own realities rather than being imposed upon by a partial, elite and standardizing group of experts. He envisages an FE curriculum steeped in engagement with the world through awe, beauty and poetry rather than compliance.

Beaumont and Wyn-Williams examine the Augar Review and explore the nature of a truly idealized FE space enhanced by the enabling power of an Access to HE Diploma, alongside a deeper understanding of the needs of the mature non-traditional student. They want their students to dance within an HE community where they are not othered, and have gained the confidence, sense of self and academic skills to enable them to learn and integrate successfully.

All these inspiring explorations of FE utopias offer the reader opportunities to engage in progressive thinking and to celebrate a spirit of hope and optimism. They illustrate how important it is to choose who we want to be, to think freely, to be creative, to weave our magic and to create unimaginable possibilities, wherever we may find ourselves. The chapters also include the common three features valuable for creating 'educational real utopias' as articulated by Webb (2016: 433–4). They are, first, *immanent* – grounded in real practices, processes and trends; second, *partial* – in that they eschew totalizing visions in favour of localized exercises of the utopian imagination; third, *processive* – as they don't posit a rational blueprint to which reality must conform but operate rather to highlight prefigurative institutions and practices.

In my 35 years of experience as an FE teacher and leader I've met versions of all the characters in *The Tempest*. Some were the rogues who compete, care only about money and prestige and often bring dishonour onto themselves and the sector. Occasionally they were Machiavellian opportunistic leaders and fools who weren't able to step up to the job as required or who danced subserviently to every passing whim of politicians. Yet mostly I encountered professionals and leaders who, like Prospero, often felt banished, betrayed and unseen, yet remained loyal, true and dedicated to building an FE utopia for students despite the tempests they regularly faced. These were magical and passionate educationalists who came into FE to improve pedagogy and the student experience, and to make the world a better place. These radical thinkers and activists are determined not to accept the outdated or toxic status quo. They are the staff who resist or make possible the confetti of policy endlessly showering down – often without rhyme or reason or steeped in ministerial whim but still expecting immediate responses. They are the many who, like Alonso, support, equip and liberate others, because they choose to. They are the teachers who have learnt to create magic whatever the circumstances – to empower, enchant and prepare our students.

Many students land in FE feeling they have gone through a tempest, maybe failing GCSEs or A levels, needing to learn a vocational skill, undergo an apprenticeship or to reskill, learn English as an additional language, change careers, gain professional qualifications. They may feel alienated from previous formal learning. They find an island of sanity, safety, recognition and comfort in FE. As Prospero liberates the spirits trapped in trees, FE liberates the lives and learning of millions of students. With our magic we transform the lives of those whom the school sector or society has disadvantaged and encourage them to realize their fullest potential.

Reviews, reports and national commissions contain the many attempts to simplify, articulate in a single purpose or capture the essence of FE, not least in the 2019/20 Independent Commission on the College of the Future. Never an easy or definitive task. Why? Because FE is beyond definition through a purely rational or economic lens. It can never exist just for commercial ends: it serves a myriad of economic, community, social and individual needs – and always will. Over many decades FE has developed a blended elixir of services for the betterment of students in whatever space or position in society they find themselves. Every college needs to find its optimal place in the skills ecosystem – locally and nationally – with an offer that is vital, relevant and inspiring to employers, students and the broader community.

I entered FE in 1980 as an optimistic – at times naive – young woman. I was deeply excited by the freedom and possibility I perceived in a sector that felt freer than primary or secondary schools and less elite than universities. As a working-class girl, FE was the perfect fit for me – my island of choice – the educational space in which I could experiment.

I wanted to be of service to those I had left behind on my Stoke-on-Trent council estate, friends who hadn't had the educational chances I enjoyed, so who were less able to find their own hopes, passions, capabilities and dreams. At times it felt magical.

I also experienced periods of disappointment, restriction, confusion and bewilderment. Yet always I experienced FE as a place of possibility. I frequently flirted with a utopian perspective; I am a pathological optimist with huge doses of pragmatism and realism. I have been preoccupied with, and resisted, abuse of power in organizations and have frequently undertaken high-risk radical experiments to explore the benevolent use of power. I've experimented deliberately with co-creating healthy, high-performing and high-spirited FE communities in colleges and national organizations (Fry and Altman, 2013; Sedgmore, 2013).

My most successful attempt was as CEO of the Centre for Excellence in Leadership (CEL), in which I led consciously with four different kinds of power – power over, power with, power for and power through other people, to achieve a balance of power (Torbert, 1991) and radical trust (Healey, 2009). We introduced a range of radical interventions to genuinely distribute power and to co-create a utopian organization through leadership steeped in explicit spirituality, virtues and values; a project to democratize strategy and decision-making to every level and function was implemented.

In my experience, remaining hopeful, utopian and magical within adversity or challenge can foster a positive orientation, an openness, availability and movement towards people, rather than against them. As in *The Tempest*, this can lead to resolution of differences without the need for revenge. The use of magic and professionalism for good ends can foster union and unity and bring about a future that turns out well for everyone.

## References

Fry, L. and Altman, Y. (2013) *Spiritual Leadership in Action: The CEL Story*, Charlotte, NC: Information Age Publishing.

Healey, J. (2009) *Radical Trust: How today's great leaders convert people to partners*. Hoboken, NJ: Wiley.

Sedgmore, L. (2013) 'Illumination of practice through research and inquiry: A spirited leader's path'. In J. Neal (ed.) *Handbook of Faith and Spirituality in the Workplace: Emerging research and practice*. New York: Springer Press, 631–46.

Simon, E. (2016) 'Five Hundred Years of Utopia'. *Jacobin*. Online. www.jacobinmag.com/2016/04/thomas-more-utopia-socialism-progress-wilde/ (accessed 12 February 2020).

Torbert, W. (1991) *The Power of Balance: Transforming Self, Society and Scientific Inquiry.* London: Sage. Online. www.williamrtorbert.com/wp-content/uploads/2013/09/PoB91.pdf (accessed 7 May 2020).

Webb, D. (2016) 'Educational Studies and the Domestication of Utopia'. *British Journal of Educational Studies*, 64 (4), 431–48. Online. https://doi.org/10.1080/00071005.2016.1143085 (accessed 7 May 2020).

*When anxious, uneasy and bad thoughts come, I go to the sea, and the sea drowns them out with its great wide sounds, cleanses me with its noise, and imposes a rhythm upon everything in me that is bewildered and confused.*

(Rainer Maria Rilke)

Teo Forbes

opposite: Eimantas Valiukenas

## Chapter 7

# Learn like witches: Gesturing towards Further Education otherwise

*Sarah Amsler*

It is the year 2020; a workshop for educators in an English town. A group of teachers is finishing a theatre activity based on the final act of Aimé Césaire's play, *A Tempest* (2002; French original 1969). 'Caliban' is walking away from his aging master, singing 'Freedom hi-day!', towards what everyone expects will be greater self-determination on a less-colonized island in the future. The rest of the group poise over giant pieces of paper, ready to imagine alternatives for Further Education, again.

*Enter a woman whom nobody recognizes. She moves like she has different priorities and tends to the four corners of the room before sitting at its centre. She runs her hands across her heart and hair and says she felt called to speak. She wasn't invited.*

'I was expecting Shakespeare', she begins. Everyone looks proud. 'No matter', she continues, 'this island is sinking. Its sisters are burning. This is not a metaphor. It doesn't care what or whose it becomes on its way down, nor what we want it to be. It only wants life and has lost much of that already. It can't abandon us, nor we it, and our entanglement has turned poison because we have lost the capacity to understand what it needs. So, if you can't imagine this reality becoming otherwise, then try like Caliban to remember it that way instead.'

*She stands up, acknowledges the room and leaves. The workshop is irredeemable. The facilitator looks around the room, naked without their normal tactics for carrying on. No one picks up a pen. Now they really don't know how to begin.*

This chapter starts from the eye of a storm for global existence. The earth is warming towards catastrophic temperatures, species are disappearing, lifestyles in the global North continue to demand extraction and death from the South, governments refuse to disinvest from white-man-capitalist development, and education is mass-producing *homo economicus* to staff, manage and secure this mode of existence. Wanting education to transform this situation raises difficult questions. What learning can interrupt the circuits of power that hold such systemic violence in place today? How can educational desire be reoriented away from sustaining harmful social relations that benefit some, and towards confronting the problem that we collectively may have no future at all?

These questions disclose challenging horizons of hope that indicate that 'the continuation of our present institutions and fulfilment of their promised benefits is ... unlikely as the sustainability of our political, economic and ecological systems appear increasingly uncertain' (Stein, 2019: 1). Moreover, as some researchers suggest, 'the way we respond to the crisis is part of the crisis' (Emergence Network, 2019). Aspirations of individual self-realization or social mobility, inclusion, equalization and empowerment within global capitalism rely upon the stability of deeper structures of global injustice. If hope now lies at 'the end of the world as we *know* it', in the promise that other ways of being exist beyond the borders of this reality, then strategies to humanize, democratize or collectivize its existing institutions cannot carry us across (Ferreira Da Silva, 2019).

There are, however, educational projects working in this world's cracks, margins and exteriors that experiment with the alternative thinking and practice of alternatives. Examples include programmes in agroecology, common and cooperative living, 'degrowth', ecological regeneration, food sovereignty, global citizenship education 'otherwise', post-capitalist transition and solidarity economy (often based in the North), and Buen Vivir, post-development, post-extractivism and healing justice (more commonly in the South). While they address the injustices of neoliberal rule and 'austerity', they reach deeper into our psychosocial fabric of existence to contend with the 'modern-colonial imaginary', a centuries-old framework for being that assumes the benevolence (or at least neutrality) of heteropatriarchal, racialized and colonial capitalism, the nation-state, the supremacy of universal reason and the hierarchical classification of human and non-human beings. All of these not only underpin modern oppressions but undermine collective efforts to dismantle them, not least within ourselves.

The vignette that opens this chapter invites us to dive into the impossibility of solving modernity's crises within this framework and to bravely lean towards what is presently unintelligible at its edge. In it, a creative exercise is facilitated to help teacher-activists organize collective action against restructuring, redundancies and exploitative labour contracts at their college – a fictional scenario, but ongoingly real in Britain today. The facilitator uses Césaire's adaptation of William Shakespeare's *The Tempest* in which Caliban signifies both the racialized anti-colonial rebel and the 'proletarian body as a terrain and instrument of resistance to the logic of capitalism' (Federici, 2004: 11).

The uninvited woman, however, suggests that there is more to Caliban than is captured by either characterization. She also observes that the group makes unexamined assumptions: that well-intentioned action will catalyse progressive improvement, that the future of the island itself is guaranteed, and that Caliban can recognize all of his own sources of power. Then, by inviting them to remember reality being otherwise if they cannot imagine it becoming so, she invites them to (re)connect with 'trashed alternatives' (Santos, 2004: 153) and 'exiled capacities' (Jimmy *et al.*, 2019) that could open radically different perspectives on the nature of the problem and its possible solutions. Trashed alternatives exist but are unintelligible within dominant paradigms of recognition, or are regarded as so worthless or dangerous that they are silenced, marginalized or quashed before they can emerge at all. Exiled capacities are humans' abilities to sit with uncomfortable knowledge and unknowable things, feel and respond to collective joy and pain, experience the world without reducing it to concepts (through emotion, sensation, aesthetic experience or movement), sense that people are connected with one another, nonhuman beings and the living planet, and openly interact with non-dominant knowledges and realities.

There is much evidence that reality is plural. Cash Ahenakew, for example, describes how 'Western frames cannot comprehend ... the way indigenous knowledge places animals, plants, and landscapes in the active role of teacher' (Marker, 2004: 106), or how knowing 'literally comes from the ground, above, and beyond, from the wisdoms of continuous metaphysical engagements and familiarity with "all our relations"' (Ahenakew *et al.*, 2014: 222; Ahenakew, 2016: 347). Within science, quantum field physics suggests that matter is energy that exists without becoming a thing, that its possible forms are infinite and that 'nothingness' is actually 'a scene of wild activities' (Barad, 2015: 394).

One consequence of trashing alternatives and exiling the capacity for connection is that we lose touch with realities that contradict and exceed the way things are (Amsler, 2016). Such 'ontological blindness' can produce debilitating feelings of anger, sadness, frustration, resentment and despair, all of which saturate educational politics in Britain today. This situation is critical in FE, for while always potentially a site of transformation it has 'shared its DNA with advanced capitalism and exists largely to provide skills for economic prosperity' (Mycroft, 2018: 95). In this context, the educator-body forms both as a 'receptacle of powers, capacities and resistances that have been developed in a long process of co-evolution with our natural environment, as well as inter-generational practices that have made it a natural limit to exploitation (Federici, 2016), and an invested labour-production machine (Federici, 2004). Here, capitalism has struggled hard to eliminate those qualities of the critical or transformative teacher that are directly 'antagonistic to the requirements of capitalist production' (ibid.: 9). These include capacities for non-transactional, non-hierarchical and non-competitive relationships; compassion and care for economically unproductive bodies, knowledges and places; erotic energies and desires; a perspective on life that 'includes suppressed, silenced, or marginalized realities, as well as emergent and imagined' ones; and a sense of entanglement between oneself, other beings and the earth (Santos, 2014: 157).

The subsumption of such life-generating and life-sustaining capacities into the (re)production of harmful economic and social systems is violent; it hurts. Subsumption is the 'process through which inherent constraints on the labour capacity of a particular section of the economy are overruled, and subordinated to the demands of capital' (Hall and Bowles 2016: 30). This – not just proximate causes like managerialism or its proximate effects like stress – is what makes market-governed educational institutions 'anxiety machines' full of physical and mental suffering (Hall and Bowles, 2016). Responses to this process in institutions – compliance, strategic compliance, survivalism, resistance, subversion, exit and democratic professionalism – are thus often inclined to protect these capacities, hide them within the system, or attempt escape from the institutions (although not necessarily its modern promises) altogether.

Yet what if we could struggle *with* and *through* these capacities rather than fighting *for* them with broken tools? What if we took guidance from our individual and collective bodies rather than being distracted by languages that numb the senses? What if our desires were guided less by the need to know 'what works' – either to sustain or dismantle the system – and more by the 'creative energy for change' that comes from 'those physical, emotional and psychic expressions of what is deepest and strongest and richest within each of us, being shared: the passions of love, in its deepest meanings'? (Lorde, 1984; Rowe, 2012)

These questions are posed in *The Tempest* (and *A Tempest*). Most interpretations of the play centre characters representing masculine colonialism and anti-colonial resistance (Prospero and Caliban) or decolonized, transcultural and multicultural subjectivity (Ariel) (Santos, 2014). Feminist readings, however, highlight the significance of Caliban's mother, a powerful witch named Sycorax, who appears as a voiceless memory throughout the play (see, for example, Cliff 1991; Collard and Dempsey, 2018; Lara, 2007). Interested in the 'absent presence' of this formidable female figure, Silvia Federici asks how the plot might change if its protagonists were not colonizing, colonized and decolonizing men, but a 'damn'd witch' and 'the sisters of the witches who, in the same years of the Conquest, were being burned in Europe at the stake' (Federici, 2004: 107).

How, indeed? Sycorax is represented as a 'racialised, sexualised and witched' memory that anxious and angry men – enemies, yet equally trapped in a common Eurocentric system of domination – use to threaten each other (Lara, 2007: 82). Yet she haunts the play with alterity. She interjects erotic power, empathic communication, a multilayered realism that exceeds what is visible and knowable, knowledge without scientific rationality, and an enchanted relationship with the world in which the cosmos is a living being and matter and spirit are unpredictably intertwined. On one level, Sycorax represents a

> world of female subjects that capitalism had [and still has] to destroy: the heretic, the healer, the disobedient wife, the woman who dared to live alone, the obeha woman who poisoned the master's food and inspired the slave to revolt. (Federici, 2004: 11)

More concretely, she is the 'actual women of color whose historical agency has been negated' (Lara, 2007: 81). On another level, however, she is not a heroic feminist archetype but a metaphor for the paradigm-defiant knowledges of which Caliban knows he has been violently dispossessed. 'You only think [Sycorax] is dead', Caliban tells Prospero:

> because you think the earth itself is dead ... it's so much simpler that way! Dead, you can walk upon it, you can pollute it, you can tread upon it with the steps of the conqueror. I respect the earth, because I know that it is alive, and I know that Sycorax is alive. (Césaire, 2002: 12)

Locating possibility not just in physical strength, cognitive intelligence or political strategy but in the indeterminate vital energy of the natural world within and beyond his own body, Caliban can ask the poisonous creatures of the island to lick him like allies 'with a gentle tongue, like the toad, whose pure drool soothes with sweet dreams the future. For it is for you, for all of us, that I go forth today to face the common enemy' (Césaire, 2002: 52). Here, Caliban demonstrates not only resistance to the colonization of his language, body, relationships and territory, but 'ontological disobedience'. He refuses to reduce reality to what is knowable, visible and intelligible on their terms. By channelling Sycorax's prohibited powers, Caliban invokes forms of intelligence that precede and exceed the colonization of reality and, even *in absentia* and *in potentia*, loosen its stranglehold on the imagination.

Globally, what is at stake is collective metamorphosis and survival. But if this is a modern problem with no modern solutions and if education still invests so much in mastering or resisting the latter, how will we learn to at least make new, 'potentially but not necessarily wiser' mistakes (D'Emilia and Andreotti, 2019)?

Sycorax teaches that the 'otherwise' is already (often absently) present within disenchanted and colonized realities. Simply loosening attachments to and acknowledging entanglements with violent modern systems, we can build 'solidarity with the Sycorax within' (Lara, 2007: 82). Honouring a body's 'natural limit to exploitation' rather than making it more 'resilient' makes tolerating resilience less possible. Experiencing ourselves as parts of an interconnected metabolism that we affect and are affected by makes all forms of separation and complicity with it more painful. What appears at these limits is not alternative 'solutions', but a visceral imperative to exercise the nerves and muscles needed for accessing other realities.

FE has the demonstrable potential to improve (particularly working-class, women's, migrants' and older people's) lives, unlock language and experience, turn 'failures' into experiments (Duckworth and Smith, 2019) and subvert individualism and commodification 'even within repressive contexts' (Petrie, 2015: 6). Yet to keep this tradition alive today also requires interrogating the limits of modern imaginaries of educational and social progress. Educators seeking to challenge anthropocentric, androcentric, capitalocentric, Eurocentric and nationalistic tendencies in teaching and learning might find 'inspiration from witches, subjects who were seen to threaten or destabilize capitalist order and discipline' (Collard and Dempsey, 2018: 1361). This is partly because the enclosure of education belongs to the long history of enclosing knowledge, the body, as the earth that has turned so many women and other counterproductive subjects into voiceless memories. It is also because witchy learning doesn't happen as abstract concept or imagination but through embodied, relational and sensorial experiences that intervene in living reality. By attuning to the Sycoraxes in our needs and desires, we may sharpen our sensitivity to trashed and exiled possibilities that, while real, are unintelligible from within prevailing critical educational identities, paradigms, imaginaries and horizons of hope.

# References

Ahenakew, C., Andreotti, V., Cooper, G. and Hireme, H. (2014) 'Beyond epistemic provincialism: De-provincializing indigenous resistance'. *AlterNative: An International Journal of Indigenous Peoples*, 10 (3): 216–31. Online. https://doi.org/10.1177/117718011401000302 (accessed 7 May 2020).

Ahenakew, C. (2016) 'Grafting indigenous ways of knowing onto non-indigenous ways of being: The (underestimated) challenges of a decolonial imagination'. *International Review of Qualitative Research*, 9 (3): 323–40. Online. https://doi.org/10.1525/irqr.2016.9.3.323 (accessed 7 May 2020).

Amsler S. (2016) Learning hope: An epistemology of possibility for advanced capitalist society. In Dinerstein A. (ed.) *Social Sciences for an Other Politics*. London: Palgrave Macmillan.

Barad, K. (2015) 'Transmaterialities: Trans*/matter/realities and queer political imaginings'. *GLQ: A Journal of Gay and Lesbian Studies*, 21 (2–3): 387–422. Online. https://doi.org/10.1215/10642684-2843239 (accessed 7 May 2020).

Césaire, A. (2002) *A Tempest*. Trans. Miller, R. New York: TCG Editions.

Cliff, M. (1991) 'Caliban's daughter: The tempest and the teapot'. *Frontiers: A Journal of Women's Studies*, 12 (2): 36–51. Online. http://doi.org/10.2307/3346845 (accessed 7 May 2020).

Collard, R.C. and Dempsey, J. (2018) 'Accumulation by difference-making: An anthropocene story, starring witches'. *Gender, Place and Culture*, 25 (9): 1349–64. Online. https://doi.org/10.1080/0966369X.2018.1521385 (accessed 7 May 2020).

D'Emilia, D. and Andreotti, V. (2019) 'Engaged dis-identifications, coLab#2: Radical tenderness me-in-you'. Online. https://decolonialfutures.net/portfolio/radical-tenderness-me-in-you/ (accessed 17 September 2019).

Duckworth, V. and Smith, R. (2019) 'Transforming teaching and learning in further education: Summative report for the University and College Union Transforming Lives and Communities Project'. Online. https://tinyurl.com/ybt38tsk (accessed 14 September 2019).

Emergence Network (2019) 'What if the way we respond to the crisis is part of the crisis?' Online. www.emergencenetwork.org/ (accessed 17 September 2019).

Federici, S. (2004) *Caliban and the Witch: Women, the Body and Primitive Accumulation*. New York: Autonomedia.

Federici, S. (2016) *In Praise of the Dancing Body*. Online. https://abeautifulresistance.org/site/2016/08/22/in-praise-of-the-dancing-body (accessed 26 February 2020).

Ferreira Da Silva, D. (2019) 'An end to "this" world: Denise Ferreira Da Silva interviewed by Susanne Leeb and Kerstin Stakemeier'. *Texte Zur Kunst*, 12 April. Online. www.textezurkunst.de/articles/interview-ferreira-da-silva/ (accessed 13 September 2019).

Hall, R. and Bowles, K. (2016) 'Re-engineering higher education: The subsumption of academic labour and the exploitation of anxiety'. *Workplace: A Journal for Academic Labor*, 28: 30–47. Online. https://doi.org/10.14288/workplace.v0i28.186211 (accessed 7 May 2020).

Jimmy, E., Andreotti, V. and Stein, S. (2019) *Towards Braiding*. n.p. Online. https://decolonialfutures.net/towardsbraiding/ (accessed 17 September 2019).

Lara, I. (2007) 'Beyond Caliban's curses: The decolonial feminist literacy of Sycorax'. *Journal of International Women's Studies*, 9(1): 80–98.

Lorde, A. (1984) 'The uses of the erotic'. In *Sister Outsider: Essays and Speeches*. Trumansburg, NY: Crossing Press.

Marker, M. (2004) 'Theories and disciplines as sites of struggle: The reproduction of colonial dominance through the controlling of knowledge in the academy'. *Canadian Journal of Native Education*, 28 (1/2): 102–10.

Mycroft, L. (2018) 'Unwritten: (Re)imagining FE as social purpose education'. *Research in Post-Compulsory Education*, 23 (1): 94–9. Online. https://doi.org/10.1080/13596748.2018.1420732 (accessed 6 May 2020).

Petrie, J. (2015) 'Crippled Cinderella: How Grimm is Further Education?' CRADLE seminar series, University of Wolverhampton. Online. www.academia.edu/12334635/Crippled_Cinderella_How_Grimm_is_Further_Education (accessed 14 September 2019).

Rowe, A. (2012) 'Erotic pedagogies'. *Journal of Homosexuality*, 59 (7): 1031–56. Online. https://doi.org/10.1080/00918369.2012.699844 (accessed 7 May 2020).

Santos, B.d.S. (2014) *Epistemologies of the South: Justice against Epistemicide*. New York: Routledge. Online. http://unescochair-cbrsr.org/pdf/resource/Epistemologies_of_the_South.pdf (accessed 7 May 2020).

Stein, S. (2019) 'Beyond higher education as we know it: Gesturing towards decolonial horizons of possibility'. *Studies in Philosophy and Education*, 38 (2): 143–61. Online. https://doi.org/10.1007/s11217-018-9622-7 (accessed 7 May 2020).

*Raise your words, not voice. It is rain that grows flowers, not thunder.*

(Rumi)

Hayley Mills

overleaf: Zoe Gardiner

## Chapter 8

# Unlearning Prospero's language: Decolonizing leadership in FE

*Rania Hafez*

*You were born with potential. You were born with goodness and trust. You were born with ideals and dreams. You were born with greatness. You were born with wings. You are not meant for crawling, so don't. You have wings. Learn to use them and fly.*

(Rumi)

 The tempest is passed. The colonizers have left the island. Caliban is at last free to determine his own destiny. How will he rule this realm he finds himself in charge of? What principles will he draw on to govern his new world? Caliban had only Prospero as an example. Will he emulate him? He once bemoaned his master's impact on him: 'You taught me language, and my profit on 't / I know how to curse. The red plague rid you / For learning me your language!'(1.2:368)

As we imagine a future Further Education liberated from its shackles, and liberating to those who inhabit it, we must look afresh at governance and leadership that eschew past practices and create new principles to govern our utopia, otherwise we will be condemned to repeat the past. But how do we construct what we do not yet know? Where can we find the building blocks for our new FE?

This chapter uses Cultural Theory (Thompson, 2008) to survey the current FE landscape and scope a potential new one. Cultural Theory creates a typology of five forms of organization – egalitarianism, fatalism, individualism, hierarchy, and autonomy – which each serve as an analytic tool in the examination of organizational cultures. It is the role and position we occupy in an organization that moulds our perceptions and actions.

This chapter sets out to explain how we must unlearn the language that has kept FE in servitude and how, unless it is fundamentally altered, it will condemn us to recreate Prospero's world. Drawing on ongoing work with existing and would-be FE leaders undertaking postgraduate study, it describes the decolonizing process they experience as they critically examine their beliefs and practices and seek to formulate a different model of pedagogical leadership. As they look to principles of liberation pedagogy and community philosophy such as *Ubuntu* (Ncube, 2010), we seek to articulate a new language with ancient roots in our collective memory.

## Learning from the past

Unlearning is the most difficult part of learning. Caliban, who only knows what his master taught him, will undoubtedly find it difficult to unravel his learning and start to weave new understandings. To do so, he must look within himself and his island to a time before Prospero's arrival. I always start by taking my students back to a time when FE was different to what they have become accustomed to. It's remarkable how little those currently leading the sector know about its history.

FE's early nineteenth century roots lie with the establishment of the Mechanics' Institutes (Turner, 1980) at a time when education was a conduit for working class emancipation. The aim of this education was to provide workers with powerful knowledge such as science and the liberal arts that until then were the preserve of the privileged few. Many of these mechanics' institutes would evolve into colleges, others into universities. Although some were controlled by well-meaning industrialists, the Prosperos of their time, several colleges came about through the efforts of radical labour and were a place of intellectual evolution and political transformation, where a collective consciousness was born and flourished (Turner, 1980). Young FE leaders I teach are invariably astonished to learn of the agency of both teachers and learners in FE's history.

If we superimpose the cultural theory model outlined by Thompson to examine the FE terrain past and present, we can see that FE has always involved a tussle between various interest groups.

The hierarchists, who established institutes with the purpose of controlling the workers, still hold sway, their philosophies having morphed into the current managerialism that plagues the sector. The philanthropic industrialists who endowed the original mechanics' institutes have become the individualist market actors who favour what they may refer to as talent and skills. Whereas the radical workers, whose successes were ultimately limited, are the egalitarians who strove for social justice and equity and who still reside in the very DNA of teaching and learning in FE. The evolving terrain of the sector from the nineteenth century to the present reflects the ongoing scrimmage between these groups, with the wider population as the fatalists, either ignorant of FE or unconcerned with its fate, while the teachers and tutors of the present subvert the system from within; Dancing Princesses biding their time in Trojan Horses (Hafez, 2017), a form of underground leadership waiting to emerge.

Cultural Theory posits that dynamic instability can allow for a new balanced order to emerge. The neoliberal regime that has fractured FE may be the tempest that offers us the opportunity to finally reshape the terrain. But first we need our FE Calibans to break out of their internalized oppression. This is the starting point for our future FE, reclaiming its old emancipatory mission, and giving voice once again to its staff and students. It is from the narratives of those who teach and learn within FE that the new language and practice of leadership and governance will be forged.

## Unlearning the present

> In all such cases of colonial conquest, language was meant to complete what the sword had started; do to the mind what the sword had done to the body. (Ngũgĩ wa Thiong'o, 2017).

The current institutional architecture of FE has been set firmly in the hierarchists' mode. Policies of marketization have restricted funding, imposed a strictly transactional target culture, and pushed colleges into mergers to become quasi conglomerates. An instrumentalist managerialist bureaucratic structure permeates colleges, with most teachers and students unaware of the times when they had power and agency (Ball, 2008). Even leaders and managers seem to labour under an acquired amnesia, induced by a necessity to adopt a performative approach.

We see this most starkly in the language of management in FE, which has been transposed from the market model. Teachers' professional autonomy has been subjugated, where they work under supervision of a line manager, a term borrowed directly from the factory floor, to deliver a uniform standardized programme, to achieve predetermined outcomes, known as KPIs (Key Performance Indicators). Language defines us, and if we construct the teaching profession in transactional terms, we reduce it to something more equivalent to a service industry as opposed to learning institutions.

Although the language of performativity and managerialism in FE gives the semblance of order, it belies a paucity of pedagogical principles and knowledge. When my students attempt to analyse educational quality, they face a tangible dilemma, as they find it exceedingly challenging to think outside the terms that have colonized their minds. 'Unequal and unjust systems are located in banal, everyday choices not to think critically, to be comfortable, and to go along with current majority choices' (Arendt, 1958: 5).

The MA leadership course creates a new semantic space where they are reacquainted with principles of knowledge and practice they had known and experienced earlier in their careers, principles and values they struggle to reconcile with the managerial regiment they currently live by. Slowly they begin to articulate a new discourse of leadership that supports pedagogical agency emanating from the classroom but extending beyond it.

Foucault remarked that dominant discourses produce knowledge and meaning and lead to 'practices that systematically form the objects of which they speak' (Foucault, 1972: 49). The current FE discourse is deeply entrenched in both minds and practices, reproducing power structures, creating the rules and criteria that have legitimized the emasculation of teachers and the reduction of knowledge to a commodity. To rebuild our new FE we must first dismantle the dialectal edifice that holds up the current structures and replace it with the language of a liberated and liberating education.

Paulo Freire (1970) wrote of the emancipatory power of education when it emanates from the pedagogy and the language of the oppressed, but that necessitated teachers who recognized the oppression and worked from its location to start the pedagogical dialogue. We have a system that has long mirrored the language and mindset of those in power and has produced knowledge that bound teachers and students alike to notions of incompetence and limited ability. This colonial process has pitted prescriptive neoliberal bureaucracy against emancipatory pedagogy, as described in the seminal book by Ngũgĩ wa Thiong'o, *Decolonising the Mind*:

> Education, far from giving people the confidence in their ability and capacities to overcome obstacles or to become masters of the laws governing external nature as human beings, tends to make them feel their inadequacies, their weaknesses and their incapacities in the face of reality; and their inability to do anything about the conditions governing their lives. They become more and more alienated from themselves and from their natural and social environment. (Thiong'o, 1986: 56)

Ngũgĩ wa Thiong'o's words ring very true of both the content and structure of FE. The alienation of students from the curriculum, teachers from sources of knowledge and leaders from both teachers and students, is starker than ever. The princesses in FE are in danger of forgetting how to dance. So how can we learn to play a different tune?

## Beyond language

Creating our new dialectic, we need to look beyond the hackneyed leadership models in the field of organizational leadership and management, and source an alternative rooted in emancipatory and ethical values. We need to delve back into the heart and soul of teaching and learning in FE to source our new vocabulary. The building blocks for our new FE are to be found in pedagogy and organization.

Pedagogy is essentially about knowledge – its construction, its legitimacy, who defines it and who controls access to it. The current orthodoxy speaks of taught knowledge as a commodity, measured by assessment, sold in the form of qualifications, anchored firmly to employment and employability. This is the language we need to challenge and replace. The debate has already started in the first two books of this trilogy; we need to take it further.

Our new FE will be a bastion for powerful knowledge (Young *et al.*, 2014), where great canons are shared with students, with the firm belief that they are legitimate heirs to that knowledge. And our FE will also be a place of unfettered pedagogical dialogue, where knowledge is co-created by students and teachers, rooted in values of intellectual flourishing, equity, and future possibilities.

This will require us to rethink what we mean by quality in teaching and learning, challenging the hegemony of Ofsted orthodoxy that seems to change periodically, to push an external perspective on what makes for good teaching and learning. We need to shift that to building the autonomy of the individual teacher as the pedagogical authority (Hafez, 2016).

Beyond the classroom, we need to look afresh at how to build organizational structures. I don't wish to speak of management structures and competitive advantage; this is the old language of hierarchy and division. I propose instead that we move to thinking in terms of networks of connectivity. I am using this term to mean the networks within an FE institution and between the institutions that make up the wider lifelong-learning sector. How do we formulate teams to work on various aspects of creating and sustaining FE? The core of that would be an ethical, equitable and communal approach to organization, where teachers are at the heart of the networks and students are invited in as co-scholars while they are there. This will be based on hedonic solidarity (Smith and Jenks, 2018). The hedonic structure is inherently equitable, eliminating the fear from hierarchical competition and encouraging creativity. Hedonic organization allows us to be 'more free to form a network of personal relations that typically offer mutual support. Then we can give free reign to our intelligence, our creativity ... because attention [is freed from] self-protective needs and can be used to explore ... [and] process information in quite different ways' (Smith and Jenks, 2018: 114).

There are many ways we can construct our hedonic education collective; one I would like to propose is *Ubuntu*.

## *Ubuntu* and the philosophy of communal leadership

> There are four cardinal principles which are derived from the values of any African community ... Morality, Interdependence, Spirit of Man and Totality. (Nzimakwe, 2014: 37)

*Ubuntu* is an African philosophy of communal leadership (Ncube, 2010). It is a term that derives from the South African Bantu Nguni language and means humanness: 'It is a way of life and stresses the importance of community, solidarity, sharing and caring' (Nzimakwe, 2014: 30).

As a philosophy of ethical leadership, *Ubuntu* puts the emphasis on communal solidarity within a humanistic network, while recognizing the importance of individuals in their diversity. As a postcolonial approach, it recognizes the inequities inherited from colonial structures and discourses and seeks to replace them with a hedonic connection based on dignity, mutual regard, reciprocity and responsiveness. As an approach to conceptualizing leadership and governance, *Ubuntu* is yet to break into the current canon of management theories – unsurprising given the hegemony of the agonic discourse of markets and hierarchies. Yet with its roots deep in African precolonial thought, it ought to claim a place among critical frameworks for educational organization.

An *Ubuntu* approach to leadership in FE means fostering networks of connectedness while recognizing and valuing what every individual brings to the collective. It encourages autonomy, not in a self-regarding every-person-to- themselves way, but by giving every individual both voice to contribute to the group, and responsibility to take their rightful place in the collective. *Ubuntu* does not assign preferential positions within a group, all parts of the institution and sector are equally valued. Neither is this a lip-service ethos, but a blueprint for a practical structure where staff and students organize in interactive units and decisions are taken collectively with a view to the interests of individuals, groups and the collective.

As for knowledge, *Ubuntu* recognizes the wisdom of history and culture. FE's history thus becomes the foundation that defines our values of powerful knowledge and intellectual empowerment. The canon is no longer divided between vocational or academic but embraced in its totality as knowledge to be passed on, built upon and co-created.

## Conclusion

In an MA class debating what makes for authentic leadership, my students raised the problem of congruence between the ideals they espoused as teachers early in their career, and the more corporate standards they now feel compelled to adopt as leaders and managers. I asked them: how can they reclaim their fundamental values and subsume them into their leadership roles? They're still working on finding the answer.

*Ubuntu* may be a model we can adapt, but it need not be another orthodoxy. What matters is that we return to the moral purpose of FE and uphold the imperative of unfettered access to powerful knowledge for all. Only when the authentic voice of FE is allowed to guide us, will we find the way to our education utopia. In the post-tempest FE, every teacher, every tutor, every student is a leader. Caliban is the island and every creature within it.

## References

Arednt, H. (1958) *The Human Condition*. Chicago: Chicago University Press.

Ball, S. (2008) *The Education Debate*. Bristol: Policy Press.

Foucault, M. (1972) *The Archaeology of Knowledge:* Trans. A.M. Sheridan Smith. New York: Pantheon Books.

Freire, P. (1970) *Pedagogy of the Oppressed*. Trans. M.B. Ramos. New York: Continuum Books.

Hafez, R. (2016) 'Professionalism without autonomy' in Hayes, D. and Marshall, T. (eds.) *The Role of the Teacher Today*, Derby: SCETT, 36–40. Online. https://derby.openrepository.com/handle/10545/621919 (accessed 27 July 2020).

Hafez, R. (2017) 'Inside the Trojan horse: Educating teachers for leadership'. In M. Daley, K. Orr and J. Petrie (eds), *The Principal: Power and Professionalism in Further Education*. London: Trentham Books, 171–6.

Ncube, L. (2010) 'Ubuntu: A transformative leadership philosophy'. *Journal of Leadership Studies*, 4 (3), 77–82. Online. https://doi.org/10.1002/jls.20182 (accessed 7 May 2020).

Nzimakwe, T.I. (2014) 'Practising Ubuntu and leadership for good governance: The South African and continental dialogue'. *African Journal of Public Affairs*, 7 (4), 30–41. Online. https://repository.up.ac.za/handle/2263/58143 (accessed 7 May 2020).

Smith, J. and Jenks, C. (2018) *Sociology and Human Ecology: Complexity and post-humanist perspectives*. Abingdon: Routledge.

Thiong'o, N.W. (1986) *Decolonising the Mind: The politics of language in African literature*. London: Currey.

Thiong'o, N.W. (2017) 'Decolonise the mind: Secure the base'. Lecture given at the University of the Witwatersrand, Johannesburg. Online. www.iol.co.za/news/opinion/decolonise-the-mind-secure-the-base-8051134 (accessed 7 May 2020).

Thompson, M. (2008) *Organising and Disorganising: A dynamic and non-linear theory of institutional emergence and its implications*. Charmouth, Dorset: Triarchy Press.

Turner, C.M. (1980) 'Politics in Mechanics' Institutes 1820–1850: A study in conflict', PhD dissertation, Leicester University. Online. http://hdl.handle.net/2381/35680 (accessed 11 September 2019).

Young M., Lambert, D., Roberts, C. and Roberts, M. (2014) *Knowledge and the Future School: Curriculum and social justice*. London: Bloomsbury.

*Now that it's raining more than ever*
*Know that we'll still have each other*
*You can stand under my umbrella*

(Rihanna)

Kyana Veiga

opposite: Lawrence Fleming

*Chapter 9*

# Voices of the isle: Towards a research utopia for FE

*Sarah-Jane Crowson, Jo Fletcher-Saxon, Samantha Jones and Amy Woodrow*

This chapter shares the perspectives of practitioners from the Further Education (FE) sector, including College Higher Education (CHE) and Sixth Form Colleges (SFC). Crucially, these perspectives are diverse and sometimes dissonant. Taken together, they present a powerful argument that FE voices, though rarely heard, are complex and, perhaps because of their diversity, have valuable insights to offer.

We open with a discussion of the tensions between FE lecturers and leaders in creating the space, agency and harmony to conduct small-scale practitioner research. This is followed by an argument that the inclusion of data from small projects alongside larger data sets creates more nuanced decision-making. Subsequently, from a college leader's perspective, a more agentic view of the practitioner-researcher is developed to argue for the facilitation and dissemination of this work between institutions and agencies. We close with an exploration of the potential for small-scale research projects to enable creative problem-seeking and problem-solving, and a wider utopian vision for FE research.

## 'The isle is full of noises' (Amy, FE)

Caliban's observation that the isle is full of noises, is a fitting metaphor for my experiences of research in a large general FE college. The isle is full of noises, but the instruments are playing different tunes, driven by different agendas and policy. From my perspective, practitioner inquiry provides the opportunity to acquire new knowledge or problem solve. Those undertaking projects will develop a greater understanding of their topic as they link theory to practice. This can lead to improved outcomes for students and imbue the researcher with high levels of motivation, a sense of satisfaction and the feeling that they have contributed to research or practice. As a highly effective CPD tool, research allows the teacher to reflect on their own practice, an essential skill in the ever-changing FE landscape.

I organized a ResearchMeet event, a space designed to bring together FE practitioner-researchers, which revealed that many of the college workforce were involved in research projects, as part of their initial teacher education or postgraduate qualifications. Interestingly, a high proportion of these projects were undertaken by staff in support occupations and were completed almost in secret. As a Learning and Development Coach, I believe that work should be shared and celebrated, and, if appropriate, disseminated among the workforce. By being research-active, practitioners are demonstrating their commitment to improvement and dedication to their profession.

The college leadership team see the value of research-active employees, but there is still a long way to go. Arguably the fear of Ofsted and a done-to culture is preventing action. External instruments are all making noise yet playing different tunes – as Eric Morecambe once told Andre Previn: 'I'm playing all the right notes, but not necessarily in the right order' (The *Morecambe and Wise Show*, 1971). Currently, the college is focused on an assumed upcoming inspection and a drive to improve the quality of teaching. Leaders need to make links between practitioner-research activity and Ofsted's new Education Inspection Framework that assesses the pedagogical knowledge of practitioners.

Research has the potential to provide a sense of autonomy and control of practice, but there is a feeling of fear. Employees, from the top down, are scared to take risks in light of the threat of job losses or a drop in student achievement rates if things go wrong. Practitioners and leaders alike need to be braver, recognize that 100 per cent compliance is not necessarily a good thing. We need to have the confidence to test new strategies and theories and think for ourselves. If we're brave, we can set our own pathway and follow it regardless of what other people think. We may get a great result and encourage our invisible research voices to be fully rounded characters on our FE isle.

## 'Every fertile inch o' th' island' (Sam, FE and CHE)

Caliban is living on the island when Prospero arrives. Prospero claims the island for himself and begins to erode Caliban's agency and power, forcing him into servitude. Caliban, the native, speaks of the 'voices of the isle' who open the clouds and 'show riches'. One set of rich voices that is arguably unheard amid the clamour for data and compliance within the sector at present is that of teachers.

The measure of research presently used by government bodies is the nationally generated data that demonstrates the effectiveness of the work of the FE sector. Practitioner-research rarely achieves this. However, as a supervisor of research within teacher education and more widely across a college, I see the practical and reflective practice of teachers, and their curriculum develops from these practitioner-led, small-scale research projects. I have seen teachers conduct action research that draws upon the findings of larger research projects, often undertaken by previous inhabitants or visitors to the island, which develops careers guidance practice for students with autism, and introduced breakfast clubs in pupil-referral units to develop social skills. Very laudable, very small scale, but also contextually relevant and, if applied correctly, potentially useful for developing knowledge and the FE island itself.

The first question I pose for the future of practitioner-research touches on accessibility. What if this small-scale research, complete with details of the larger projects it drew on, were stored and searchable? The second question looks to challenge governmental bodies' definition of what constitutes good research. What if the only work stored was that which met the college's own measure of research: a joint endeavour by academics and senior leaders designed to ensure that the knowledge stored would reflect the potential of the island and have appropriate rigour? What impact would answering these questions have on subsequent projects and management decision-making?

Imagine the scene: a department is choosing an awarding body and each has different assessment pathways. The team accesses the practitioner-research database and is able to access studies on both their subject and the different assessment methods. Or, if financial pressures force the senior management team to decide which one of two initiatives to cut, they search the database to find work around both areas. They consequently make different types of decisions – that are informed by college practice, along with other forms of data, not solely that which measures a narrow range of metrics.

In this future the research of the practitioner is enmeshed in the development of the college. In order to understand the potential riches and fertility of the island, all voices will need to be heard.

## 'O brave new world' (Jo, SFC)

Introducing a research culture into the life of a college can leave one feeling all at sea. The notion of a research culture, although gaining much attention and traction among FE edu-gurus, is not the classroom reality of most sixth-form teachers. These are teachers who, I might add, get excellent results – without necessarily reading the outputs of research schools, bodies and universities. So, what's the point? As a senior leader, my driving force to pursue this voyage was my individual conviction. It was about offering colleagues an opportunity to embody agency in their professional development, rather than being limited to passive attendance at college-prescribed continuous professional development (CPD) sessions.

Sycorax, Caliban's exiled mother, lacked choice and agency over her future. Sixth form colleges as a subset of FE have been forced into change through area reviews. Some chose to stay as individual islands, whereas others (including my home college), opted to become academies – perhaps forming an archipelago of new islands. The rhetoric underpinning academization often includes references to the benefits of the wider grouping, working together on CPD. This connected landscape must be called upon to inform, support and contribute to a culture of research that should sustain and nourish post-16 learning.

We're at sea as far as research culture in SFCs is concerned. Discovering that other SFCs are engaged in formally developing research engagement I feel the way Caliban must have felt on seeing other people on the island. Research active institutions often have no idea of each other's existence until the intervention of fortune, fate, or a chance meeting. Then, the rhizome develops, ripples are generated, and changes may occur. What *is* clear is that the SFCs engaged in research activity are largely dipping their toes in other people's waters rather than owning their own research areas. Examples might include hosting conferences organized by external organizations, or participating in SFC leadership programmes that have research projects within them. These approaches, however, make it more difficult for individual waves of activity to form a tidal wave together.

My vision for the future of research in SFCs is for an established (action) research programme to be created and articulated as a celebrated and well supported arm of the CPD on offer in SFCs. Rather than individual islands of activity, I would suggest the need for a systemic cross-sectoral response to research activity that is supported and disseminated by bodies associated with SFCs. However, support need not come only from sector-specific bodies and can involve collaboration with other subsects of FE and Higher Education Institutions (HEIs). Thus, SFC teachers might be redefined as both academics and professional experts, as much engaged in their subject as their practice. Therefore, as members of a recognized, wider archipelago that includes FE, CHE and HEIs, an ingrained habit of passive participation in CPD might be challenged, and replaced with a research culture that is nourished and enabled to have impact across this seascape.

## 'When I waked, I cried to dream again' (Sarah-Jane, CHE)

Postcolonial readings and retellings of *The Tempest* suggest that the island is an unseen character, its voices hint of a past for the island before the arrival of Sycorax and, later, its appropriation by Prospero (Ridge, 2016: 231). This reading of place as character relates to post-humanist understandings of our world and object-oriented ontologies (Harman, 2018), which argue that non-human objects have as much cultural and social importance as humans do in our meaning-making.

Centring the island hints at future potentials for an unruly place-based FE research landscape no longer in thrall to policy, or the magic of Prospero; no longer dismissive of Caliban – perhaps creating agency from dissonance, messiness and its place-based nature. We must embrace critical, radically creative solutions to global problems if we are to sustain ourselves. I would argue that such solutions are as likely to germinate in smaller scale, low-stakes projects as in formal, highly articulated, well-funded initiatives. Practitioner research is untidy, iterative and rooted in practice – this leads to valid critiques of it as disharmonious. However, it is in this dissonant openness that creative ideas might flourish.

It is worth considering how smaller, place-based research might not only provide creative solutions to local problems but be recontextualized to have value in different places. Therefore, in my vision of future FE, practitioner-research projects hold social and cultural capital for the Higher Education Institution (HEI) – Prospero and Caliban work with the Island rather than inhabiting it as a transient space to be colonized. Consequently, the full potential of small-scale projects might be used to problem-seek and problem-solve in the wider landscape.

Place counts. It's easy for the practitioner-researcher in a small town to consider that their possible project might not be feasible because much existing research has already taken place. But it's worth asking: has a project designed to improve understanding of this problem been carried out in that space and with those students before? Practitioner-research projects can also support community social action and individual empowerment – individuals or small groups are given agency to inquire into highly context-specific issues that are meaningful to them. Action research is holistic rather than competitive.

In my imaginary future, the particular practice and knowledge of FE teacher-researchers are valued as a combination of rare and fragile creative skill sets; the sounds from the isle are not considered as unimportant or as a threat to established hierarchies but are recognized as different voices and respected as such. So, rather than make front-line practitioner-research unseen because of its scale or complexities, let us instead recognize its powerful potential; consider how practice-based, place-based creative thinking might support the wider educational ecosystem.

## Conclusion

In our shared future imagining of practitioner-research in FE, we remove the fear from the practitioners owning and developing practice. At an institutional level we see active, dialogic practitioner-research CPD events offered as one alternative to training days. In this model, practitioners have agency to problem-seek and problem-solve, and to develop their personal praxis. Within the uncontrollable and exciting messiness – the complexities – of practice there also exist moments of potential for creative problem-solving with students. Indeed, rather than being transient, mysterious and perceived as largely binary (either full of delight or full of discord) the richness of practitioner and other voices might be made accessible and searchable, alongside related key literature, to enable critical, contextualized readings of small, individual projects.

At a sector level, the research should embrace the diversity of contexts on the island and encourage a collaborative and networked approach to supporting practitioner research within the SFC and the FEC, echoing the call for collaborative practice in *The Principal* (Crawley, in Daley, Orr and Petrie, 2017). This requires support and respect from professional bodies associated with both SFC and FEC. Thus, the isle is no longer isolated, but part of an archipelago of research practice, within which its particular voice can be critically addressed and understood by institutional and sector leaders as part of a wider collaboration.

In our utopian future, the creative potential of these smaller, localized projects is recognized and utilized by institutions. They are afforded respect by sector institutions through the creation of a body of knowledge that is used to inform practice and policy. Thus, we present a future focused on the critical awareness and promotion of agency for the individual practitioner, and the development of the sector and its institutions as a whole.

# References

Crawley, J. (2017) 'Principalities of people: Destabilizing the prince's power through acts of connection'. In Daley, M., Orr, K. and Petrie, J. (eds), *The Principal: Power and professionalism in FE*. London: Trentham Books.

Harman, G. (2018) *Object-oriented Ontology: A new theory of everything*. Harmondsworth: Pelican.

'The Morecambe and Wise Christmas Show' (1971) Broadcast 25 December. London: BBC Television.

Ridge, K. (2016) '"This Island's Mine": Ownership of the island in *The Tempest'*. *Studies in Ethnicity and Nationalism*, 16 (2), 231–45. Online. https://doi.org/10.1111/sena.12189 (accessed 7 May 2020).

*Scaramouche, Scaramouche, will you do the Fandango*
*Thunderbolt and lightning, very, very frightening …*

(Queen)

Gabi Mind

opposite: Bronek Kutereba

*Chapter 10*

# 'You taught me language.' Educating Caliban: Brokering citizenship in ESOL

*Rob Peutrell and Melanie Cooke*

## Introduction

Citizenship is a significant issue in the UK today. Although centred on immigration, its many concerns include: sovereignty and national security; the real or imagined tensions between migrant and established (white, British) communities; identity and language. Language testing for migrants seeking residency or citizenship, along with the common (mis) perception that migrants aren't interested in learning English has reaffirmed the status of the language as a key marker of national belonging. ESOL (English for Speakers of Other Languages) has consequently found itself at the centre of policy discourse as the means by which migrant-outsiders can acquire the language and cultural knowledge they need to integrate into UK society. In the process, multilingualism has been stigmatized as a measure of lost cohesion and a risk to national well-being.

This chapter is about ESOL and citizenship learning and draws on our recent edited collection, *Brokering Britain, Educating Citizens* (Cooke and Peutrell, 2019). The collection is framed by two simple arguments: first, ideas of citizenship are implicit in ESOL; second, ESOL teachers broker or mediate citizenship discourses through their pedagogy and professional identities. As brokers, ESOL teachers are not policy ciphers, but have agency (albeit conditioned) to decide whether and how to resist, accommodate or implement citizenship policy mandates. This agency means that ESOL can be a site not only for the transmission of prescribed ideas of citizenship, but also for the formation of new discourses and configurations of citizenship.

We discuss citizenship and brokering below. In the discussion, we introduce the notions of *discitizenship* and *acts of citizenship*, which we illustrate with reference to two contrasting representations of Caliban – the colonized Caliban, seen through the eyes of Prospero's daughter Miranda in Shakespeare's *The Tempest* (Lindley, 2002), and Caliban reimagined in Aimé Césaire's anticolonial version of the play (2002; French original 1969). If recent policy and public debate are the immediate setting for thinking about ESOL and citizenship, the Caliban metaphor reminds us of a much longer history. *The Tempest* has been widely read as a colonialist text (Lindley, 2002); a colonial imaginary still shapes popular and political attitudes towards citizenship, migration and language.

In the original Caliban, we see the projection of colonial fantasies and fears: fantasies of the strange, but also fear of strangers and of the uncertainty their presence is felt to portend. Arguably, ESOL policy reflects a desire to assuage these fears by making ESOL a 'technology for domesticating the Other' into a prescribed idea of nation (Luke, 2004: 28). This view of ESOL is not uncontested, however. Within the sector, there are practitioners and researchers trying to promote participatory and emergent ideas of citizenship against the prescriptive grain of policy and public discourse. Their initiatives show the possibility of an ESOL that embodies the ideals of democratic – and (apropos Caliban) decolonized – citizenship learning. We discuss some examples below – but first, let's look at citizenship itself.

## Citizenship

Citizenship concerns the relationships between individuals, communities and the state within a political community: in modern times, the nation-state. Citizenship is also a field of struggle, an argument over the nature of that community and the relationships that constitute it: what is a citizen? What rights and responsibilities do citizens have? What forms of community are consistent with citizenship? What does citizen participation amount to? Is citizenship a legal status that pertains by definition to the nation-state or are local, transnational and global iterations of citizenship possible? Can migrant residents and refugees act as de facto citizens without being citizens in a narrower, legal sense?

Different interpretations of citizenship have emerged in response to changing social conditions and reflect different ideological stances. Thus, there are tensions between the liberal ideal of rights-bearing individual citizens pursuing their private interests; communitarian claims that citizenship should be rooted in shared community, culture and language; republican aspirations for a democratic public constituted by an actively-engaged citizenry; arguments that social rights and a welfare state are preconditions of equal citizenship in market economies; and neo-liberal consumer-citizens and a marketized public realm. In addition, there are the contemporary tensions between national citizenship and emerging forms of post-national and cosmopolitan citizenship that reflect a world that seems (paradoxically) both more integrated and increasingly fragmented. For some, the nation-state protects the solidarities and democratic affiliations of citizenship against their globalized erosion; others see the revival of national citizenship as anxiety-driven and outmoded, if not blatantly reactionary.

Finally, perhaps more contentiously, there is the matter of who counts as a citizen when deciding on the citizenship we want. It is in citizenship's dual nature that it excludes as well as includes. National citizenship implies a binary of citizen-insider–non-citizen stranger. But within the national political community also, the *ideal* of equal citizenship masks the inequalities citizens experience in *practice*: class, gender, race, disability, sexuality, language, are all implicated in making '"second class" insiders' (Lister, 2007) and 'internal exclusion' (Balibar, 2015).

Within a political community, education remains the most important public mechanism for inculcating citizenship norms – the values, behaviours, knowledge and skills expected of citizens and would-be citizens. Citizenship learning does not necessarily mean an explicit curriculum (e.g. the *Citizenship Materials for ESOL Learners* (NIACE / LLU+ 2005, 2010)) or curriculum requirement (e.g. the statutory teaching of British Values). More typically, ideas of citizenship are tacitly embedded in the taken-for-granted classroom practices and curriculum choices that constitute the hidden curriculum. It is this tacit suffusion of citizenship discourses that makes brokering particularly significant.

## Brokering

The term brokering originated in anthropology to refer to those who bridged between colonial administrators and colonized communities. More recently, brokering has been used to refer to the process of interpreting or translating the culture of the 'host' community to newcomers, and *vice versa* (Jezewski and Sotnik, 2001).

As brokers, ESOL teachers use their language skills to mediate learning and communication with non-native speakers (Bass, 2012). They similarly draw on their knowledge and beliefs to broker discourses of citizenship for their students. Importantly, brokering is more than translating in a literal sense, it also involves interpreting the social and cultural practices in which linguistic and other activities are embedded.

As brokers of citizenship, there are three key issues that ESOL teachers might reflect on: first, how ESOL students are positioned and represented within dominant citizenship discourses; second, how teachers' own (tacit) beliefs and practices confirm or contest this positioning and representation; and third, how ESOL can assist students to resist *discitizenship* and develop the capacity for *acts of citizenship*. By *discitizenship*, we mean the ways in which the capacity for citizenship can be stripped away by non-recognition, stigmatization or discrimination (Ramanathan, 2013) and so result in second-class citizenship or the full or partial exclusion of individuals or groups. In contrast, *acts of citizenship* are public acts through which individuals or groups contest their exclusion and claim new citizenship rights (Isin, 2008). These divergent tendencies draw attention again to the dual nature of citizenship: discitizenship excludes and objectifies; subjective acts of citizenship are (potentially) inclusive and transformative. They can be illustrated by the contrasting Calibans referred to above.

## Which Caliban?

In scene one of *The Tempest*, Miranda remarks to Caliban, the 'abhorred slave ... capable of all ill!' (Lindley, 2002: 119):

> I pitied thee,
> Took pains to make thee speak, taught thee each hour
> One thing or other: when thou didst not, savage,
> Know thine own meaning, but wouldst gabble like
> A thing most brutish, I endow'd thy purposes
> With words that made them known. But thy vile race,
> Though thou didst learn, had that in't which good natures
> Could not abide to be with; therefore wast thou
> Deservedly confined into this rock,
> Who hadst deserved more than a prison. (1.2:357–67)

Through Miranda's eyes, Caliban appears grotesque, lacks virtue, and is incapable of coherent language or thought. Initially an object of pity, then of resentment and violence, this Caliban foreshadows contemporary discourses of dis-citizenship – the positioning by aid agencies, for instance, of refugees as 'merely objects of ethical care' (Nyers, 1999); the deliberate creation of hostile environments for undocumented migrants; the stigmatization of speakers of other languages through linguistic xenophobia

In contrast, Césaire's Caliban confronts the colonialist Prospero with a critique of colonial domination that inverts their relationship of dependency and power. Prospero's position depends on his expropriation of Caliban's island and on the symbolic violence of his non-recognition of Caliban's autonomy, language and identity. There is a message here for all teachers about power and position, but ESOL teachers might particularly reflect on Caliban's response to Prospero's claim to have given him language and education. 'You didn't teach me a thing!' he says:

> Except to jabber in your own language so that I could understand
> your orders: chop the wood, wash the dishes ... (ibid.: 17)

Caliban's riposte presages Auerbach and Burgess's seminal critique of the 'hidden curriculum of survival ESL': English-language teaching that prepares migrants for low-status roles and hierarchies in and outside the classroom (1985: 475). Césaire's Caliban draws attention further to the internalized violence and loss of self-identity that non-recognition results in:

> Prospero, you're a great magician:
> you're an old hand at deception.
> And you lied to me so much,
> about the world, about myself,
> that you ended up by imposing on me
> an image of myself:
> underdeveloped, in your words, undercompetent
> that's how you made me see myself!
> And I hate that image ... and it's false! (ibid.: 61)

Resisting this violent othering, Caliban's act of citizenship is a transformative demand that exposes Prospero's hidden vulnerability:

> But now I know you, you old cancer,
> And I also know myself!
> And I know that one day
> my bare fist, just that,
> will be enough to crush your world!
> The old world is crumbling down! (ibid.: 61)

Of course, acts of citizenship don't always succeed, they can dissipate or lapse into conflict and violence (Isin, 2008). Colonialism did not crumble as Césaire's Caliban anticipated. Rather, its power relations shifted and partially relocated, struggles against colonial domination were taken up by movements for civil rights and racial equality in post-colonial capitalist societies. Thus, Césaire's (2000) demand for decolonizing consciousness in the anti-colonial struggle presages contemporary calls for decolonizing the curriculum, and what Phipps (2019: 8) describes as the messy business of '(un)learning habits of oppression and inequality'. This asks us to consider the implications for ESOL of the long association between language ideology, language education and colonial and postcolonial systems of power (see Pennycook, 1998). These power-relations are visibly embodied in ESOL – mostly white, British, native-English speaking teachers; students who represent a diverse, diasporic 'Other' (Luke, 2004). In this chapter, we are simply acknowledging the connections between the notion of decolonizing the curriculum and participatory citizenship learning and their shared concerns with issues of power, ideology, voice, access and recognition. In the following section, we outline the case studies from *Brokering Britain, Educating Citizens* to show how these concerns already inform the work of some ESOL practitioners and researchers.

## Practices and principles: *Brokering Britain, Educating Citizens*

The discussion in this section is framed by four principles – guides for assisting Caliban to resist discitizenship and to develop the capacity for acts of citizenship – that emerged from the contributions to our collection. These principles are not new, but like all principles, need restating.

The first principle is that ESOL should be ethnographically informed: students' situations, meanings and real-life linguistic demands should be at the centre of classroom practice and curriculum design. The Leeds-based Refugee Education and Training Advisory Service's Steps to Settlement project (Callaghan, Yemane and Baynham, 2019) is an innovative example of ethnographically-grounded ESOL provision. The project draws on the knowledge of students, teachers, organizers and others of the linguistic and other challenges students face as they transition from asylum seeker to refugee. Rather than training in the language someone else has decided Caliban needs, the provision is designed with students' experience at its core. Its ethnographic stance is evident in the project's argument for authentic real-language materials, and in its view of the classroom as a place where stories are shared and empathy built in order to nurture the capacity for active and activist citizenship. Roberts' (2019) similarly ethnographic exploration of job interviews shows how migrant interviewees are judged by their native-English speaking interviewers on the basis of assumptions made about their linguistically-coded attributes (e.g. adaptability, initiative, trustworthiness) rather than their job-related competencies. In this way, interviews become mechanisms for measuring Caliban's deficits and rationalizing his or her exclusion.

This ethnographic analysis of the interview highlights the second principle: ESOL needs a broad understanding of language. Language is more than a formal system and a set of transactional conventions that ESOL students must acquire. As the different Calibans show, language is also a social and cultural practice through which ideology is enacted and identity recognized or recognition withheld (see Kramsch, 1998; Norton, 1997). Linguistic identity was a key theme in the Our Languages project, undertaken by the London-based English for Action (Cooke, Bryers and Winstanley, 2019). Our Languages engaged with students' experiences of language and multilingualism as English-language learners and speakers of other languages. The notion of sociolinguistic citizenship was used to validate a multilingual citizen identity, so positing ESOL as a site for challenging conventional understandings of citizenship rights and identities.

Challenging conventional meanings of citizenship introduces the third principle: ESOL is political. ESOL exists in a contested political space, ideas of citizenship are implicit within it. With or without formal citizenship status, ESOL students are not just objects of policy or public discourse but social agents, whose everyday relationships and actions (including the act of migration) shape the wider experience and meaning of citizenship. This is evident in Vollmer's (2019) account of digital citizenship among Syrian refugees in Leeds. Volmar points out that citizenship is increasingly mediated by digital technology as state agencies routinely interact with citizens via digital platforms. However, digital technology also enables different kinds of citizen identities and practices. Smartphones and Facebook assist the Syrian refugees to participate in local community life, including with established Leeds-based communities. They also help recreate relationships with communities in Syria. In this way, diasporic locals challenge state-centric notions of citizenship, not by resisting integration but by actively constructing an integration that accommodates both local and transnational citizenship identities and practices. Volmar argues that these different digital-citizenship experiences are a resource for ESOL teachers to draw on.

Another example of ESOL as a site for pushing the meaning of citizenship is the 'Queering ESOL' seminar series (Gray and Cooke, 2019). This British Council-sponsored project addressed the cultural politics of LGBT issues in ESOL, in response to the requirement under the 2010 Equality

Act that teachers address the needs of LGBT people. Many ESOL teachers felt unprepared for brokering this policy by addressing issues of sexuality and gender. Some felt strongly that religious and cultural sensitivities among ESOL students made gender and sexuality inappropriate topics for the ESOL classroom – acting, by default, as if Caliban was straight, or if not, at least delicately closeted. 'Queering ESOL' recognized that sexual citizenship contested the discitizenship that resulted from the prevailing heteronormativity. It also acknowledged the tensions between the rights of different groups, including religious believers and LGBT people, that teachers and students in multicultural societies (and ESOL classrooms) need to navigate. Assisting Caliban to resist discitizenship and claim citizenship rights clearly requires an intersectionally sensitive pedagogic approach.

Similar political commitment motivates Beyond The Page (MacDonald, 2019). Established in Thanet in Kent, an area of the UK with a reputation for anti-immigrant activism, Beyond the Page provides a space in which migrant and local women learn together, exploring common experiences despite differences of language and culture to shape a shared curriculum. This illustrates the fourth principle: ESOL practices should reflect the democratic citizenship we aspire to; participatory citizenship requires participatory learning. In Moon and Hussain's (2019) account of a photography and ESOL project with students with mental health needs, an explicit link is made between participatory learning and the idea of resisting discitizenship. In the project, students learned language and photography skills, while collaboratively exploring aspects of their lives in a visual way. Although neglected in the managerialized learning cultures of contemporary further education, the notion that adults should participate in the decision-making about their learning has long been a mainstay of democratic citizenship education. From this perspective, ESOL should be dialogic and responsive, *'bring-the-outside-in'* and enable students to *'talk from within'* about their own experience (Baynham, Roberts *et al.*, 2007). For Moon and Hassan, resisting discitizenship is integral to the practice of negotiated learning; they see the public exhibition of the students' work at the end of their project as an act of citizenship.

The four principles inform all the case studies, but they are compellingly brought together in Hepworth's (2019) account of classroom argumentation. His chapter is an ethnographic study of classroom interaction that explores both the potential for developing the communicative skills of citizenship through participating in debates over controversial political issues, and the position teachers should adopt in classroom discussions of this kind. Hepworth believes that teachers should (where possible) be participants rather than disinterested facilitators in such discussions. Drawing on the metaphor of the *agora*, a site of public deliberation in the classical Greek *polis*, Hepworth further argues that we should see the classroom as a discursive space of citizenship in its own right.

## Conclusion

This chapter concerns ESOL and citizenship learning. We argue that, as brokers of citizenship, ESOL teachers should consider the implications for ESOL students of dominant citizenship discourses. We make the case that ESOL teachers are not policy ciphers, but have a capacity for agency, and that ESOL can be a site for the formation of new, democratic citizenship discourses and configurations – not simply for the transmission of prescribed ideas of citizenship. We illustrate our argument with examples of current practice and research to show how ESOL can assist (indeed is assisting) Caliban's capacity for resisting discitizenship and for engaging in empowering acts of citizenship.

## References

Auerbach, E.R. and Burgess, D. (1985) 'The hidden curriculum of survival ESL'. *TESOL Quarterly*, 19 (3), 475–95. Online. https://doi.org/10.2307/3586274 (accessed 8 May 2020).

Balibar, E. (2015) *Citizenship*. Cambridge: Polity Press.

Bass, T.L. (2012) 'Cultural brokers in classrooms and the new literacy studies'. In Dupuy, B. and Waugh, L. (eds) *Intercultural Competence and Foreign/Second Language Immersive Environments: Proceedings of the third international conference on the development and assessment of intercultural competence.* Vol. 2, 1–10.

Baynham, M., Roberts, C., Cooke, M., Simpson. J., Ananiadou, K., Callaghan, J. McGoldrick, J. and Wallace, C. (2007) *Effective Teaching and Learning: ESOL.* London: National Research and Development Centre for Adult Literacy and Numeracy. Online. https://dera.ioe.ac.uk/22304/1/doc_3341.pdf (accessed 8 May 2020).

Callaghan. J., Yemane, T. and Baynham, M. (2019) 'Steps to settlement for refugees: A case study.' in Cooke, M. and Peutrell, R. *Brokering Britain, Educating Citizens: Exploring ESOL and citizenship.* Bristol: Multilingual Matters, 85–102.

Césaire, A. (2000 [1955]) *Discourse on Colonialism*. Trans. Pinkham, J. New York: Monthly Review Press.

Césaire, A. (2002) *A Tempest*. Trans. Miller, R. New York: TCG Editions.

Cooke, M., Bryers, D. and Winstanley, B. (2019) '"Our Languages": Towards sociolinguistic citizenship in ESOL'. In Cooke, M. and Peutrell, R. *Brokering Britain, Educating Citizens: Exploring ESOL and citizenship.* Bristol: Multilingual Matters, 137–55.

Cooke, M. and Peutrell, R. (2019) *Brokering Britain, Educating Citizens: Exploring ESOL and citizenship*. Bristol: Multilingual Matters.

Gray, J. and Cooke, M. (2019) 'Queering ESOL: Sexual citizenship in ESOL classrooms'. In Cooke, M. and Peutrell, R. *Brokering Britain, Educating Citizens: Exploring ESOL and citizenship*. Bristol: Multilingual Matters, 195–212.

Hepworth, M. (2019) 'Argumentation, citizenship and the Adult ESOL classroom'. In Cooke, M. and Peutrell, R. *Brokering Britain, Educating Citizens: Exploring ESOL and citizenship*. Bristol: Multilingual Matters, 103–20.

Isin, E. (2008) 'Theorising Acts of Citizenship'. In Isin, E. and Nielsen, G. (eds) *Acts of Citizenship*. New York: Zed Books, 15–43.

Jezewski, M.A. and Sotnik, P. (2001) *Culture Brokering: Providing culturally competent rehabilitation services to foreign-born persons*. Buffalo, NY: Center for International Rehabilitation Research Information and Exchange. Online. http://cirrie-sphhp.webapps.buffalo.edu/culture/monographs/cb.php (accessed 31 December 2019).

Kramsch, C. (1998) *Language and Culture*. Oxford: Oxford University Press.

Lindley, D. (ed.) (2002) *The Tempest*. The New Cambridge Shakespeare. Cambridge: Cambridge University Press.

Lister, R. (2007) 'Inclusive Citizenship: Realizing the Potential'. *Citizenship Studies* 11 (1), 49–61. Online. https://doi.org/10.1080/13621020601099856 (accessed 8 May 2020).

Luke, A. (2004) 'Two takes on the critical'. In Norton, B. and Toohey, K. (eds) *Critical Pedagogies and Language Learning*. Cambridge University Press: Cambridge, 21–9.

MacDonald, D. (2019) 'Migrant women, active citizens'. In Cooke, M. and Peutrell, R. *Brokering Britain, Educating Citizens: Exploring ESOL and citizenship*. Bristol: Multilingual Matters, 173–94.

Moon, P. and Hussain, R. (2019) 'Using participatory photography in English classes: Resisting silence, resisting dis-citizenship'. In Cooke, M. and Peutrell, R. *Brokering Britain, Educating Citizens: Exploring ESOL and citizenship*. Bristol: Multilingual Matters, 121–36.

NIACE/LLU+ (2005/2010) *Citizenship materials for ESOL learners*. Leicester: NIACE. Available at https://tinyurl.com/yctxpxm8 (accessed 8 May 2020).

Norton, B. (1997) 'Language, identity and the ownership of English'. *TESOL Quarterly*, 31 (3), 409–29.

Nyers, P. (1999) 'Emergency or emerging identities? Refugees and transformations in world order'. *Millennium: Journal of International Studies*, 28 (1), 1–26. Online. https://doi.org/10.1177/03058298990280010501 (accessed 8 May 2020).

Pennycook, A. (1998) *English and the Discourses of Colonialism*. London: Routledge.

Phipps, A. (2019) *Decolonising Multilingualism: Struggles to decreate*. Bristol: Multilingual Matters.

Ramanathan, V. (ed.) (2013) *Language Policies and (Dis)Citizenship: Rights, access, pedagogies*. Bristol: Multilingual Matters.

Roberts, C. (2019) 'From the outside in: Gatekeeping the workplace'. In Cooke, M. and Peutrell, R. *Brokering Britain, Educating Citizens: Exploring ESOL and citizenship*. Bristol: Multilingual Matters, 213–26.

Vollmer, S. (2019) 'Digital citizenship for newly arrived Syrian refugees through mobile technologies'. In Cooke, M. and Peutrell, R. *Brokering Britain, Educating Citizens: Exploring ESOL and citizenship*. Bristol: Multilingual Matters, 157–72.

*Walk on through the wind*
*Walk on through the rain*
*Though your dreams be tossed and blown*

(Richard Rodgers and Oscar Hammerstein II)

Jake Forrest

opposite: Olivia Kelly

*Chapter 11*

# 'Stranger in a strange land': Reclaiming the terrain for a disorientating dilemma and the possibility of forgiveness

*Pete Bennett, Howard Scott and Julie Wilde*

## 'Our revels now are ended'

In *The Tempest* Shakespeare exiles Prospero to an island in order that he and we might learn something, a propitious starting point for our conversation here about education. Prospero is allowed to keep his 'powerful knowledge' (which cost him everything else) for as long as it benefits him, which is to say: until he learns better. The play finds him after seven years 'hard at study', dragged from his books by outside events. He is not yet woke but in causing the storm he is catalyst for the play and agent for Biesta's 'learning as a reaction to a disturbance, as an attempt to reorganize or reintegrate as a result of disintegration' (Biesta, 2005: 62).

Shakespeare challenges us to respond to 'what is other or different, to what challenges, irritates and disturbs us' (ibid.: 62), a parallel to Mezirow's disorientating dilemma, which precipitates learning transformations. This is what this chapter proposes – Further Education as a space to *become*: a humanist view. Yet instead, we have built institutions that are designed solely to sign on, zoom in, and churn out, where a college is a machine for conditioning 'reflexive impotence' (Fisher, 2009: 21) – an institutionalized sterility and self-fulfilled pathological apathy among FE youth that essentially prohibits personal transformation in order to preserve a particular state of things.

Against this is authority's view of knowledge as capital, which can be stuffed inside students to open up their worlds, with no regard for students' apprehension of being in that world or for their own agency to act on this world. Prospero, arguably the ultimate omniscient and omnipotent author of reality, perceives learning as the acquisition of something external. Yet he comes to discover that learning can also be a cumulative cycle of disorientating and orientating states, symbolized by the storm that brings the sailors to the island. The island in *The Tempest* is sanctuary for ludic experience: a holding environment (Winnicott, 1971) where learning as becoming thrives in an ongoing process of inner- and outer-exploration. Here there is plenty of evidence of the risk that has been cleaned out of contemporary FE: 'the risk that you will learn something that you rather didn't want to learn, something about yourself, for example' (Biesta, 2005: 61). Of course, all learning – including that realization of our own powerlessness – represents a risk of entering new territories. In the play, for example, Trinculo and Stephano are bewildered and 'afear'd' (though hardly assured by the knowing Caliban) of the foreign domains they enter. They resist the strange. As in our current sector, the terrain has been designed by those furthest from its boundaries and alien to its intrepid navigators (teachers *and* students).

Caliban and Miranda are symbols of subjugation – to become civilized. One is bred to be harnessed, the other to station the colony, but both are subjects of an education predicated on procedure and predestination. Caliban, bred to serve, is being tamed by force ('By sorcery he got this from me') in a tradition that pits culture against anarchy and aims to tame the savage breast of the beast that sought to 'violate my child'. It seems that time has caught up with Prospero and it is time told on a body clock by Nature. His focus on the derangement of Caliban is pure projection, damning him as generations of the poorest sort of kids have been damned for generations: suitable cases for treatment, yet unsuited for instruction, since 'human beings may be equally endowed with dignity and rights, but they are not academically equal and do not have the same academic needs' (Johnson, 2006). Three hundred and fifty years before a sociology of education emerged, Shakespeare manages to find the pertinent vocabulary for Caliban: 'A devil, a born devil, on whose nature nurture can never stick' (4.1:179–80). Moreover, in a heartfelt plea perhaps to those who have given of their best before and failed with these kinds of kids, the ne'er-do-wells, Prospero continues: 'on whom my pains / Humanely taken, all, all lost' (4.1:180–1).

## 'Your future dream is a shopping scheme'

Caliban is neatly cast as the peripheral participant (Lave and Wenger, 1991), he is other people's children, NEET (Not in Education, Employment or Training): the ultimate outsider. The role of Caliban, like the threat of the uneducated and disenfranchised, is both real and created, an apparent problem of civilization that we have both the right and the responsibility to fix. For Miranda, whose fate is constructed as the very antithesis to this (she is bound to succeed, though passivity is the price she must pay), Caliban is that which she does 'not love to look on' (1.2: 315). He is the NEET peripheral participant pushed outside – where they may well be happy to be, given the state of the inside.

Like generations of young people, Caliban struggles to find a place: he is of the underclass who understands all too well what is offered him and his refusal to accept is a beautiful negation of what others value. And so he lurks, watching, waiting. Caliban stands not only for young people undernourished by the profligacy of an instrumentalist education system, but for those distinctly underwhelmed by what society's instrumentation has on offer for them. Every college is the same and why work hard, anyway, if every right that others had is withdrawn, then scornfully labelled as an entitlement if it's demanded? Why work hard at all if you will never secure even basic foundations, because Power has given everything to those with the most capital? Caliban stands for those students who have trained for trades, only for apprenticeships to undermine their enterprise; students who trained for health care, only for agencies to undercut their prospects; or students who trained for the creative industry, only to face paying for an internship. This is to say nothing of those who studied in order to study Higher, only for tuition fees to mount ever higher. They learn to become the underclass, silent at the underbelly with no means to protest, except by non-compliance, divergence and refusal to participate.

Caliban is the challenge to any system of education or individual teacher whose first responsibility is to enable the student to be unique and become individual. Peim writes about the notion of education as a 'gift', as 'an offer that you cannot refuse' when for 'certain segments of the population it is also, at the same time, an offer you can't accept' (Peim, 2013: 38). Because it is represented as 'a gift that keeps on giving', those like Caliban, who lack engagement 'may be represented as being in need of reorientation, salvation and realignment' (ibid.: 38). While this sounds alarmingly like dystopian reprogramming of the mind, Fisher sees students as caught in a double bind of 'business ontology', where they are 'stranded between their old role as subjects of disciplinary institutions and their new status as consumers of services' (2009: 22). Students' disorientation in this holding place of FE must lead to them rejecting the continual pursuit of ephemeral pleasure and self-fulfilment they have been promised and instead they should seek the boredom of self-improvement that comes from intellectual labour. Education may not set them free on their terms, they are told, but it can set you free (on our terms).

Miranda remains open to the new, the possible and the transformational. Where the traditionalists reconstitute this narrative as a tale as old as time, Miranda might be expected to take her place in the natural province of the privileged, wherein being educated just means being who you are and knowing what you know. However, she is first cast into a wilderness where this status becomes meaningless as the curriculum is lived, not invented. Prospero invokes a formal Masque to mark the transition from one illusion (an isle full of noises as the music of youth) to the no less illusory world of *Realpolitik*, ('news from the Rialto' as Shakespeare memorably coined it elsewhere). The play exemplifies Žižek's notion that 'the fundamental level of ideology is not an illusion masking the real state of things but that of an (unconscious) fantasy structuring our social reality' (1989: 33).

Students are subordinated to an order that is assumed to be real and, as Fisher (2009) explains, they have long since given up thinking Reality (®) can be anything other than that which is proffered them. The student must relinquish agency to play a part (a role) in a marketized world and their undignified duty in FE is to reify the impossible dream of capital:

> The role is a consumption of power. It locates one in the representational hierarchy ... at the top, at the bottom, in the middle but never outside the hierarchy ... The role is thus the means of access to the mechanism of culture: a form of initiation. (Vaneigem, 1972: 132)

The GCSE resit in FE represents this rite of passage into society, the qualification an unwanted ticket to ride. You can only escape the mechanism by embracing the mechanism, otherwise you churn around again or become NEET – and capital barely affords you that option, nowadays.

Marx said that 'Every emancipation is a restoration of the human world and human relationships to man himself' (Marx and Engels, 1978: 46) and that is our premise here for a renewal of the project of FE as the home of the genuine second chance. It must be so much more than the repetition of what was performed in school. If all can be emancipated, as are all those who experience *The Tempest*, then who knows what might be achieved?

> Emancipating students requires only a supply of emancipated teachers, but conversely, what is similarly required for the intellectual enslavement and control of students is a reliable supply of teachers prepared to be themselves controlled. (Bennett, 2019: 19)

## 'What's Past is Prologue'

The present state of FE is as *The Tempest*: on paper static, flat and monochrome, but easily transformed if imagined into a more exotic space. And what should this space be? Biesta has argued:

> if education is indeed concerned with subjectivity and agency, then we should think of education as the situation or process which provides opportunity for individuals to come into presence, that is, to show who they are and where they stand. (Biesta, 2005: 62)

Like Miranda, Caliban himself is entirely engaged with his education, though his is in a beautiful resistance of active defiance, taunting Prospero: 'You taught me language ... I know how to curse.' Caliban is an anomaly to the narrative of compliance: an underachiever who refuses to know his place. He is claiming a right to respond and thus taking part in educational discourse with a subjectivity that is thoroughly social. This is what is missing from college education: the freedom to learn to become ... in good time. The freedom to learn to make choices, to make mistakes, to become active, to resist and to exist without limits and restrictions.

Characters in *The Tempest* illustrate irreducibly unique personhoods that echo a diversity of lived experiences in FE. So as we move towards the end of our conversation, for now, what might we learn from *The Tempest* about a humanist view of the purpose of education? How can FE reclaim its dance in the space of appearance between inner and outer explorations? The space of appearance ebbs between education as a process of socialization and learning towards subjectification (Biesta, 2013). Here, education is more than business ontology, it's a place to learn about being an authentic and active person in an existing world, a world that we might choose to conserve (through the hopeless inaction of reflexive impotence) or to change. And how does *The Tempest* challenge us to respond to that which disturbs us? It seems that the experiences that disturb or disorientate us can indeed become quite powerful in nudging the imagination away from that which is proffered to us.

The first step is to overcome the imposition of fear in a conditioned and mythical world. Miranda does this in the play. She is seen to be innocent and naïve and yet she is aware of her worth and what she has to offer. Miranda knows that she has a choice; being passive to Caliban's heartless demands would be dangerous, as would a simple acceptance of her father's ignorance. In her actions we witness the implications of strategic compliance and resistance. Despite the despotic power of those around her, she calls on her humanist view of the world to initiate change and freedom. She cares enough to act and challenge the empty words of Prospero and the brutal deeds of Caliban, because she values fairness and justice and realizes this through her agency to take action upon the world. Miranda takes notice to act in light of her disorientating dilemma and disturbing experiences. She sees the importance of promise and forgiveness in safeguarding human relationships and her own emancipation. Higgins asserts that 'by offering promise, teachers hedge against the risk and unpredictability of human action and with forgiveness they are able to release others from the irreversibility of their actions' (Higgins, 2011: 100).

So it is Miranda's care for human affairs and associations that echo hope for the purpose of education and allow FE to reclaim its dance without restrictions or fear. In FE, every individual ought to hold the promise of a new beginning where to act means to be able to seize an initiative, bring about change and begin anew. FE can hold the promise of transformation so that students and teachers can move away from being peripheral observers. There is scope for students and teachers to take risks and dance: to be redeemed, as Caliban is; to self-actualize and learn to become oneself, as Miranda does.

Sadly, trepidation emerges with uncertainty and, like the chaos of a shipwreck, students and teachers wonder what happens should they get the dance wrong. Too often students and teachers in FE are conditioned through fear, anxiety and concerns about vengefulness. Bureaucracy, the onset of professional regulation and the demise of thinking space create circumstances where it is safer to be tamed than to act with initiative and integrity. How can teachers consciously promote self-determination, agency and self-actualized becoming in their students, when it is hamstrung in their own everyday working practices? Abhorrent environments impact the sense of self and close down consideration of different ways of being. Students and teachers become weary and wary of the fantasies structuring their realities. They must not let go of their freedom and, like Miranda, they must use their capability to act in order to choreograph their own dance, so resisting ridicule and regress.

FE is a beautiful risk that is rich with lived experiences from various agents who act in unpredictable ways. It is renowned for offering transformative educational experiences with responsibility for social and moral justice. FE must not merely supplement wider political agendas towards churning out servants for the labour markets and capital gain. Like Miranda, those who truly care for education must safeguard what is precious to them: the moral purpose of education from a humanist standpoint. Students are part of the FE dance too. What we need are teachers who are prepared to engage in the risks and are well informed about education, society and moral justice (Ball, 2016). FE needs teachers who offer hope for change through engaging in critical reflexivity and through relational contexts to initiate new beginnings. It needs those who are committed to the heart and the head, who provide time for the imagination to play, who create safe spaces (the solace and refuge of an island) for students to disclose unique selves in an old, existing world. Educationally this means that the responsibility of the FE teacher, like Miranda, needs to be directed to the maintenance of a space in which, through promise and forgiveness, freedom can appear (Biesta, 2013). A brave new world where thinking students and teachers become agents that can challenge the dangerous distortion of perceived reality (Allen, 2002) and contest the external powers that remove the space in FE for thinking, acting and dancing.

## References

Allen, A. (2002) 'Power, *subjectivity, and agency: Between Arendt and Foucault.' International Journal of Philosophical Studies*, 10 (2), 131–49. Online. https://doi.org/10.1080/09672550210121432 (accessed 8 May 2020).

Ball, S.J. (2016) 'Education, justice and democracy: The struggle over ignorance and opportunity'. In Montgomery, A. and Kehoe, E. (eds) *Reimagining the Purpose of Schools and Educational Organisation*s. Cham: Springer, 189–205.

Bennett, P. (2019) 'Why we must never become classroom managers'. In Robinson, D. (ed.), *Classroom Behaviour Management in Further, Adult and Higher Education: Moving beyond control?* London: Bloomsbury.

Biesta, G. (2005) 'Against learning. Reclaiming a language for education in an age of learning'. *Nordisk Pedagogik*, 25, 54–66. Online. https://orbilu.uni.lu/bitstream/10993/7178/1/NP-1-2005-Biesta.pdf (accessed 8 May 2020).

Biesta, G. (2013) *The Beautiful Risk of Education.* Boulder, CO: Paradigm.

Fisher, M. (2009) *Capitalist Realism: Is there no alternative?* Ropley, Hants: John Hunt Publishing.

Higgins, C. (2011) *The Good Life of Teaching: An ethics of professional practice.* Chichester: Wiley-Blackwell.

Johnson, B. (2006) 'The Future of Higher Education' [speech]. Online https://conservative-speeches.sayit.mysociety.org/speech/600062 (accessed 8 September 2019).

Lave, J. and Wenger, E. (1991) *Situated Learning: Legitimate peripheral participation*. Cambridge: Cambridge University Press.

Marx, K. and Engels, F. (1978) *The Marx-Engels Reader*, ed. R.C. Tucker. New York: Norton.

Peim, N. (2013) 'Education as Mythology'. In Bennett, P. and McDougall, J. (eds) *Barthes' Mythologies Today: Readings of contemporary culture*. Abingdon: Routledge, 32–41.

Vaneigem, R. (1972, French original 1967) *The Revolution of Everyday Life*. London: Action Books.

Winnicott, D.H. (1971) *Playing and Reality*. New York: Basic Books.

Žižek, S. (1989) *The Sublime Object of Ideology*. London: Verso.

To make the sea your own, to watch over it, to brood your very soul into it, to accept it and love it as though only it mattered and existed.

(Jack Kerouac)

Winter Bourner

overleaf: Kaice Walker

*Chapter 12*

# Red plagues, dust storms and death to utopia

*Peter Shukie*

**Miranda:**
I pitied thee,
Took pains to make thee speak, taught thee each hour
One thing or other: when thou didst not, savage,
Know thine own meaning, but wouldst gabble like
A thing most brutish, I endowed thy purposes
With words that made them known. But thy vile race,
Though thou didst learn, had that in 't which good natures
Could not abide to be with; therefore wast thou
Deservedly confined into this rock,
Who hadst deserved more than a prison.

**Caliban:**
You taught me language, and my profit on 't
Is, I know how to curse. The red plague rid you
For learning me your language! (l.2:358–70)

Encased in this short exchange between the privileged and the dispossessed is the howl of a frustration that echoes across four hundred years. Reverberating injustice, the subjugation of minoritarian voices in favour of the force-fed language of the powerful, continues to characterize contemporary Further Education (FE) landscapes. Exiled on an island that they colonize, brutalize and where they subsequently enslave the existing residents, the crux of Prospero and Miranda's power lies in mysticism, fantastical books and tyrannical power. Punished by being denied the fruits of his own labours, Caliban signifies how oppression relies on ridicule and mockery of, and false charity to, those it strips of agency. Whatever relief from toxic imperial cruelty emerges comes only from a tarnished education meted out from a pitying condescension of the same imperial class. Caliban might easily fit the popular image of a brutal outsider set against with the cultivated beauty and nobility of those that enslave him. As he curses, he reveals more, that his magnificence and wisdom is of necessity crushed to allow his domination, the only voice he has to respond with is that forced upon him and that seeks only to erase his own. Cast adrift in the language of others, he can never be more than a poor imitation that serves to justify the supremacy of the civilization that enslaved him.

We might find our turning to a classical drama as a framework for this volume as privileging elite concepts, and revealing that my own clumsiness is much the same as Caliban's. In response, a gonzo education is proposed in this chapter. Gonzo emerges from my own narrative around exile and subsequent establishment of a new approach that empowers rather than destroys.

## I / We as Caliban

What if we see ourselves as Caliban, rather than be encouraged to see through the eyes of others? Reflecting on my educational experiences, of standing in free dinner queues, being mocked when suggesting university applications, having my accent the subject of every response to my queries in lectures after getting there, I see a mild exile, always made to feel an outsider. After university, now homeless, a visit to the housing department saw me instructed to sit in a waiting area for a whole day; I did briefly consider that the chair was the solution being offered me. What later became my home was a flat among a hundred others, most single males, many from incarceration in justice or mental health establishments, others with complex stories of loss, or being found surplus. The whole place had a nightmare reputation, Locally, Durham Street was the end of the line, the bottom of the barrel. I worked in many places, temporary contracts, warehouses, offices, labouring. I was not alone in finding this location crept with us, somehow permeating every encounter even when wandering beyond its corrugated iron grasp. Yet, among these flats I found brilliance. I started to paint there; we had a lively exchange of books on philosophy, politics, New Age thinking, art and history. There were parties, music from all eras and many backgrounds, and these came with detailed histories from multiple lives. Our existence felt vital and much of what I learned there informs my practice as an educator now. Our lives were not some artistic haven, our collective exiles were tinged with desperate anger, loss, health issues and too frequent self-destruction. We lived what I later recognized in Paulo Freire's observation that:

> self-depreciation is another characteristic of the oppressed, which derives from their internalization of the opinion the oppressors hold of them. So often do they hear that they are good for nothing, know nothing and are incapable of learning anything – that they are sick, lazy and unproductive – that in the end they become convinced of their own unfitness. (Freire, 1996: 45)

We became experts at finding the diamonds in our own souls, while recognizing sustained exposure here would make even that essential search too hard. Yet we learned to survive, to incentivize and support each other, to create new models of existence that happened beyond the usual spaces. I was acutely aware that this micro-society was forgotten, marginal and actively resisting integration by authorities. I was equally aware it was vivid, creative and innovative. It was not silent, though it was most certainly unheard. But I couldn't wait to get out.

Being considered a brute, as lesser and outside society is not altogether a bad thing. It has its intense mental and emotional costs, it kills people, it kills friends. But it also means that once experienced, you never fall into the trap of seeing others as they are described. This place needed love, support, direction and dialogue. It got instead dawn raids, bailiffs, evictions and authoritarian contempt. I may be a contemporary Caliban, but unlike him, I found another storm that revealed new possibilities not bound by insistence on the common senses of imperial power and beholden to a classical canon.

## Fear and Loathing in FE

In place of Shakespeare's watery maelstrom in *The Tempest*, Hunter S. Thompson (1971/2005) uses the parched dirt of a Nevada desert to reveal possibilities for a future in which the treachery of power can be challenged. Sent to cover a desert motorcycle race, Thompson discovered that scores of wheels churning up scorched sand generate an impenetrable curtain, impossible to report on and pointless to try. Yet for almost every other reporter, the race was reported from partially heard accounts, blind impressions and guesswork; guesswork that became the definitive account when these partly imagined events made the newspapers. For Raul Duke, Thompson's character in *Fear and Loathing in Las Vegas* (1971; 2005), something more developed. In place of speculative objectivism, his reportage developed into a personalized account of the wildness experienced in a Vegas dust cloud. Out of this storm we can see gonzo journalism, a seeker of some truth as a truth realized, lived and real. Subjective and responsive, gonzo journalism realized the agency and significance of the author. Like the crushed and ignored poets, artists and philosophers of Durham Street, gonzo reveals a desire to be, to exist and to participate in terms we can contribute to and help define. Rather than be loathed, feared and discarded, we might instead consider the benefits of love, inclusion and respect.

This chapter will explore how the development of gonzo might help us see a different educational purpose. Rather than building knowledge factories based on a Miranda curriculum designed to create mini-Mirandas, thwarted simulations that serve only to reify the original power, we might see a space in which we create and realize our own realities – a gonzo education.

## Travels in the hyperreality of FE

Gonzo education insists on an intensified awareness of ourselves, it is not louche or undisciplined but instead courageous and insistent on authenticity, of lived experiences. As with gonzo journalism, this can create blurred lines, when what we represent is not clear or universally agreed, resisting a powerful common-sense census that decides what is permissible. Shortly after Thompson's initial American Odyssey, an Italian linguist offered insight into distorted realities. In *Travels in Hyper Reality* (1986) Umberto Eco describes an America characterized by imitation, of Hearst's Castle, Disneyland, of perfect copies of classical art, and recreations like Van Gogh in 3D model form sitting on one of his own impressionistic chairs. He links such classical reappropriation with natural-world counterparts, of otters taught to sip martinis in San Francisco and Bengal Tigers petted by children in San Diego. This slippage between real and fake, of imitation and natural, Eco characterizes as 'universal taming' (Eco, 1986: 51). Immersed in cultures of copies of copies of copies, the power of any originality is lost.

As Caliban is removed from his own reality and programmed with another preferred reality he, like the martini sipping otter, is tamed and through gauche imitation becomes a parody of the original. In FE, and specifically college-based Higher Education (CBHE), the insistence on imitation and exact copy is enshrined through validation, quality measures and inspection.

The struggle of we CBHE teachers to achieve academic brilliance, establish an alternate yet equal space for research, study and achievement is already thwarted. Doomed to copy and follow, our replication seems always lesser, faked, part of a lower order. Becoming tamed not by the lesser value of action and encounter, creation or academic purposefulness, but by always being the Other, measured by the degree to which we demonstrate our tameness. All of this cannot generate assertiveness or confidence, so, like the desire to leave the bullied and brutalized landscape of Durham Street, new perceptions of possibility are required. Rather than being the last line of condemnation, the final whip crack of the tamer's power, we might realize that a different creative potential exists. We can consider FE as the first line in establishing a means for realizing the potential of diverse and complex communities, and layers of communities within them. Not for us the authoritarian condemnation and generalization of hard to reach and marginal, but the gonzo educators that light up and promote the value of diversity.

## Gonzo, power and alternative action

There may be dispute over the authoritative narrative of *The Tempest*, whether Prospero's or Caliban's version takes precedence. No such dispute rages in FE; power and the voice of authority unmistakeably lie elsewhere, not in colleges. Seeking to empower agents of change in the colleges from positions of relative powerlessness requires a radical reimagining of pedagogy and the ways we teach and learn in FE. Just as gonzo journalism found authenticity through conscious subjectivity rather than 'bogus objectivity' (Elborough, 2005: 9) the experiences of gonzo education require a shift in perspective. Gonzo is an appeal to see beyond binary logic. In educational terms, we are transfixed by lecturer and student, of expert and not.

Widely, beyond the campus, we see simple binaries that present either meek acceptance of distant authority on one hand, or populist rabble-rousing on the other. What Freire (1996) defines as sectarianism is the division of society by assemblages of atomized selves and separated-out micro-communities, creating division and perpetuating disadvantage. What we might create in gonzo education is a means of educating that values the input of all and creates growth through participation, knowledge through action, and community built on dialogue. Not as theoretical assemblages concocted in university seminar rooms, but as real and lived encounters within, and necessarily between, diverse communities.

## Making gonzo real

The examples described here are not pedagogical parlour games that invite educators to try alternate activities to engage and amuse. Instead, they are attempts to place the educator in a less hierarchical relationship in which agency is transferred and expertise, choice and knowledge-creation become distributed. They might be read as my own efforts to realize an educational experience that is inclusive and respecting of diversity, not seeking a centralized vision and allowing each of us to find our diamonds and to be supported in the attempt. The act of creating learning beyond the campus is not new and it is the purposefulness of these acts that distinguishes these activities from service learning and university outreach programmes. Only by establishing a clear shift in perspective toward goals that students and informal educators help decide, does this realignment of power become possible.

## My context: Education Studies, a critical not compliant space

The context of our work is an Education Studies programme at an FE college. A beautiful diversity characterizes our student body, where A-level access is a minor route to participation and courses attract a wide range of ages, experiences and backgrounds. Most students are the first in the family to attend university and they carry a wealth of cultural capital. This is not, however, the type of capital endorsed by Ofsted's (2019: 43) adoption of Matthew Arnold's problematic nineteenth-century definition. A Caliban-like resistance to simply appropriating elitist concepts of 'the best that has been thought and said' (ibid.: 43) is not to call, like Caliban, for a 'red plague'. Instead, the response of our educators and students, communities and collaborators has been the establishment of educational activity rooted in purposefulness, social justice and meaningful experience. The remainder of this chapter outlines three positive and powerful gonzo responses in which those involved write themselves into theory, action and, yes, assessment.

## Technology and community projects
### Art Brut

Art Brut, or 'raw art', defines an approach to artistic creativity and expression that come from diverse and unrepresented sectors of society. Marcuse (1978: 72) considered that 'art breaks open a dimension inaccessible to other experience, a dimension in which human beings, nature and things no longer stand under the law of the established reality'. Following this concern that a new dimension is necessary, we ran classes where students arrived with a canvas and I provided the paints. We converted a seminar room into a studio space for the afternoon and we painted. This was not an art class, I did not act as teacher and the creations were open and without instruction. From this, students generated paintings but far more importantly we engaged in discussion of purpose and our own rationales. I took part and as we talked, the theories from other parts of the course merged with our experiences, of art, of life, of feeling for purpose rather than responding to a clear and articulated dominant purpose.

The emphasis on art proved powerful in generating actions that reflected our distinct positions and offered a framing for dialogue. Without academic measures, or distinct roles, we encountered a new series of interactions, spoke differently and behaved in ways we otherwise would not. Imagination is what Greene says can allow us, 'to break with the taken for granted, to set aside familiar distinctions and definitions' (Greene, 1995: 3). Even as students began with trepidation, some talking about a sense of loss or futility, we could start to rebuild the purpose by relating to what we did expect.

In the final evaluation of this module, every student related the experiences in this session – all of them positively. We made films of ourselves painting and talking, displayed the work, wrote about the experience and several people have taken this activity to other places in primary education, teacher training, lectures in counselling, on a business degree and in staff development. Through seeking alternatives to existing power structures, we disrupted what was expected and found a more vibrant space beyond the norm.

### Psychogeography / The *Dérive*

*It was just exciting, brilliant and I wanted to read every book I'd ever read again, to see again what I might bring to my wandering. I was initially uncertain about what this might be for, and I even thought, what if I just spent time on my assignments. Now I know because I felt different, saw differently and want to do so much more of this. It was that feeling that made me see new, lost but not lost, finding and feeling things at the same time.* (participant on *dérive*)

*Taking the group around my own area was terrifying but the most rewarding presentation I could have ever made. Every question made me see my own streets differently and that would not happen sat in a room and talking.* (Student leader of community *dérive*)

Psychogeography has developed since its inception by Guy DeBord and the situationists but at its core it offers a means of accessing the familiar and seeing with new eyes. A key function of our sessions was to take people somewhere unfamiliar, to blend theoretical reflection with experiential wanderings. From this, the students created their own *dérives* in spaces we had not considered. This led to cross-cultural encounters that broke down barriers and led to new conversations and further encounters. The *dérive* was an excellent indication of the desire of people to generate awareness of their isolated communities and bring others to them, on equal terms as friends and peers. Both the initial *dérive* and the several student and community created ones that followed highlighted two things:

1.  The generation of knowledge through an unknown and unknowable set of circumstances generates experience and excitement. Learning is valued because of unfamiliarity and alternate views become a necessary response – no model answer is available.
2.  People choose the *dérive* as an assessment method to recreate the sense of discovery, but in places they themselves value and are invested in. This is beyond what can be read about or measured against and requires engagement on a deep level that requires awareness of planes of knowing that outweigh any prescribed measures.

## Conclusion

Shakespeare created a complex web of supremacy through Prospero's mysticism and nobility interwoven with Caliban's natural, living power. 'Absolute Milan' (I.2:107–9) invests a royal order from an alien landscape. Yet Caliban remains a power, a living reality that counters the ethereal force generated through Prospero's fantastical books. From wild existence, the presence of Caliban's story, another voice is heard even though Prospero's is 'such a convincing and ample historian that other histories have to fight their way into the crevices of his official monument' (Hulme and Sherman, 2004: 237). Just as Caliban's voice is necessary to challenge the tyranny of a mono-narrative of wealth and power, it is from FE that we might generate new voices, alternate narratives and lived experiences that shape contemporary society.

Gonzo education implies that we must do this through action aligned with theory, reflection and courage. The risk of seeming a 'treacherous slave' (Hulme and Sherman, 2004: 237) should be no deterrent as we collectively insist our narratives are included. Courageous activism permits education that is inquisitive and vital; we must also recognize our opportunity to be the instigators. The necessity of gonzo is speaking truth to power, avoiding stereotyping such that, 'sane is rich and powerful. Insane is wrong and poor and weak. The rich are free, the poor are put in cages' (Thompson, 2003: 9). Escaping caged existence comes through our recognizing the spirit of gonzo education as not a method, but a necessary writing of ourselves in the work we do. Providing opportunities for ourselves and for those we work with generates the power of the multiplicity that is not easily squashed by magic or elitist power.

## References

Eco, U. (1986) *Travels in Hyper Reality*. New York: Harcourt Brace.

Elborough, T. (2005) 'P.S. Ideas, Interviews and Features'. In Thompson, H.S., *Fear and Loathing in Las Vegas*. London: Harper Perennial.

Freire, P. (1996) *Pedagogy of the Oppressed*. Revised edition. London: Penguin.

Greene, M. (1995) *Releasing the Imagination: Essays on education, the arts, and social change*. Hoboken, NJ: Wiley.

Hulme, P. and Sherman, W.H. (2004) *The Tempest*. Norton Critical Editions. New York: Norton.

Marcuse, H. (1978, German original 1977) *The Aesthetic Dimension: Toward a critique of Marxist aesthetics*. Trans. Marcuse, H. and Sherover, E. Boston: Beacon Press. Online. www.marginalutility.org/wp-content/uploads/2011/10/aesthetic-dimension-_-marcuse.pdf (accessed 8 May 2020).

Ofsted (2019) *School Inspection Handbook: Ofsted guidance on inspecting maintained schools and academies in England under the education inspection framework*. 14 May. London: Ofsted. Online. www.gov.uk/government/publications/school-inspection-handbook-eif (accessed 8 May 2020).

Thompson, H.S. (2003) *Kingdom of Fear: Loathsome secrets of a star-crossed child in the final days of the American century*. New York: Simon and Schuster and London: Penguin.

Thompson, H.S. (2005, original publication 1971) *Fear and Loathing in Las Vegas*. London: Harper Perennial.

*Marxism … is at its best when butting heads in self-criticism, and in historical thunder and lightning, it retains its strength.*

(Rosa Luxemburg)

Natene Larty

overleaf: Aran Quinn

## Chapter 13

# The sorcery of academic skills
*Casey Beaumont and Rhian Wyn-Williams*

From a tempest of political confusion so deep it seems 'a thousand furlongs of sea', it is the Further Education sector that appears to offer that 'acre of barren ground, long heath, brown furze' (1.1:65). This, at least, is one reading of the government's Augar, or Post-18 Review of Education (Augar, 2019), which promises reform of post-compulsory education through increased support and funding of technical and vocational courses, skills formation and lifelong learning. Whether this represents a clever political policy that speaks to the 50 per cent of school leavers who haven't engaged in higher education, a group often equated with disenfranchised working-class voters, or a means of ensuring parity with European education and industry, or a timely rebalancing of education towards an evolving employment market shaped by next generation technology, this focus represents a shift in favour of the FE sector.

This is also apparent in the review's recommendation to withdraw financial support for foundation-year programmes, most of which are delivered within Higher Education Institutions (HEIs), and to encourage take-up of Access to HE (AtoHE) Diplomas, that are provided mainly by FE colleges (FECs) (Augar, 2019). In 2017/18, 77 per cent of foundation years were taught in HEIs, whereas 90 per cent of AtoHE Diplomas were taught within FECs. But it is really in the recognition of the need for more robust collaboration between HEIs and FECs that this idealized educational landscape begins to take form: in the development of technical and vocational qualifications that can lead to higher-level study, and in the design of effective AtoHE programmes that support students in their lifelong development of skills.

Arguably, however, such a brave new world is possible only if it is underpinned by an ideological and pedagogical understanding of what an AtoHE Diploma offers the individual student and the HE student body, rather than it being driven by political posturing, international competition or fiscal saving. True, AtoHE Diplomas are ripe for challenging the pragmatic notion of education as little more than a technical training. While AtoHE explicitly challenges educational disadvantage and promotes opportunities, it can also offer a transformative experience that guides students towards self-actualization. AtoHE students are mostly between the ages of 21–35 with a greater proportion of Black and minority ethnic students and people who have disabilities than in the comparable HE population in the UK (QAA, 2019). HEIs, looking at them through a lens of othering, categorize them as non-traditional students.

Here is where we can envisage the AtoHE student as Caliban and FE as his island. FE and the AtoHE classroom are places in which he is not the other but instead part of a community that shares his lived experiences rather than highlighting his differences. While there is a paucity of research on the experiences of AtoHE students, Jones's (2006) case study offers us a glimpse into experiences on the island. The study's participants spoke of initial trepidation and a tendency to recall past negative educational experiences, but noted that, by the time they transitioned to HE, they had an advantage over other students because of their academic skills.

Interviews with previous AtoHE students from a local FE college who have transitioned into Liverpool John Moores University extend such findings. Interviewees spoke of Access as having been a boot camp for university, of recognizing their own skills as independent students and effective academic communicators when compared with classmates from a traditional route into HE through A levels. Unlike A-level students, the Access student has regular summative assessed coursework as well as exams and doesn't have a course-specific textbook to rely on. This may encourage them to use a wider range of source material, thus mirroring undergraduate study and preparing them more successfully than an A- Level course. Above all, AtoHE students feel enthused about and equipped for undergraduate learning. Mature students on a foundation programme within an HE environment may have less-positive experiences as they struggle with the process of academic acculturation (Webber, 2014). A level-three qualification within the FE sector offers benefits for developing academic skills but also, more importantly, for self-efficacy.

Being a mature student in FE may be a more transformative experience because the student isn't othered in this environment. It's a space in which Caliban can dance, where he can 'embrace the joy and power of thinking itself' (hooks, 2009: 8) outside an HE environment that might shackle him to an image of deficiency. In the FE classroom, the Access student owns the space and is free to realize the value of their contribution to the learning process, and thus gain the confidence to acquire and deepen their academic and personal skills. The Access student is able to successfully embark on a degree programme because of the skills-first focus of the QAA validated provision in colleges. The QAA places less importance on subject content and more on the development of independent learning, critical analysis, academic communication and applying academic skills (QAA, 2018). It is on Caliban's island, therefore, that students can learn the skills associated with successful study in HE most effectively.

If we imagine the figure of the academic as Prospero and HE as his mainland home, we can start to comprehend academic skills as nothing more than the spells the sorcerer learnt during his own education. Yet these spells do not exist in isolation from the social and cultural capital that so frequently underpins notions of academic convention, such as what constitutes critical thinking, academic literacies and points of reference. As Prospero considers his library a 'dukedom large enough' (1.2:10), we can place him within the context of a sixteenth and seventeenth century elite education that valued natural philosophers and intellectual necromancers such as John Dee. These men were given the opportunity to not only build a library but also be educated on how to use it – and through this knowledge they learned their spells were learnt. Prospero then, can be viewed as a representation of the social and cultural capital acquired through traditional education from which AtoHE students may have been excluded. Just as Caliban was born of a 'blue eyed hag' whose 'earthy and abhorred commands' are synonymous with the contemporaneous common cunning folk whose magic was considered symbolic of their deviance, and are contrasted by Prospero to his own 'art', the spells that Caliban's heritage and culture have given him are considered deficient and inferior. This Prospero-culture leads many academics to consider mature students as being most in need of targeted support upon their transition to HE. This, however, runs counter to students' own perception of their newly-acquired academic skills and their potential for future attainment, as evidenced by their being as likely to get a first-class degree as non-access students (QAA, 2019). Indeed, some of the students interviewed spoke of being aware that negative assumptions were being made about their capabilities but that they also found the culture they were now in to be alien.

Academic literacy and in particular critical thinking are socially constructed and through academe's perpetuation of what the ideal student looks like, an environment emerges in which the other has to work harder to be seen as possessing such capabilities, which often makes them feel insecure. This stands in contrast to the AtoHE classroom where the central academic skill of critical analysis is encouraged and developed alongside academic writing and research skills, but which is potentially more accepting of alternative images of what that looks like. For this reason, once in the HE environment, previously confident and motivated Access students can begin to display traits of imposter syndrome, reverting to their initial feelings of negativity and trepidation from the start of their diplomas. This may be exacerbated by their minority position, with the largest number of Access students studying in any HEI standing at just 3.5 per cent (QAA, 2019).

AtoHE students may also experience intersectional othering, not only as mature students, but also because of minority characteristics such as ethnicity or disability. Given the relatively high proportion of AtoHE students with such characteristics, challenging negative feelings of difference and deficiency is essential, especially as imposter syndrome may be a dominant factor in the decisions of first-year undergraduates to withdraw from studies. So, once Caliban has left a space in which his own culture and lived experiences were valued and where he consequently began to learn Prospero's spells, he needs to be reminded that those experiences are not deficient or less artful than Prospero's and that the spells Access has taught him are adequate to successfully transition. Once the Access students recognize that the academic culture, which can appear designed to isolate them, is nothing more than a set of skills they can learn. Prospero no longer holds a power over them. Instead, they can meet him with a sense of parity and belonging. As Caliban insightfully recognizes in Act 3 Scene 2 (87–9), Prospero's books are the source of his power but 'without them / He's but a sot, as I am, nor hath not / One spirit to command'.

If we agree that understanding the culture and conventions of academia enables both students and their instructors to prosper within HE, then we must surely concede that it's incumbent on all FECs and HEIs to offer explicit instruction on these cultures and conventions. This is an argument for an approach that elucidates, illuminates, and draws back the veil on academic convention. Educators who focus on embedding learning and developing skills within subject teaching arguably share such an approach. We also require an academic literacies pedagogy, which acknowledges that the practices of academic disciplines are grounded within the broader social discourse of academic institutions, and that students are required to develop and deploy a range of literacy practices that are accepted within the cultural community they are in (Lea and Street, 2006). In other words, if we are to give students access to Prospero's books, we must also give them the skills to use them in ways defined by the particular context, and thereby attain that sense of belonging and empowerment.

The development of skills is a complex process that requires careful scaffolding as students move from one context to another. Indeed, the Gestalt theory of learning notes that transfer of knowledge or skills from one situation to another can only occur when similarities between the two, be they in content, method or attitude, are clearly perceived by the students (Leberman, McDonald and Doyle, 2018). The presence of a more knowledgeable other in this process of realization is clearly fundamental, also clear is that the gap between educational experiences and cultures have to be bridged. Much of this may already be understood: calls for greater collaboration in easing students' transition into and through FE and HE are not new and have in some cases led to important theoretical and practical studies into the causes of poor transition between institutions and levels of study and thence to resolution. However, focusing on the problems of transition is neither systematic nor sustained and sometimes leads to problematizing students, particularly non-traditional students, rather than problematizing the often implicit institutional practices against which these students are measured. Accordingly, the new governmental call for wider skills development, greater facilitation of lifelong learning, and for collaboration between educational providers, may offer opportunities to build a bridge, between not only FE and HE provision but also between the students' self-perception, as being capable, skilled and valued, and their cognisance of the need for further learning and skills development.

In this idealized landscape, the bridge between Caliban's island and Prospero's mainland must enable freedom of movement in both directions. To develop partnerships and programmes of study that illuminate these cultures and conventions, and actively help students along their journey, HE should not be in the all-powerful position. Transition events should not take place only in HEIs as this reinforces the perception that Prospero's position is the locus of power. Furthermore, the existing and unique capabilities of AtoHE students entering HE must be recognized to avoid Caliban again becoming the other: engaging with students in their pre-transition environment would encourage Prospero's enlightenment and, therefore, Caliban's sense of belonging.

Ultimately what is required is a pedagogically-grounded skills-first curriculum, designed within an FE-HE community of practice in which each can benefit from the others' expertise. This might take the form of, for example, regular cross-institutional transition fora or distinct transition roles that work to facilitate the transfer of knowledge and practice between students *and* practitioners in both areas, and to build a community of more knowledgeable others in both FE and HE. For this to be achieved, we educators need to step back from negativity and cynicism about the political landscape in which we are working and instead focus on the possibilities that policy can offer. In our current context, the strongest possibility seems to be that the value of the FE classroom is recognized, and particularly its potential to enable Caliban to dance on the mainland as freely as he does on the island. We need to encourage a letting-go of the sense of powered authority that exists within HE, much as Prospero relinquishes control by casting his books, the symbols of his power, into the sea when he leaves the island.

For the tempest to be truly calmed, therefore, we need to work collaboratively rather than competitively, to provide students with an empowering education in not only their specialist subject but also in developing the sociocultural, educational and personal skills they require to inhabit any space successfully. Fostering a multiplicity of skills and an appreciation of the diversity of creative and critical thinking, problem solving and reflexive resilience in our students will arguably enable us all to traverse different worlds and to challenge the elite's dominance of intelligence. If not shipwrecked by future political storms, this vision augurs well for future Calibans' self-actualization to be magicked into being and for FE and HE to keep in step with the dance to come.

# References

Augar, P. (2019) *Post-18 Review of Education and Funding: Independent Panel Report* (The Augar Review). London: Department for Education (DFE). Online. www.gov.uk/government/publications/post-18-review-of-education-and-funding-independent-panel-report (accessed 1 June 2019).

hooks, b. (2009) *Teaching Critical Thinking: Practical Wisdom*. New York: Routledge.

Jones, K. (2006) 'Valuing diversity and widening participation: The experiences of access to social work students in further and higher education'. *Social Work Education*, 25 (5), 485–500. Online. https://doi.org/10.1080/02615470600738866 (accessed 11 May 2020).

Lea, M.R. and Street, B.V. (2006) 'The "academic literacies" model: Theory and applications'. *Theory Into Practice*, 45 (4), 368–77. Online. https://doi.org/10.1207/s15430421tip4504_11 (accessed 11 May 2020).

Leberman, S., McDonald, L. and Doyle, S. (2018) *The Transfer of Learning: Participants' perspectives of adult education and training*. London: Routledge.

QAA (2018) *Access to higher education*. 'The grading scheme handbook: Section A'. Online. www.qaa.ac.uk/docs/qaa/about-us/access-grading-scheme-handbook-section-a-2018.pdf?sfvrsn=8d3bc581_4 (accessed 28 September 2019).

QAA (2019) *Access to Higher Education*. 'Data report'. Online. www.qaa.ac.uk/docs/qaa/about-us/access-to-he-data-report-19.pdf?sfvrsn=322cc581_6 (accessed 28 September 2019).

Webber, L. (2014) 'Accessing HE for non-traditional students: "Outside of my position"'. Research in Post-Compulsory Education, 19 (1), 91–106. Online. https://doi.org/10.1080/13596748.2014.872936

*Timid men prefer the calm of despotism to the tempestuous sea of liberty.*

(Thomas Jefferson)

Robby the Robot from *Forbidden Planet* – MGM Art Department

overleaf: Sean Jeal

# Act 3 Introduction: 'Set it down with gold on lasting pillars': In search of FE's golden age

*Stephen Exley*

*'Our escape / Is much beyond our loss'*

(*The Tempest*, Act 2, Scene 1: 3–4)

Has there ever been a golden age for FE? There has been no shortage of attempts to map-out what one might look like in England, not least through the litany of government-commissioned reports churned out since incorporation. From Leitch to Lingfield, from Moser to Foster, there have been isolated examples of astute analysis. But the success in achieving parity of esteem (a tired cliché that deserves packing off to an isolated island, along with its cousin 'the Cinderella sector') between the gilded citadels of higher education and the paupers of further education in the public consciousness has been virtually non-existent. The addition to the pile of every new official report has merely served to reinforce the toothlessness of its predecessors.

The latest effort, the so-called Augar Review, set out a bold reimagining of post-18 education in England – and a fundamental rebalancing of the relationship between HE and FE. At the launch of the report, Prime Minister Theresa May managed to pledge to 'boost further education spending and put right the errors of the past' – shortly before being ushered out of Number 10 by her party.

The government that followed, led by old Etonian Boris Johnson, made the long-overdue announcement that the 16–18 base funding rate was to be raised for the first time in seven years, thanks to a £400 million cash injection (a modest sum, in the context of the cuts that had preceded it).

The news was delivered by the chancellor (and former Filton Technical College student) Sajid Javid, who pledged: 'I'll continue to look at what more we can do to help, just as my FE college opened my horizons and set me on my way.' Within six months, he had resigned from the Cabinet, claiming he had been left with 'no option', after being ordered to sack his trusted advisers. Another false dawn.

So, after decades of being battered and tossed around by changing political winds, the tempest has brought FE to the Isle of Wonder, a (seemingly) safe haven caught between its painful past and fluid, fluctuating visions for its future. But whether one is looking at the sector's history, its present or what is yet to come, it's worth bearing in mind one of the most-cited quotations from another of Shakespeare's plays, *The Merchant of Venice*: 'All that glisters is not gold.'

## Past

The simple message from the aphorism above is that appearances can be deceptive; not everything that looks precious or true turns out to be so. But within the context of both *The Tempest* and the history of the FE sector, the role of gold is more complex. Take 'Yellow Sky', the 1948 film starring Gregory Peck, Anne Baxter and Richard Widmark, which is loosely based on the plot of *The Tempest*. In Shakespeare's play, magic becomes the source of Prospero's growing power. In this Wild West reimagining, it comes down to gold and greed. The characters vie for ownership of the precious metal, which is both the cause of a violent power struggle, while simultaneously being perceived as what is needed to come out on top – and stay there.

This motif, cynics might suggest, takes us neatly back to arguably the single political change that genuinely and irrevocably changed the nature of the English FE sector: incorporation in 1993. For its supporters, this was when colleges gained their freedom: freedom from LEA control, freedom to set higher pay, and freedom through greater autonomy. In the years that followed, participation, retention and success rates increased. And that was just the start of the radical redefinition of the college landscape. In 1993, there were almost 450 FE and sixth-form colleges; today, there are barely half that number.

The next great change came with the coalition government (elected in 2010) and the advent of austerity. In the years 2010/11 and 2018/19, per-student funding for 16- to 18-year-olds fell by 12 per cent in real terms. Even after Javid's investment outlined in 2019, per-student funding in 2020/21 will remain 7 per cent below its level in 2010/11.

For adult education, the situation is even bleaker: total spending (excluding apprenticeships) dropped by almost half between 2009/10 and 2018/19, largely driven by student numbers collapsing from 4.4 million in

2004/05 to 1.5 million in 2017/18. Predictably, the main victims of this decade of cuts have been FE staff. A 2017 report by the Education and Training Foundation revealed that the college workforce in England had dropped by 9 per cent – the equivalent of 12,000 full-time roles – over a three-year period. For those who remain, average teaching salaries in colleges are now £7,000 less than in schools (ETF, 2017: 3). In one case, Amersham and Wycombe College, staff went over a decade without an annual pay rise.

For those on the front line, the conclusion is clear: incorporation has failed. In the words of Stuart Rimmer (2019), the principal of East Coast College in England:

> There are too many old-thinking college principals holding to the glory days of freedom from LEA control, higher pay and promises of autonomy that have never truly materialized. Incorporation has failed to protect the security of colleges, of staff and students. It has failed to protect continued investment, it has failed to protect high standards, it has failed to protect support from those in high government since 1992.

Colleges may have won their freedom – but the cost has been profound.

## Present

The storms of Brexit may place the UK in peril, but the prospect of the tide of immigration (cynically inflated and exploited by Brexiteers) being turned back by Boris Johnson, Brexit Britain's answer to King Cnut, has dragged FE into the political limelight. Speaking at the 2019 Conservative Party Conference, Education Secretary Gavin Williamson vowed to 'super-charge further education' over the next decade. Could the golden age finally be here?

In Act 5, Scene 1 of *The Tempest*, Gonzalo reflects on how misfortune can ultimately lead to happiness and fulfilment:

> *Was Milan thrust from Milan, that his issue*
> *Should become kings of Naples? O, rejoice*
> *Beyond a common joy, and set it down*
> *With gold on lasting pillars.*

Engraving these tidings in gold is portrayed as a means of achieving their permanence. A clear parallel can be drawn with the language being used by government to describe its latest flagship FE policy: the introduction of 'gold-standard' T levels. These two-year qualifications will, the Department for

Education (DfE, 2019) proclaims, 'provide the knowledge and experience needed to open the door into skilled employment, further study or a higher apprenticeship'.

Yet the confidence and certainty coursing through this statement belies the challenges the initiative has faced from its infancy. The challenges posed by tight timescale for the design and delivery of T levels were of such magnitude that Jonathan Slater, the most senior civil servant in the Department for Education, felt compelled to take the unusual step of publicly raising his concerns (Slater, 2018) over the 'ambitious' project, requiring a formal ministerial direction for the project to be continued in spite of these objections. Most embarrassing of all, the former skills minister Anne Milton admitted before the House of Commons Education Select Committee that, as a mother, she would advise her own children to 'leave it a year' before taking the very qualifications she had been tasked with championing (see Ryan, 2018).

Let's not forget that introducing a mainstream, technical post-16 qualification that will win the confidence of students, parents and employers is something that no government has managed to carry out successfully. The most recent attempt – New Labour's 14–19 diploma – was scrapped by the coalition government after two years – and £300 million in investment. Nonetheless, T levels have repeatedly been described in government statements as one of three 'gold-standard' routes open for post-16 students, alongside A levels and apprenticeships. So what evidence is there to back up this claim? The answer is simple: none whatsoever. As former City & Guilds Group chief executive Chris Jones put it in 2019 (quoted in Exley, 2019: 8):

> As of today, we have no student that has studied a T Level. No student has been examined in a T Level. No student has progressed into a job with a T Level. No student has progressed to university with a T Level. How on earth can we say it is a gold standard?

Yet, as Education and Training Foundation chief executive David Russell pointed out (ibid.: 8–9), 'gold-standard' is simply a metaphor, an inference into the quality of a qualification that is impossible to prove or disprove. The act of describing T levels as 'gold-standard', he suggests, can actively play a role in their being perceived as such.

# Future

Whether or not you accept this argument, it brings the question back to the tensions at the heart of the FE sector's identity crisis. Can a sector that is defined by being other to the more established and recognized parts of the education system – schools and universities – ever be regarded as gold-standard by the public at large?

For those who have lived, breathed, even bled for FE, its maltreatment at the hands of successive governments feels like wilful abuse of the worst kind. Reports on FE almost always fall back into comparisons with life before the coalition, as if FE prior to austerity was a land of plenty. It may, in many respects (not least funding), have been better than what followed, but it was by no means utopian. And this deficit model does the sector a disservice.

Another unfortunate consequence of the battering of the FE sector's morale during the decade of disappointment is the pervading sense of gratitude that emerges from sector bodies when any scraps are tossed in FE's direction. Make no mistake: the extra £400 million funding package for 16–18 education last summer was badly needed. But it was a mere step in the right direction – and a modest one at that. The FE sector changes lives. Receiving proper funding should be seen as its entitlement, not a favour.

The University and College Union has undoubtedly played a valiant role in fighting for the FE sector's right to dance but its 2017 petition, calling on the government to recruit 15,000 staff to restore the college workforce to 2009 levels, missed the point. FE's ambition should on no account be limited to simply returning to a past when things were not quite as bad as they are now. It can do better.

Further education is a community of survivors and visionaries – one that has survived the tempest and earned the right to dream, to dance. To return to the words of Gonzalo:

> Beseech you, sir, be merry. You have cause,
> So have we all, of joy, for our escape
> Is much beyond our loss. Our hint of woe
> Is common. Every day some sailor's wife,
> The masters of some merchant, and the merchant
> Have just our theme of woe. But for the miracle,
> I mean our preservation, few in millions
> Can speak like us. (2.1:1–9)

The Dancing Princesses continue to cavort – and their number is growing. From #ukfechat to #FEresearchmeet, they are carving out new spaces to explore, to reflect, to share. And the sector is theirs for the taking. Take the example of the redoubtable members of the National Association for Teaching English and Other Community Languages to Adults, representing the ESOL sub-sector's practitioners and supporters. Rather than waiting for a national strategy to be created for them, they took matters into their own hands and drafted their own. As I write, civil servants are hastily following suit. When FE sets the agenda, others follow.

The golden age of further education will not be enabled by a white paper, pronounced by a press release or enacted by legislation. Dancing is no longer enough; it's time for FE to call the tune.

# References

Department for Education (DFE) (2019) 'Guidance: Introduction to T Levels'. Online. www.gov.uk/government/publications/introduction-of-t-levels/introduction-of-t-levels (accessed 2 March 2020).

Education and Training Foundation (ETF) (2017) *Further Education Workforce Data for England: Analysis of the 2015–2016 staff individualised record (SIR) data*. Online. www.et-foundation.co.uk/wp-content/uploads/2018/04/FE-workforce-data-2017-FINAL_new.pdf (accessed 3 March 2020).

Exley, S. (2019) 'Burden of Proof: Is evidence really the key to good policy design?' Manchester: Further Education Trust for Leadership. Online. https://fetl.org.uk/wp-content/uploads/2019/07/2829-TES-Stephen-Exley-Provocation-v6.pdf (accessed 3 March 2019).

Rimmer, S. (2019) 'College incorporation: "An experiment that has failed"'. *TES*, 12 November. Online. www.tes.com/news/college-incorporation-experiment-has-failed (accessed 2 March 2020).

Ryan, G. (2018) 'Milton: "Leave it a year" before taking T levels'. *TES*, 17 July. Online. www.tes.com/news/milton-leave-it-year-taking-t-levels (accessed 3 March 2020).

Slater, J. (2018) Letter to Secretary of State for Education, Damian Hinds, 17 May. Online. https://assets.publishing.service.gov.uk/government/uploads/system/uploads/attachment_data/file/710831/180517_Request_for_Ministerial_Direction_-_T-Levels.pdf (accessed 3 March 2020).

*What to do with such a sorrow? It was like an enormous black cloud boiling up over the horizon … He had to transform it, or at the very least enclose it.*

(Margaret Atwood)

Emily Ransley

opposite: Erin Brett

## Chapter 14

# A new enlightenment: Scottish FE as a source of emancipation

*Steve Brown*

## Introduction

In *The Tempest*, Caliban expresses regret for allowing Prospero to take control of the island, lamenting his own loss of power and effective enslavement:

> All the charms
> Of Sycorax, toads, beetles, bats,
> light on you!
> For I am all the subjects that you have,
> Which first was mine own king; and
> here you sty me
> In this hard rock, whiles you do
> keep from me
> The rest o' th' island. (Act 1, Sc. 2: 340–5)

Prospero's decision to enslave Caliban is motivated by lack of trust, but also by an assumption that he, Prospero, knows how to rule the island better than Caliban. In the same way that Prospero uses his ill-gotten magic to exploit Caliban and the entire island, recent policies have transformed the Scottish further education (FE) sector from something intended to empower civil society into something that seeks to 'create an individual that is an enterprising and competitive entrepreneur' (Olssen *et al.*, 2004: 136). This shift in focus from the societal to the individual gives the illusion of promoting individual autonomy, but is in fact indicative of a deeply neoliberal conceptualization of education that Gillies has described as a 'subtle, insidious form of governance where ends can still be aimed at merely by shaping actors' own choices' (Gillies, 2011: 215).

This chapter explores the impact of the neoliberal tempest on the Scottish FE sector and ways in which the prioritization of corporate needs over the wellbeing of communities has inhibited the sector's potential to benefit society. It then presents a reimagining of Scottish FE in a world that regards education as more than a source of human capital. A return to classical liberal values, embellished with the emancipatory overtones of critical pedagogy, can allow the sector to scratch out a new tune – one that allows FE professionals to dance again, unfettered by the indoctrinatory chains of work-readiness.

## Historical background

Scotland had its own formal education system in place before the United Kingdom was formed. The post-reformation project of having a school in every parish was more or less achieved by the end of the seventeenth century, driven by what Smith describes as 'a conscious effort to create a literate and informed public who would be able to take responsibility for their own religious and civil life' (Smith, 2016: 7). This desire to use education to develop autonomous rational thought across all social classes became a key tenet of classical liberalism, and led to Scotland achieving such high status as the centre of eighteenth-century philosophy that Voltaire declared 'it is to Scotland that we look for our idea of civilization' (Skowronski, 2014: 1075).

Liberal philosophers regarded universal education as an essential means of allowing individuals to become freed from the guardians who control both their thoughts and actions. In his essay 'What is Enlightenment?', Kant argued that the development of capacities for individual rational autonomy would lead to a society that is naturally more accommodating of free thought, leading in turn to increased equality and social justice: 'At last free thought acts even on the fundamentals of government and the state finds it agreeable to treat man, who is now more than a machine, in accord with his dignity' (Kant, 1784).

Despite its role as a provider of vocational training, the influences of classical liberalism on the Scottish FE sector were evident until very recently. Throughout the pre-devolution Thatcher years and the post-devolution New Labour era, attempts to introduce neoliberal reforms in FE were made through a managerialist approach to policymaking – one that sought to retain government control while removing government accountability (for examples see Mulderrig, 2015). However, Scottish Labour's commitment to social justice, equality and inclusion in the first few years of the twenty-first century ensured that the FE sector retained its role of serving local communities through the provision of part-time programmes, with funding available to cover childcare or travel expenses in order to facilitate access for harder-to-reach individuals.

The continued provision during the 2000s of a wide range of non-vocational evening courses (also known as leisure courses) embodies the liberalist view of education as a source of human flourishing. A deliberate lack of instrumental focus allows people to learn for the sake of learning, with the autonomy to choose to study what interests them rather than what might benefit future employers. It can also be argued that part-time vocational courses, despite having the clear instrumental purpose of attaining a qualification and developing employability, were at least made accessible to such vulnerable members of society as single parents or people on low incomes, thereby promoting social inclusion.

## The neoliberal tempest

Caliban speaks of Prospero's kindness towards him when he first came to the island:

> When thou camest first,
> Thou strok'dst me, and mad'st much of me; wouldst give me
> Water with berries in't, (Act 1, Sc. 2: 334–6)

Prospero seduced Caliban into thinking that he would look after him, developing an unequal, yet mutually beneficial, relationship based on respect and the valuing of each other's knowledge and expertise. In a similar way, recent education policy gives the impression that it seeks to benefit society by addressing the problem of youth unemployment. However, closer scrutiny suggests otherwise, with recent FE policy implying an agenda that isn't concerned about community learning needs, forcing the sector instead into a narrow, employability-focused remit. A Scottish Government report of 2011 claimed that 'the fundamental role of further education is to provide people with the skills they need to get a job (however far they are from the labour market), keep a job, or get a better job and develop a good career' (Scottish Government, 2011: 10). A subsequent policy document entitled *Developing the Young Workforce* (DYW) called on colleges 'to reduce the level of youth unemployment … by 40% by 2021' (Scottish Government, 2014: 46). This policy explicitly directs colleges to 'deliver learning that is directly relevant to getting a job' (ibid.: 15), encouraging stronger links with employers to allow colleges to adapt their curriculum so it is more closely aligned with industry needs.

This policy clearly advocates an approach grounded in Human Capital Theory, a neoliberal conceptualization of education that regards learning as the development of human capital, which increases 'capacities that contribute to economic production' (Little, 2003: 438). While there is, of course, a societal benefit in addressing problems of youth unemployment, the all-pervasiveness of the employability agenda in the DYW policy has led to developments in the FE sector that seriously undermine classical liberal values. The call for colleges to provide full-time, vocational programmes that meet the specific requirements of employers led to the number of college students dropping by 152,000 between 2008 and 2016, and this was widely attributed to the axing of part-time courses.

Furthermore, the range of study options available has narrowed, with a greater proportion of programmes available in the STEM subjects (Science, Technology, Engineering and Mathematics), as they are perceived as more likely to lead to employment. This was achieved at the expense of subjects less clearly associated with the workplace, or of courses aimed at mature students who are already in work or retired. The practice of conceptualizing education as a commodity that can be acquired for economic gain is, in Robeyns's view, 'severely limiting and damaging, as it does not recognize the intrinsic importance of education, nor the personal and collective instrumental social roles of education' (Robeyns, 2006: 74).

This disregard for the value of education in its own right directly conflicts with classical liberal values. Perhaps even more concerning, though, is the way in which DYW hands control of FE programme content directly to employers. Employers will naturally value a specific and limited set of skills and capacities in their staff – those that allow them to do their job well. They have no interest in developing capacities that might allow their staff to question or challenge employment practices, or even capacities to enhance people's knowledge, skills or development beyond the workplace. The application of Human Capital Theory to education policy leads to a curriculum with a high level of instrumentalism, a narrow range of focus, and a disregard for criticality and autonomous thinking that strengthens the position of employers. This is ultimately disempowering for students as it merely indoctrinates them into the limited workplace opportunities presented within the parameters of the status quo.

In the same way that Prospero seduces Caliban before enslaving him and forcing him into a life of mundane drudgery, recent FE policy in Scotland ultimately forces the FE sector to prioritize the needs of industry over communities. Furthermore, the preoccupation with employability has led to not only the demise of non-instrumentalism and student autonomy within FE programmes. The prioritization of full-time programmes and the consequent loss of part-time places has limited opportunities for vulnerable or disadvantaged members of society to gain access to FE programmes. While attempts to reduce youth unemployment are certainly commendable, it is necessary to question the benefit of pursuing this goal if it comes at the expense of the wide range of learning opportunities that local communities have previously benefited from.

Another feature of neoliberal policymaking in the Scottish FE sector is the development of an increasingly performative culture that requires colleges to demonstrate their effectiveness according to over-simplistic performance criteria such as retention and attainment rates. The use of these statistics to measure quality naturally encourages colleges to become more risk-averse in their student recruitment practices, favouring students who are unlikely to drop out or struggle to succeed. Coupled with a funding model that encourages colleges to pack as many students as possible into a single class (Scottish Funding Council, 2018), the system is not one that encourages the recruitment of harder-to-reach or vulnerable students who require additional support in order to achieve success. These risks to accessibility, inclusion and support reflect Coffield's concerns that the application of Human Capital Theory in lifelong learning creates a 'moral economy' (Coffield, 1999: 485), in which individuals with greater capacities to learn are valued more highly than those with fewer, leading to the exclusion of individuals who have little potential to make an economic contribution.

## A new enlightenment?

Just as Prospero uses his power to relegate Caliban to a role of servitude, neoliberal policymaking has reconfigured the FE sector so that it is no longer concerned with the needs of those whom it educates, but is now required to '...enhance sustainable economic growth [by providing] a skilled workforce' (Scottish Government, 2014: 7). The existential crisis this creates for FE professionals has, understandably, led to considerable resentment among college lecturers, and to several instances of industrial action in recent years. Like Caliban lamenting his enslavement by Prospero, FE professionals feel that their position has been usurped, as they are forced to alter their praxis to address the needs of the powerful, at the expense of the vulnerable.

It is, however, possible to envision an alternative FE landscape in Scotland – one in which the constraints of neoliberal managerialism have been removed. For this to happen, though, the source of the current crisis needs to be exposed for what it is. Neoliberal policymaking works on the materialistic and unethical assumption that individuals exist in order to serve an economic need, and are therefore valued according to the potential economic contribution they can make. Removing this assumption would allow a return to previous liberal values, in which students are no longer regarded simply as workers or future workers, but instead as citizens within society. Prioritizing societal development over economic growth allows the three classical liberal tenets of breadth, autonomy and non-instrumental purpose to return to the fore, elevating social and community values above corporate priorities.

In addition to evoking the principles of classical liberal education, an FE landscape unfettered by neoliberalism would also benefit from the introduction of progressive pedagogies that aim to go beyond individual empowerment and towards social emancipation. Following the work of Freire (1996), Giroux (2011) describes critical pedagogy as being 'rooted in a project that is tied to the creation of an informed, critical citizenry capable of participating and governing in a democratic society' Giroux, 2011: 7). Such a project aims to raise the critical consciousness of students by exploring how locations of power affect their position within society. Rather than encouraging compliance with the inequalities of the neoliberal status quo, a critical-emancipatory approach can instead develop capacities to identify and challenge neoliberalism's inherent injustices, with a view to implementing change. Rather than creating a society that works for the economy, critical pedagogy prioritizes social justice over economic growth. This takes learning beyond the narrow, financially-driven limitations of neoliberalism, and also goes beyond the classical liberal goal of individual empowerment. Guided by the principles of critical pedagogy, FE can exceed the classical liberal ambition of empowering students to be more successful within existing social structures. It can also give students the capacities to engage critically with these structures, identify inequality and injustice, consider alternatives, and become actively involved in the positive transformation of society.

## Conclusion

Neoliberal ideology, as the name suggests, appears at first to be merely an extension of the invisible hand proposed by the classical liberal economist Adam Smith during the Scottish Enlightenment – the idea that market forces act as a form of self-regulation. However, Smith never envisioned the application of capitalist principles to a field such as education that, from a classical liberal perspective, functions as a common good and a source of empowerment for individuals within society. The Scottish government's neoliberal approach to FE policy has consigned the sector to a servitude comparable to Prospero's enslavement of Caliban, and leaves those who work in the Scottish FE sector feeling disillusioned and resentful about being co-opted into a neoliberal project that promotes inequality and incorporation.

The prioritization of industry needs over community needs, as described in this chapter, the concomitant deprioritization of learning opportunities for the more vulnerable members of society (Coffield, 1999), and the breakdown in industrial relations resulting from recent reforms and funding crises (for example McIvor, 2019), all imply that Scottish FE is in dire need of a reboot. The sector would benefit from a return to the values that existed before the implementation of the current neoliberal project – when education sought to empower individuals to become successful and autonomous members of society. However, it would be even more beneficial to society for FE to extend its ambition by seeking to empower *beyond* existing social structures. The structures themselves need to be challenged and ultimately replaced by a new imaginary, a structure that sets out to address – rather than perpetuate – power imbalances. In the same way that Prospero's return to Milan frees Caliban from the magical bonds that forced him into slavery, removing the neoliberal constraints from Scottish FE would allow the sector to prioritize its societal role once again and consider how it can benefit – rather than facilitate the exploitation of – the communities it serves. Scotland's first minister, Nicola Sturgeon, has recently referred to Scottish enlightenment philosophy, arguing that: 'the objective of economic policy should be collective well-being – how happy and healthy a population is, not just how wealthy' (Sturgeon, 2019). Perhaps this signals a revised approach to policymaking – an approach the Scottish FE sector desperately needs.

# References

Coffield, F. (1999) 'Breaking the consensus: Lifelong learning as social control'. *British Educational Research Journal*, 25 (4), 479–99. Online. https://doi.org/10.1080/0141192990250405

Freire, P. (1996) *Pedagogy of the Oppressed*. Revised edition. London: Penguin.

Gillies, D. (2011) 'Agile bodies: A new imperative in neoliberal governance'. *Journal of Education Policy*, 26 (2), 207–23. Online. https://doi.org/10.1080/02680939.2010.508177 (accessed 11 May 2020).

Giroux, H.A. (2011) *On Critical Pedagogy*. London: Bloomsbury.

Kant, I. (1784) 'What is enlightenment?'. Trans. Smith, M.C. Online. www.columbia.edu/acis/ets/CCREAD/etscc/kant.html (accessed 30 September 2019).

Little, A. (2003) 'Motivating learning and the development of human capital'. *Compare: A Journal of Comparative and International Education*, 33 (4), 437–52. Online. https://doi.org/10.1080/0305792032000127748 (accessed 11 May 2020).

McIvor, J. (2019) 'College lecturers to stage two-day strike over pay', *BBC News*, 15 May. Online. www.bbc.co.uk/news/uk-scotland-48274102 (accessed 07 November 2019).

Mulderrig, J. (2015) '"Enabling" participatory governance in education: A corpus-based critical analysis of policy in the United Kingdom'. In Smeyers, P. Bridges, D., Burbules, N.C. and Griffiths, M. (eds), *International Handbook of Interpretation in Educational Research*. Dordrecht: Springer, 441–70.

Olssen, M., Codd, J. and O'Neill, A.-M. (2004) *Education Policy: Globalization, citizenship and democracy.* London: Sage.

Robeyns, I. (2006) 'Three models of education: Rights, capabilities and human capital'. *Theory and Research in Education,* 4 (1), 69–84. Online. https://doi.org/10.1177/1477878506060683 (accessed 11 May 2020).

Scottish Funding Council (2018) 'Credit Guidance: Student activity data guidance for colleges in AY 2018–19'. Online. www.sfc.ac.uk/web/FILES/guidance_sfcgd102018/SFCGD102018_Credit_Guidance_-_Student_Activity_Data_2018-19.pdf (accessed 6 October 2019).

Scottish Government (2011) *Putting Learners at the Centre: Delivering our ambitions for post-16 education.* Online www.webarchive.org.uk/wayback/archive/20170701072502mp_/http://www.gov.scot/Resource/Doc/357943/0120971.pdf (accessed 29 September 2019).

Scottish Government (2014) *Developing the Young Workforce: Scotland's youth employment strategy.* Online. www.gov.scot/publications/developing-young-workforce-scotlands-youth-employment-strategy/ (accessed 29 September 2019).

Skowronski, S. (2014) 'Enlightenment, Scottish'. In Gibbons, M.T. (ed.), *Encyclopaedia of Political Thought.* 8 vols. New York: Wiley. 3: 1075–81. Online. https://doi.org/10.1002/9781118474396.wbept0316 (accessed 11 May 2020).

Smith, C. (2016) 'Reforming Scotland: The Scottish liberal tradition'. Edinburgh: The Melting Pot. Online. https://reformscotland.com/wp-content/uploads/2016/06/Craig-Smith-The-Scottish-Liberal-Tradition.pdf (accessed 11 May 2020).

Sturgeon, N. (2019) 'Why governments should prioritize well-being' (video lecture), *TED Summit 2019.* Online. www.ted.com/talks/nicola_sturgeon_why_governments_should_prioritize_well_being?language=en (accessed 07 November 2019).

*Those who profess to favour freedom and yet deprecate agitation, are people who want crops without ploughing the ground; they want rain without thunder and lightning; they want the ocean without the roar of its many waters.*

(Frederick Douglass)

Tia White

overleaf: Ella Benson

## Chapter 15

# 'I urge you to hear me': Changing prison education for the better

## *Vicky Butterby, Claire Collins and David Powell*

There is a tradition of prisoners writing letters. It remains an important part of prison culture and is one way for prisoners to communicate their experiences of being imprisoned, presenting their ideas, concerns, fears, and hopes. Our chapter seeks to add to this tradition by conjuring two new prison letters about prison education: the prisoner Caliban's letter to Prospero, his jailer, and Prospero's reply. Then we employ the theory of practice architectures (Kemmis *et al.*, 2014b) to illuminate the messages raised within them. We conclude by arguing that if we want to reimagine and change prison education for the better, we could start with a sincere, genuine and democratic 'conversation' (Kemmis *et al.*, 2014a: 149) with prisoners about their hopes for a better life upon release.

> *Dear Prospero,*
>
> *You think you know me, you think you know what's best for me – that you know my heart and my mind and my spirit. But I know this place, the beating heart of this island, its magic and its mayhem, the rhythm to which it dances. I, Caliban, too have knowledge that I can share.*
>
> *For my (past) actions I am deeply sorry, for I have come to understand meeting violence with violence will never a happy union be.*
>
> *I, Caliban, hurt people.*
>
> *I, Caliban, did wrong.*

*I make no bones about the mistakes I made. And now I urge you to walk in my shoes, come hide with me under my cloak and peer out at my world as I see it. For you speak of distant lands, opportunity and possibility. You speak in metaphors and use miracles and magic tricks ... yet I, Caliban, do not have the liberty of your view. You gave me a map I cannot read, spells I cannot conjure, words I cannot say.*

*And in this, I, Caliban, have too been wronged.*

*I, Caliban, have been mistreated. I have been oppressed and marginalized and abused and hurt. I am at the margins, I am clinging on to the cuff of your coat. I need you to understand my story too. I need you to 'always ask why'.*

*Others who share my story tell me: 'you don't do it because you want to, you do it because you have to'. At the time, I, Caliban, also saw no other way, for me all hope was lost.*

*I, Caliban, write this letter to share something of my life with you, to help you understand what I need and how I can make different choices now that the Tempest's storm has passed. Please hear me. For too long I have felt unworthy of voice, I have communicated only in curses, I urge you to put aside your preconceptions. I urge you to hear me, Caliban, as I speak to you.*

*Help me see the wonder in learning, help me put it to good use. Don't tell me there is hope for the future if there is nothing but old bones to hang my new clothes on. Bring with your hope a sense of realism, let me put what you teach me to good use now. Help me understand the purpose behind what it is you wish me to learn.*

*I, Caliban, do not want to be part of your system – a number, a payment by results, a box to be ticked. Share with me the wonders and the whys, link what I learn to my aspirations, even when they do not fit with those you hold for me. Do not underestimate my insider knowledge. You are merely a visitor to this isle – this is my home.*

*Do not give me new clothes if you will not teach me how to wear them, if you will not help me find those places where wearing them brings me hope. Remember my new robes may not mean so much in my world, they are easily discarded, disregarded, they are easily stained. The hope I feel can easily become a mirage if there is nowhere for me to wear them with meaning and with pride. Do not ask me to journey to foreign lands if you are not prepared to challenge the inequalities within my world that hold me captive.*

*I, Caliban, cannot be boxed. I am everything and nothing and my mind rocks back and forth with the pain of what I have done. If you want me to learn your ways, give me first the space to learn myself, to understand my emotions, to process past hurts and to understand how I have come to be the Caliban that resides here in this place. Understand that we do not share the same experience of the world, of the land that we inhabit together. The calm waters you enjoy can be a tempest for me. The privilege you possess has awarded you many long years in study, your head lost in your books, the magician of your craft. You taught me how to say your words, but understand this, I am still learning how to speak your language. Accept and own your privileges, acknowledge we were not born equal, you and I, and envision your role as one that challenges inequality in all its forms – doing so will serve you well if you truly want to bring me hope.*

*I, Caliban, am a person.*

*I, Caliban, am human.*

*Treat me as a person. Treat me as a human being, treat me as one of your kind. Ask me how goes my day when you pass me by. Small gestures such as these can mean a lot to me. Give me opportunities where I do not need to choose learning over a higher wage – please understand that whilst I am captive in this land, immediate gains will outweigh future plans, they are what keep me going, what I look forward to most.*

*Too many times I have had to tell my story, repeat myself again and again to those who do not talk amongst themselves. Do not fragment me and my experience in this place, for I, Caliban, am whole, I am more than the sum of my parts. Collaborate across this land and put plans in place with me – in doing so you will understand the big picture of my experiences and the things that will help me most. Ask me my opinions, ask me how I feel, ask me what I think could help. Remember, I know this place like no other, and in ways you never will. Get me actively involved and I will teach you to use your nails to dig for nuts, to engage with your senses, to feel your way in this mysterious land. Approach my time with you holistically and I will share all that is hidden, the subtleties of my experience, my hopes, my joys, my* expectations. *You do not know this place as I do, but if you are open to what I have to share, then let me help you understand.*

*I, Caliban, humbly await your response.*

Dear Caliban,

There was a time when your words and ideas would have appeared to me naive, coming not from my once-beloved books, but from your uneducated mind. I would have asked: what could you know of the route to civility and a good life? What could you tell me about of which the literatures did not speak? I was wrong, I see this now, and I wish to learn from our time together and your wisdom so that the future I help to create back in my homeland does not fall foul of such lack of understanding.

What then can I learn from you?

I still believe that knowledge and understanding can unlock new ways of seeing and being in the world. You have helped me see that the value of this learning cannot be assumed or enforced; it is only when you are able to imagine your own future that learning can contribute to that dream. Ah, to dream with unfettered optimism – am I so naive? No, I see now that your world will not change through your or my agency alone. Our lives are interconnected, our dreams made or broken on our own and others' volition.

I sent you to learn and told you that you could only earn a wage when you had proven your learning achieved. Did this mean that to learn felt like a punishment to you? I believe that to be so, and I wish that you knew how lucky you were to have this chance to learn from a civilized man about a civilized world. But, again, I assume we share an idea of 'civility' and I assume that this is good in and of itself. How easy it is to forget what you tell me, and remember only my own ideas of good living.

How can we seek to influence one another in ways that nurture and shape our dreams? Perhaps our greatest gift is to listen, not with minds full of our own ideas of goodness and justice, but with open minds, seeking to understand the paths we have each taken, the robes we all wear and the tasks we must do to fulfill our many obligations and achieve our dreams. Did I listen to you while you were my captive? I fear not, and not Ariel who was so compliant in pursuit of her freedom, or Miranda, who could have helped me understand your crimes better. I attended only to my

*books, not to anyone who could have helped me understand the
island life we all shared. But despite my previously closed ears,
I ask that you hear me now as I try to explain what I will do to
atone for my ignorance. I will take not the stance of an enemy as
you had previously felt, but of a fellow traveller, seeking to make
the world a better place. I will speak to everyone and make time
to understand what they say and do and feel and why. I will try
to play my part in changing all our lives and I do this in the hope
that we may all have a brighter tomorrow.*

*Thank you for helping me understand what learning can mean,
outside my books and scholarly ways. You taught me how to use
my nails to dig for nuts, to engage with my senses, to feel my way
in that mysterious land and this, this is what civility means in the
island life you will continue to have now that I am gone.*

*Goodbye Caliban and fare you well. I hope we meet again in
the next life, when perhaps we can walk as brothers through a
fairer land.*

*Prospero*

The theory of practice architectures is a contemporary, site-based theory of practice that can help us better read the messages in Caliban and Prospero's letters. It does this by illuminating the three arrangements of a prison – the ideas and language of the social-cultural arrangements, the resources (physical, spatial and temporal) of the material-economic arrangements and the relationships of the socio-political arrangements – and how they shape the practices of its education projects (Kemmis *et al.*, 2014b). This architecture reveals how the practices of prisoners' learning, teaching and training, and prison leadership more generally, are shaped.

Caliban's letter suggests he is being shaped by his social circumstances and external factors: 'you don't do it because you want to, you do it because you have to'. However, he recognizes that prison education too is being shaped by paternalistic ideas that know what's best for the Calibans in our prisons. The teaching and instructing practices of prison education staff are dictated by government policy so, like Caliban, they can argue that 'you don't do it because you want to, you do it because you have to'. It seems it is not only the prisoners who might feel powerless in our prison education system.

Caliban is asking for a number of things from the prison staff, educators, and leaders. First, he asks that the relationships with prison staff and education staff are respectful: 'Treat me as a human being, treat me as one of your kind. Ask me how goes my day when you pass me by. Small gestures such as these can mean a lot to me.' Then, he wants prison staff and education staff to demonstrate the idea of patient hope (Webb, 2013) with him: 'If you want me to learn your ways, give me first the space to learn myself, to understand my emotions, to process past hurts and to understand how I have come to be the Caliban that resides here in this place.' He also asks that he is told 'the purpose behind what it is you wish me to learn', he understands the economics of prison capitalism and its payment by results (Collins, Powell, and Wilkinson, forthcoming). In addition, he wants prison leaders to imagine and implement forms of prison education that offer opportunities, so 'I do not need to choose learning over a higher wage', because 'whilst I am captive in this land, immediate gains will outweigh future plans, they are what keep me going, what I look forward to most'. Most importantly, he is asking for prisoner-centred learning. A form of prison education that offers Caliban and all other prisoners transformative hope (Webb, 2013), a realistic and hopeful new future, even if his hopes 'do not fit with those you hold for me'. And, when Caliban is released, he wants support to be in place that removes 'the inequalities within my world that hold me captive', so he can begin his new life with hope and confidence. More than anything, he wants prison staff to listen and learn from him.

What is so powerful about Prospero's response is its reflexivity; an openness to listening. We assert that if prison education is to be reimagined, the process must start with prison leaders, teachers, and instructors listening to and learning from the Calibans of this world. By jointly reflecting 'on the character, conduct and consequences of their practices' (Kemmis *et al.*, 2014a: 16) and the development of open communicative spaces in which a sincere, genuine, and democratic conversation will be generated about what constitutes good prison education from a prisoners' perspective. We recognize this may be a very different way for prisons to work, though we assert that this 'morally and ethically committed' (ibid.: 27) praxis could change for the better the lives of those who live, learn, and work in prisons. We hope by pursuing such an approach it would not only be 'history-making' (ibid.: 27) but also meet the goal of prison education that, in our view, is to prepare prisoners to live well in a world worth living in.

# References

Collins, C., Powell, D. and Wilkinson, J. (forthcoming) *Studying Educating, Learning, and Skills at Prison 23 Through the Lens of Practice Architectures.* Huddersfield: University of Huddersfield Press.

Kemmis, S., McTaggart, R. and Nixon, R. (2014a) *The Action Research Planner: Doing critical participatory action research.* Dordrecht: Springer.

Kemmis, S., Wilkinson, J., Edwards-Groves, C., Hardy, I., Grootenboer, P. and Bristol, L. (2014b) *Changing Practices, Changing Education*. London: Springer.

Webb, D. (2013) 'Pedagogies of Hope'. *Studies in Philosophy and Education*, 32, 397–414. Online. https://doi.org/10.1007/s11217-012-9336-1 (accessed 11 May 2020).

*All at sea again*
*And now my hurricanes*
*Have brought down*
*This ocean rain*

(Echo and the Bunnymen)

Erin Wilby

overleaf: James Harris

*Chapter 16*

# Spalpeens on the Isle of Wonders: Reflections on work, power and collective resistance in Irish Further Education

*Fergal Finnegan and Jerry O'Neil*

This chapter is crafted from an extended dialogue between two practitioner-researchers recorded on a walking inquiry (O'Neill, M. and Roberts, 2019) around Dublin City in 2019. The discussion is grounded in their common interest in Irish Further Education and Training (FET) and, in particular, working conditions and futures for FET practitioners. As they walk, they explore power and precarity in their own occupational biographies and the state of the wider field inspired by a critical, historical account of labour and resistance in, and behind, *The Tempest*.

They begin their think-walk close to Dublin's medieval centre and meander across the city towards the ever-expanding financial centre in the Docklands where the Liffey spills into the sea ...

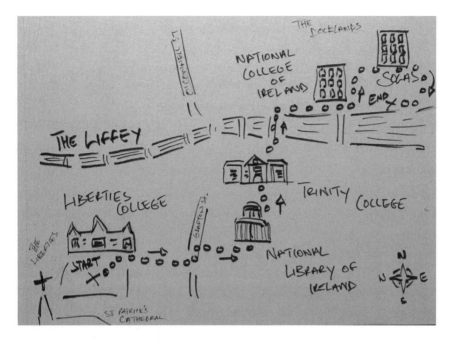

**Figure 16.1.** Map of walking inquiry

## Invisibility and taking liberties

> *Be subject to no sight but thine, and mine: invisible*
> *To every eyeball else: go take this shape*
> *And hither come in't: go: hence with diligence.* (1.2:204–307)

*Late summer 2019, we sit on a sun-drenched bench in a park in Dublin's city centre between St Patrick's Cathedral and Liberties College of Further Education. The sound of birdsong, almost electronic in its timbre and rhythm, interrupts the low but persistent noise of traffic. The Liberties is a curious area that was originally a space outside the city walls, granted to Augustinian monks by King Henry II, to live, pray and work within their own 'liberty'. It was later incorporated into the city and became famous as an area of artisans and a centre of democratic rebellion in the 1790s. Over time it evolved into a close-knit working-class community which is now shrinking through gentrification. It is the FE college that brings us here today, as the starting point of our walk…*

Jerry    So, Liberties College is one of few FE colleges in the city centre … but FE remains marginal for official Ireland.

Fergal      Yes, adult education's invisibility is reflected in the spatial
            organization of the city. FE colleges don't usually occupy central
            or high-prestige locations in Dublin ...

Jerry       ... they are hard to see all right

            – not even subject to your sight or mine ...

*East, away from the Liberties, down Golden Lane and Stephen Street.*

Jerry       ... our student teachers speak about this ... they find it hard to
            visualize placement spaces. They can point to a primary school or
            secondary school. But ask, 'Where is FE? ... where can I go?'

            FE in Ireland is certainly not as visible as it is in the UK.

Fergal      And even when centres are physically visible they are not culturally
            legible, you know? Not readily associated with solid professional
            groups or the state.

Jerry       Then there's the invisibility in terms of career paths for emerging
            practitioners ... it's tricky occupational terrain to navigate. And
            that's the thing that I struggle within my work with ITE for FE ...
            the entry points ... professional pathways are near-invisible ...

*Chatham Street ... getting closer to the centre. We hear, before we see, the
sound of a busker competing for the tourist shilling. We continue to talk
about the poor working conditions of FET practitioners: the long years
spent by so many people, including ourselves, on short-term contracts.
Just how widespread this is has become clearer in recent research (O'Neill
and Fitzsimons, 2020; Bryman, 2012) and another research project we've
worked on has made us very aware of the personal damage of extended
precarity (Finnegan et al., 2019).*

Fergal      It's not just about poor working conditions and bad pay, it's also
            the lack of any meaningful professional development.

Jerry       Absolutely ... and this is the issue for me now, with the new FET
            national policy on professional development (SOLAS, 2017).

            Surely the very notion of professionality is based on the idea, of
            the possibility, of an occupational future to develop into (The
            Teaching Council, 2012).

I see professional development working across temporal domains and being part of our ever-emerging career storytelling (Del Corso and Rehfuss, 2011). Something that is ultimately, future-facing … but to not have that … to not have a future …

*As we enter Grafton Street, the noise of pedestrians and a lone fiddler playing what may be 'The Spailpín Fánach' swells, then, as we pass, recedes. We cut across and down South Anne Street. We are, for a moment, at the heart of the Ireland that makes it onto postcards and airplane magazines.*

## Work discipline, resistance and hope in *The Tempest*

All things in common nature should produce
Without sweat or endeavour. Treason, felony,
Sword, pike, knife, gun, or need of any engine,
Would I not have. But nature should bring forth
Of its own kind all foison, all abundance,
To feed my innocent people. (2.1:134–9)

*Down Dawson Street, towards Molesworth Street, and onto Kildare Street – weaving our way through civil servants and tourists. We find an island of calm on the steps of the National Library. This highly visible space of knowledge is nestled up against the Dáil and the other grand buildings from a colonial past.*

Jerry    So, I thought we might pass this way to get to Shakespeare through *Ulysses* …

Fergal   Ah, where Stephen pontificates about Hamlet … well how can we move towards *The Tempest*? Sideways maybe?

Jerry    Yeah, how else? … I was reading the chapter you sent me from the *Many Headed Hydra* (Linebaugh and Rediker, 2000).

Fergal   What did you make of it?

Jerry    Very interesting … there are so many ways you can go with it … enclosures and the commodification of the commons …

Fergal   … Oh yeah … a stirring book, a very imaginative book which explores the history of the Atlantic from below, between the sixteenth and nineteenth centuries.

'The sea is history' to use Derek Walcott's lovely phrase ... describes the Atlantic as a fundamental space in the making of capitalism and colonialism. The flow of people and commodities between Europe, West Africa and the Americas was based on the imposition of a vicious, often deadly, work discipline.

But at same time new kinds of cooperation and culture emerged across this vast sea. Slaves, sailors, workers, soldiers and servants from different cultures and nations thrown together created cultures of solidarity. Often they went further – resisted, rebelled and even created free communities. Their stories and ideas circulated around the Atlantic along with sugar, cotton, iron, gold and human cargo, feeding further resistance and democratic experiment ...

Jerry      ... which Linebaugh and Rediker link to *The Tempest* ...

Fergal      Yeah. They say this history of oppression and resistance saturates *The Tempest*. There is an absolute obsession with authority and order in the play ... but it is a fretful obsession.

Prospero, the circus master, the magician, the Lord and Duke ... never lets control slip out of his grasp, yet we know the Atlantic was in constant ferment, the scene of repeated rebellions and multiple experiments in equality and mutual aid. The scene with Trinculo, Stephano and Caliban is a fascinating rendering of these very real social tensions as a hapless comedy ... as toothless.

*By now we are moving again – past The Lincoln Inn where Joyce met Nora Barnacle, and slipping through one of the backways into Trinity College Dublin.*

Jerry      A comedy but it's quite a sad comedy ... there might be a sense of revolt in that scene ... but we know it's not going to happen.

Fergal      Yeah, it's true, it all follows Prospero's script but of course Shakespeare was a shareholder in the Virginia company, which had a vested interested in making Caliban, Stephano and their like seem incapable ... the very idea of resistance comic ...

Jerry      ... the venture-capitalist dramatist couldn't stomach a revolt on his stage or page but maybe in a sideways manner he did acknowledge that people can resist ...

Fergal   Yes … and live different lives, flourishing lives … .

It's these tensions that make the play so interesting.

## Workplace organizing, solidarity and cultural change

In this bare island by your spell,
But release me from my bands
With the help of your good hands. (5.10)

Jerry   So when we think about work and resistance in FE … I don't see a lot of collective action, resistance – maybe that's where the work needs to be done …

Fergal   I couldn't agree more.

Jerry   I would like to see more of a kind of critical professional development, a politicized community of practice …

*We are using Trinity as a shortcut to the quays but an unexpectedly locked gate means we are momentarily trapped within the walls of the elite university.*

Jerry   So I am thinking about possible loci for collective organization …

*Finding a way out through the Science Museum, we cross Pearse Street, past Joyce House on Lombard Street – once the state's registration office for the newly living and the dead.*

Fergal   I guess it makes sense for people to engage with unions that already have a presence in their workplace. But in a way that looks outwards and builds alliances with students and communities. I think the UCU strikes in the UK and the north of Ireland were really inspiring – the way students and lecturers supported each other … I was up in Belfast during the first one … your old stomping ground.

– have a look at this on my phone it is a picture of Queen's university at that time …

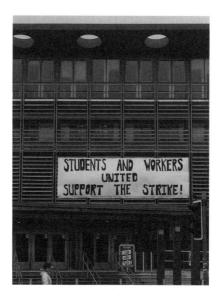

**Figure 16.2.** UCU protest at Queen's University

... the sense of collective power and hope was very strong and they made gains. The success of the teachers' strike in California last year was based on alliance building with communities and students beforehand.

Unions are not strong in Irish adult education. My guess is we will need organizational and research networks alongside unions to help us change how we imagine ourselves.

We are so habituated to focusing on students' needs we sometimes forget about effective workplace organization. My colleague Elaine Murphy is doing research on this.

What's interesting is that students in FE talk about the care they get and FE as nurturing spaces but FE practitioners often experience the same institutions as profoundly careless towards them ...

It is tricky ... there are so few places where people come together ... people have quite individualized and very fragmented work experiences. Across a vast sea and different cultures? ...

*Now on City Quay, a gust of fresh air reminds us we are near the sea now. The Jeanie Johnson is moored nearby – a replica 'coffin ship' built to commemorate the Great Famine of the 1840s. Close now to our destination, we cross Sean O'Casey Bridge as the Liffey seems to murmur beneath us ... to us ...*

Jerry      ... but with practitioners working across various institutions in precarious conditions, it's hard for them to organize at work when they are so invisible there – even to each other .... but I like what you are saying about reimagining organization and research ...

             It needs to be practitioner-led but maybe with, at times, the need for help of the good hands of folk like ourselves who can make connections across the field ...

             I often wonder should we be doing more as a university department that prides itself on its critical pedagogic practice.

Fergal     Yeah you're right ...

Jerry      ... when I work with practitioners I do try to ensure that reflexivity is ignited by some degree of criticality ... but it's not enough ... we need to do more ...

*Up Excise Walk and left up to Mayor Square.*

Jerry      ... I have been experimenting with using Twitter – curating some of the experiences of precarious workers in further and higher education – harvested from research and my own reflective practice ... some are retweeted, poetically-rendered experiences of others (@precariouspoet1, 2019).

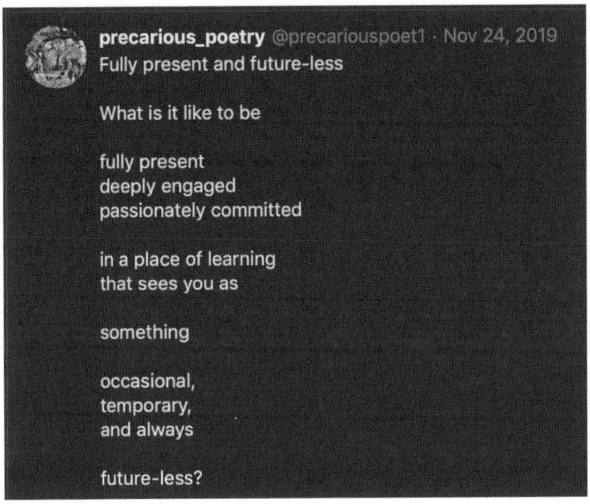

Figure 16.3. Tweet by @precariouspoet1

Jerry    But at the moment it's little more than faint electronic birdsong ... I'm not sure that a tweet ever started a revolution ... but it's one way of trying to connect, organize in other ways ... and there's a safety in the anonymity and an openness granted by a creative form and persona ... maybe it casts a kind of digital spell into the spaces where we need to organize ... part of the work of hidden transcripts ... (Scott, 1990)

## Walking the boundary of the new enclosures

In a poor Isle: and all of us ourselves,
When no man was his own (5.1:218–19)

*And so we find ourselves somehow in a very different Dublin from where we started. Somewhere in here, among the shiny metallic structures of the Docklands, are the offices of SOLAS. Founded in 2013, SOLAS is responsible for policy formation and funding allocation in FET and co-authors of a recent national policy document on professional development in the sector (SOLAS, 2017).*

Jerry    We are walking on the sea – or it would have been in Shakespeare's time ... I was just listening on the radio this morning about Ireland's role as a tax haven ... a kind of Bermuda in Europe ...

Fergal   Yeah ... the level of corporate tax dodging facilitated by the Irish state is gobsmacking. For so long we produced labouring bodies and cattle for export as part of an Atlantic economy ... now its financial services, services which include arcane ways of ensuring the wealthy become wealthier.

         Behind the magick garments of modern-day dukes eh?

         Anyhow, this place is closely associated with this but it was a dockers' community. Now it's a kind of JG Ballard landscape ... homogeneous, sterile ... and so perhaps where SOLAS is situated is significant ... when you leave your office here, I wonder what kind of Ireland are you imagining yourself a part of ...?

Jerry    Well I don't know but I do know the policy shifts – the mania for metrics, the obsession with employability and the low-trust culture this creates has worsened working conditions in a new way ... by disconnecting practitioners from their good sense, their

156

sense of purpose... dispossessed from the knowledge commons if you like.

*Off Mayor Street, up Castleforbes Road and then behind an innocuous, almost hidden doorway: SOLAS.*

Fergal     This is it ...

*We enter the foyer. Printed on the wall that leads up to the foyer, Mandela's words ... 'Education is the most powerful tool to change the world' ... As we ponder these words in this context, the disembodied voice of a security guard echoes down the hall ...*

A guard    Are you lads ok?

Jerry      We're grand ... just two educational spalpeens looking for a start ...

A guard    What?

Fergal     Just looking at the writing on the wall.

*And with that we leave again.*

Jerry      Hmm ... that was a long walk for ...

Fergal     I don't think it was ever about the destination ...

*Back towards North Wall Quay, back to the life-giving water of Anna Livia Plurabella, the muse of so much that has been creatively and critically disruptive in this once colonial outpost (Smyth, 1989). And, as if just thinking about her is enough, she is suddenly with us ...*

LP         'Riverrun Woman through whom meanings flow.

           Site of passage, carrying (away) fantasies, dreams, desires, uncertain insecurities; contradictions, paradoxes, dangers, fears, terrors' (Smyth, 1989).

Jerry      But what about hope, ALP?

ALP        Hope? Maybe ... hope in the possibilities of creative deconstruction and construction ... Hope? You are walking it ...

Jerry      What do you mean?

*But she is gone as suddenly as she appeared ...*

*And so we find ourselves with nothing to do but peer into her glittering, moving mass from the concrete riverbank of North Wall Quay. We lapse into stillness and silence – leaning over the rails looking down river to the ferry terminal and Poolbeg. And beyond that again, somewhere, the familiar destinations of Liverpool and Holyhead. What do they think about these days as they stand there on their disused docklands and look westward?*

*The Central Bank of Ireland and the National Treasury Management Agency are behind us. And a piece of public art entitled* Flow *(created by Martin Richman in 2007) – an art which comes to life after dark. A work that honours the disappeared labouring life of the docks.*

*Flow ... maybe there is something in the possibility of a disruptive creativity in amongst the chaos of life and work in advanced and accelerated capitalism ... maybe this movement, our flow here, is in itself, an act of resistance, a kind of infrapolitics (Scott, 1990) ... that the knowing is in the doing in acts of creative disruption ... and maybe the process and action-orientated ways of adult education might conspire, somehow, with workplace organization as a way forward ... maybe ...*

*We are unsure ... but we are resolved to walk that doubt through ... another day ...*

*For now, we just stare into the river ... slowing down ... catching our breath ... breathing it in ...*

# References

@precariouspoet1 (2019) 'Fully present and future-less', 23 November. Online. https://twitter.com/precariouspoet1/status/1198417627565174784 (accessed 15 December 2019).

Bryman, A. (2012) *Social Research Methods*, 4th ed. Oxford: Oxford University Press.

Del Corso, J. and Rehfuss, M.C. (2011) 'The role of narrative in career construction theory'. *Journal of Vocational Behavior,* 79 (2), 334–9. Online. https://doi.org/10.1016/j.jvb.2011.04.003 (accessed 11 May 2020).

Finnegan, F., Valadas, S., O'Neill, J., Fragoso, A. and Paulos, L. (2019) 'The search for security in precarious times: Non-traditional graduates perspectives on higher education and employment'. *International Journal of Lifelong Education* 38 (2), 157–70. Online. https://doi.org/10.1080/02601370.2019.1567613 (accessed 11 May 2020).

Linebaugh, P. and Rediker, M. (2000) *The Many-Headed Hydra: Sailors, slaves, commoners and the hidden history of the revolutionary Atlantic.* London and New York: Verso.

O'Neill, J. and Fitzsimons, C. (2020) Precarious professionality: Graduate outcomes and experiences from an Initial Teacher (Further) Education programme in Ireland. *Research in Post-Compulsory Education* 25 (1), 1–22. Online. https://doi.org/10.1080/13596748.2020.1720143 (accessed 11 May 2020).

O'Neill, M. and Roberts, B. (2019) *Walking Methods: Research on the move*. London: Routledge.

Scott, J.C. (1990) *Domination and the Arts of Resistance: Hidden transcripts*. New Haven, CT: Yale University Press.

Smyth, A. (1989) 'The floozie in the Jacuzzi'. *The Irish Review,* 6, 7–24.

SOLAS (2017) *FET Professional Development Strategy*. Dublin: SOLAS. Online. www.etbi.ie/wp-content/uploads/2016/12/FET-Professional-Development-Strategy-2017-2019.pdf (accessed 11 May 2020).

Teaching Council (2012) *Code of Professional Conduct for Teachers*. 2nd ed. Maynooth: Teaching Council. Online. www.teachingcouncil.ie/en/_fileupload/professional-standards/code_of_conduct_2012_web-19june2012.pdf (accessed 11 May 2020).

*Books have the same enemies as people: fire, humidity, animals, weather, and their own content.*

(Paul Valéry)

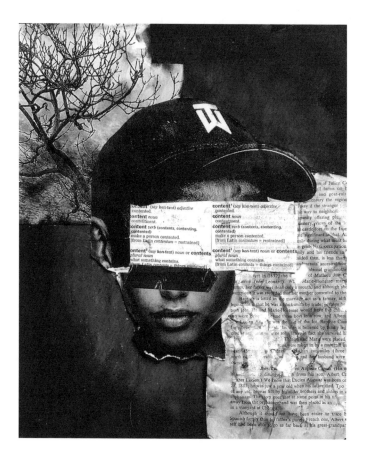

Megan Willby

opposite: Edward Cockell

## Chapter 17

# Prospero's books and the official utopias of further education

*Paul Smith*

Since the 1944 Education Act the policies of successive governments towards further education (FE) have (like Prospero in *The Tempest*) engendered periods of calm and storm. During this era, governments have created a library of sector pamphlets, reviews and papers that have articulated aspirations for FE. These visions are a response to their times and, arguably, refashioned FE in response to what had gone before. These texts can be read in various ways. Some cast the sector, the subjects taught and those who study within it, as Caliban, something base and other, having no understanding of what happens inside Colleges of FE or the people who study there. Others seek to imbue the sector with power, to make Caliban king of his own isle.

Drawing on a range of historical documents, this chapter will review some of these plans that pertain to England, the effect, if any, they had, and attempt to draw from them a notion of a utopian ideal for a sector haunted by past official visions for FE, and how they continue to affect those who study and work in the sector.

If Prospero were to conjure FE using pamphlets and reports, published officially as policy guidance, would the FE we see today be recognizable? This chapter offers an analysis of some of this literature. First, *Youth's Opportunity* (Ministry of Education, 1945) and *Further Education* (Ministry of Education, 1947), from the 1940s, and, second, '*15–18: Report of the Central Advisory Council for Education – England*' from 1959, more commonly known as the *Crowther Report* or *Crowther*. All were utopian schemes and proposals put forward for FE from official sources. They carry an authenticity and credibility due to being official government publications (Scott, 1990); they carry with them their biases of ideology and time, and 'can be interesting precisely because of the biases they reveal' (Bryman, 2012: 550). These historical publications contain debates that have continued to obsess FE since 1945, including debates on the justification of compulsory attendance until the age of 18 and the role and purpose of FE. This piece will discuss these, using later government publications and reports regarding or relating to FE, and how utopian ideals written in the 1940s and 1950s were still being debated in 2019.

First, we need to understand how FE developed in the early twentieth century. As noted by Bailey (2002) the role FE could have in developing citizens goes back to the early decades of the twentieth century, as did the drive for compulsory attendance in some form of education past statutory school leaving age. The 1918 Education Act made provision for attendance at day continuation schools between the ages of 14 and 18. However, this was not enacted due to resistance from employers, plus the financial position of the country after World War I (ibid.: 59). This state of affairs largely continued until the passing of the 1944 Education Act legislated for provision of FE, making it the statutory duty of every Local Education Authority (LEA) to provide facilities for full and part-time FE for those over compulsory school age.

The 1948 Act made clear the desire for those aged over 15 to continue to attend education and for FE to provide vocational training, cultural learning and recreational activities. This vision was comprehensively articulated in two Ministry of Education pamphlets published during the immediate post-war period. The first appeared in 1945, entitled *Ministry of Education Pamphlet No.3: Youth's Opportunity: Further Education in County Colleges*. This largely concerns compulsory part-time education for all young people, up to the age of 18, who were not already in training. A second pamphlet, published in 1947, was entitled *Ministry of Education Pamphlet No.8: Further Education, The Scope and Content of its opportunities under the Education Act, 1944 (Further Education)*. It covers a broad spectrum of FE, including part-time day release and vocational courses.

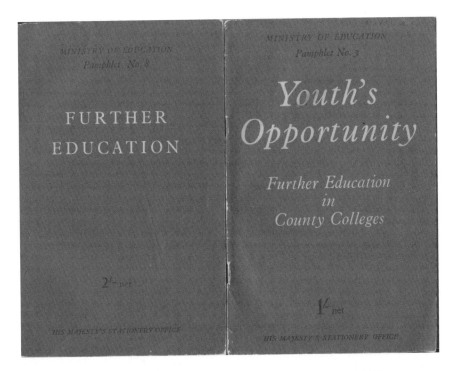

**Figure 17.1.** Further Education (1947) and Youth's Opportunity (1945)

*Further Education* goes into detail about the many considerations needed for the future development of FE, including accommodation and teacher training. It discussed types of institutions, that were to include county, local, regional and technical colleges, some of which would offer a part-time technical education or day release to apprentices. This was an attempt to bring clarity to a sector that had its roots in a range of institutions and traditions, and was a plan for a brighter future.

> 2. To-day there is a palpable need for fully-trained citizens, and we have the opportunity to train them. The need is implicit in the responsibilities of a democratic society. The opportunity is provided by the greater leisure of a scientific age. There is here a vital challenge to our educational system. For the training and preparation appropriate to the times must and can extend far beyond the statutory school-leaving age. There are no frontiers to education, a truth that has now become a guiding principle in the public service of education.

**Figure 17.2.** Further Education and post-war optimism (1947)

Although Further Education has greater breadth, it is the earlier *Youth's Opportunity* that is of interest here. It describes new county colleges that were to be attended part-time by those who transitioned into employment on leaving school at aged 14 or 15, and were not studying technical subjects at college. Study was to be compulsory until aged 18. *Youth's Opportunity* begins by stating that the establishment of these institutions will be 'one of the most important of the many tasks set before Local Education Authorities' (Ministry of Education, 1945: 2). Noting the previous failures of attempts at compulsory continual attendance, it states early-on the purpose of bringing in compulsory attendance of some form until the age of 18. It argued that 'more education would increase the happiness and welfare of the individuals to whom it was given' and that it 'would be for the good of the country and the communities that compose it' (ibid.: 3).

This would be facilitated by delivering a wider curriculum including physical and cultural activities, aiming to teach young people to live a healthy life, learn effectively, use their leisure time productively, gain enjoyment of art, literature and music and an appreciation of their responsibilities to the wider community. Importantly, it declared the hope that by the age of 18, a young person would have learned what is 'necessary for good citizenship in a democratic community', and 'to have developed their character so that they will (a) be honourable, tolerant and kindly in dealing with their fellows; (b) have an independent and balanced outlook on life' (ibid.: 31).

Compare this to the current description by the Association of Colleges (AoC) of the purpose of FE as providing 'students with valuable skills for the workplace, helping to develop their career opportunities and strengthen the local, regional and national economy' (AoC, 2019). While respecting the fact that many colleges deliver well-rounded tutorial provision, along with extra-curricular activities, it is the words and the intent of the two guiding principles: the happiness of the young people who were given the opportunity to develop their skills as workers and citizens of *Youth's Opportunity* compared to the instrumentalist view that FE Colleges are places for developing skills for the workplace, that makes the earlier pamphlet appear utopian.

However, utopia can be dystopian for some. County colleges were aimed at low-skilled young people moving into employment without training. As with many plans for FE aimed at young people who are unemployed or have low attainment, there is a sense that this was to be done to, not with or by consent of, the young people; that FE would educate this cohort of Calibans to be good and happy citizens. Although provision was made so that periods of 'comparative rigidity ... are relieved by periods in which there is the largest possible opportunity for them to choose what they want to do and how they do it' (Ministry of Education, 1945: 28), they were in effect to be captured, like Caliban, and given little choice or agency. Non-attendance at a county college would have been punishable with a fine and possible imprisonment for the young person, employer or parent (ibid.: 54). This could make Prospero's isle Caliban's dystopia. County colleges, and compulsory attendance until 18, met the same fate as the plans under the 1918 Education Act. Although legislated for, they were never realized. By 1959, Crowther was still arguing for county colleges and for each LEA to be legally required to set them up, to be reaffirmed.

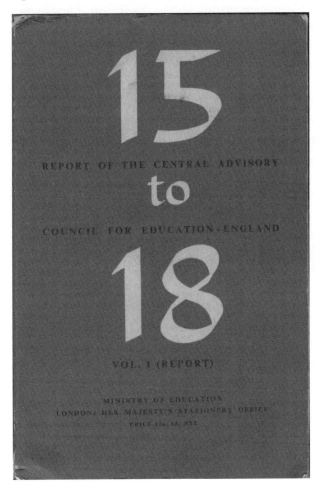

Figure 17.3. 15–18: Report of the Central Advisory Council for England (1959)

The FE sector of the 1940s was made up of a diverse range of institutions including technical, local and area colleges. Further Education hoped that the county college would be the 'focal point' for an FE sector with a range of institutions (Ministry of Education, 1947: 10). This diversity of institutions continued into the 1950s, with Crowther arguing that the term 'Further Education' was an 'imperfect definition' (Crowther, 1959: 318) covering a range of institutions. The *Crowther Report* was wide-ranging and it examined the education of young people aged 15 to 18 in relation to changes in society and industry. Within its scope was secondary education, raising the school leaving age, county colleges, sixth forms, technical education and the wider FE system.

Crowther discusses county colleges, noting their failure to materialize. As no date for implementation was set, the report stated that the intention for county colleges should be reaffirmed, especially as contact was lost with the least skilled as soon as they left school. The curriculum of county colleges was also to be of importance but had shifted in emphasis to 'an appreciation of the adult world in which young workers suddenly find themselves; guidance for them in working out their problems of human relations and moral standards; development of their physical and aesthetic skills; and continuance of their basic education, with a vocational bias where appropriate' (ibid.: 195).

Crowther also recommends an 'alternative road' (ibid.: 398) of full-time practical courses for able pupils aged 16 to 18, in place of part-time courses or full-time academic courses in sixth forms. Here we see the FE we have today beginning to emerge. Yet Crowther arguably goes further, with recommendations on broadening the curriculum to 'come closer to the ideal of what a balanced education should be', while 'still serving their vocational purposes' (ibid.: 369).

The discussions outlined so far relate to two themes: keeping young people in education for longer so that they can become skilled active citizens through a balanced curriculum, and the clarity of purpose of FE in achieving this aim. First, both *Youth's Opportunity* and *Crowther* argue that it is good for society that these young people stay in education, advocating a compulsory system until a young person is 18. *Crowther* was driven partly by concerns of 'juvenile delinquency' and 'the rejection of traditional authority' (ibid.: 38); raising the age at which young people would need to stay in education (ibid.: 42), along with county colleges, would be part of maintaining 'moral standards' (ibid.: 175). More recently, Colley, Wahlberg and James refer to this as the 'problem of youth', where FE is seen to be a response to social issues (2007: 47).

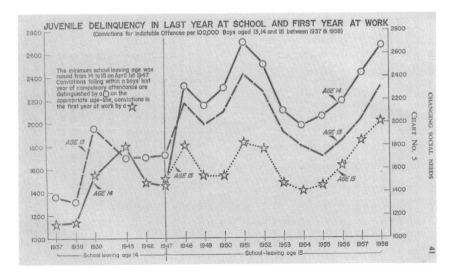

**Figure 17.4.** Crowther: Measuring Delinquency (1959)

Reports from the 1990s and 2010s make claims to the difficulties in gaining employment and other social issues if a young person does not achieve GCSEs (Kennedy, 1997; Wolf, 2011). *Bridging the Gap: New opportunities for 16–18 year olds not in education, employment or training* (2007) feared the impact that unskilled and unemployed young people might create for society, citing as possible outcomes offending, drug use and relationship difficulties.

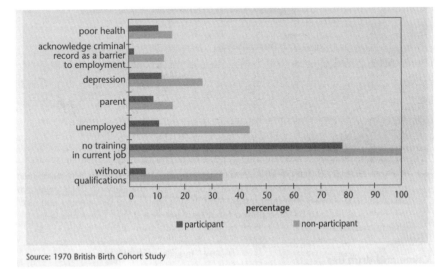

**Figure 17.5.** Bridging the Gap: Measuring Delinquency (1997)

It wasn't until 2013 that the age of participation was raised, meaning that those who entered FE at 16 would have to stay to until the academic year in which they turned 18. This has had varied success (Widdowson, 2018), with a cohort of young people still remaining NEET (not in education, employment or training).

What all of these reports have in common is the identification of the potential of FE to improve the life chances of a young person. It is telling to counterpoint the language used in the 1940s and 1950s; happiness, well-being, citizenship, and a wider or balanced curriculum, to the 1990s and beyond, which sought to manage social problems with a mixture of basic skills and personal and social development qualifications.

Second, questions about the purpose of FE still torment the sector. FE was the term used to describe the diversity of institutions that was 'both stimulating and bewildering' (Ministry of Education, 1947: 6), with unfulfilled plans being made for an even more complex sector with county colleges at the centre. Crowther argued that the term Further Education was an 'imperfect definition' covering a diverse range of institutions (Crowther, 1959: 318). The post-war FE system was so diverse that Crowther had difficulty establishing how many types of institution there were (Richardson, 2007: 389). This lack of clarity continued into the 1960s, with Peters (1967) taking nine pages to give a definition of FE to use as a basis for an account of the sector, and a further 23 pages to describe all the institutions it covered. This ill-defined purpose continues into the twenty-first century. In 2005, *Realising the Potential: A review of the future of further education colleges* (Foster, 2005) argued that the main issue facing FE was that it 'lacks a clearly recognized and shared core purpose' (Foster, 2005: vii). Foster also stated that an FE college must 'be absolutely clear about its primary purpose', namely: 'to improve employability and skills in its local area' (ibid.: 3) and that this itself will bring about social well-being. More recently, this was cited and reaffirmed in the independent panel report to the *Review of Post-18 Education and Funding* (Augar, 2019: 117), indicating that officially the sector should be defined by an output of skills rather than the utopian ideals of earlier plans that also included cultural activities and developing active citizens.

22. Our need is twofold : to produce both skill and social leadership. It is necessary that workers should be skilled to meet the highly specialized demands of industry and commerce in a scientific age. Thus our colleges must be staffed with teachers who are familiar with current industrial and commercial methods, and equipped with machinery and apparatus that is up-to-date. In addition to possessing technical knowledge, however, men and women must also have an understanding of everyday human relationships. For industry to-day is a large-scale social organization, and success in it will depend upon qualities of personality no less than upon acquired knowledge. To a very much greater degree than in the past, therefore, it is necessary to foster a corporate life in our colleges ; and through self-governing student societies and the assignment of responsibilities, to extend the students' range of interests and their social powers.

## THE FE COLLEGE OF THE FUTURE

**11.** To achieve the positive vision set out in this report, the FE college of the future must:

- Be absolutely clear about its primary purpose: to improve employability and skills in its local area contributing to economic growth and social inclusion.

Figure 17.6. The purpose of FE? (1947 and 2005)

The recommendations from *Youth's Opportunity* and *Crowther* about county colleges were not implemented. Other later reports such as the 'damp squib' (Cantor and Roberts, 1969: 10) *Henniker-Heaton Report* (1963), the 'lost opportunity' (Simmons, 2009) of the *Macfarlane Report* (1980) and the 'missed opportunity' (Nash and Jones, 2015: 37) of the *Tomlinson Report* (2004) had a similar fate. These documents, when read, create a lost future for the sector, the ghosts of ideals not met. They lead us to ask: what would the further education sector look like if some of these ideals came to pass? What would happen if Prospero were to open these magic books of utopias and see these imagined futures? It would reveal the optimism of the sector of the 1940s for the young people who study at FE colleges. It would offer a curriculum that allows young people to develop both skills for employment and new interests away from their aspired careers, and values the wider role that FE can have in producing a fair and balanced democratic society. Most importantly, it would be a sector with a clearly defined purpose: to enhance the happiness and well-being of young people, improving their lives, while giving them training for sustainable employment. I would argue that this imagined sector exists in the work we all do each day, evoking the spirit shown in the 1940s.

## XII. CONCLUSION

154. This pamphlet about the future has been written under the shadow of events which lie " between the desire and the fulfilment ". Only when they are past will it be possible to translate the suggestions made here into action. When that time comes the pioneering instinct which has always been strong in the British people will be given many opportunities and, doubtless, the very newness of the county colleges will make an appeal to vigorous and original minds. Considerable emphasis has been laid upon this newness but it is equally true that the colleges will derive much from the experience and traditions of the past. The aims that have been formulated for them are as old as liberal education itself. The educational traditions of the country, individuality, craftsmanship, scholarliness, and freedom from rigid codes, will meet and influence each other in a way that has never been possible before. They will provide an opportunity for the young people of this country to make better use of their powers and to give better service to humanity; to learn, in short, the real relationship between rights and obligations and between work and happiness.

Figure 17.7. Youth's Opportunity 'between the desire and fulfilment' (1945)

## References

AoC (2019) 'About colleges'. Online. www.aoc.co.uk/about-colleges (accessed 24 September 2019).

Augar, P. (2019) *Post-18 Review of Education and Funding: Independent Panel Report* (the Augar Review). London: Department for Education (DFE). Online. www.gov.uk/government/publications/post-18-review-of-education-and-funding-independent-panel-report (accessed 1 June 2019).

Bailey, B. (2002) 'Further Education'. In Aldrich, R. (ed.) *A Century of Education*. Abingdon: Routledge, 54–74.

Bryman, A. (2012) *Social Research Methods*, 4th ed. Oxford: Oxford University Press.

Cantor, L. and Roberts, I.F. (1969) *Further Education in England and Wales*. London: Routledge and Kegan Paul.

Colley, H., Wahlberg, M. and James, D. (2007) 'Improving teaching and learning in FE: A policy history'. in Biesta, G. and James, D. (eds) *Improving Learning Cultures in Further Education*. London: Routledge 41–59.

Crowther, G. (1959) *15 to 18: A report to the Central Advisory Council for Education (England)*. 2 vols. London: HMSO.

Foster, A. (2005) *Realising the Potential: A Review of the future of further education colleges*. Annesley, Notts: DFES Publications. Online. https://dera.ioe.ac.uk/5535/1/realising06.pdf (accessed 11 May 2020).

Greenaway, P. (1991) *Prospero's Books*. [Film]. United Kingdom: Miramax Films.

Henniker-Heaton, C. (1963) *Day Release: The report of a committee set up by the minister of education*. Stanmore: DES.

Kennedy, H. (1997) *Learning Works: Widening participation in Further Education*. Coventry: Further Education Funding Council. Online. https://core.ac.uk/download/pdf/9063796.pdf (accessed 11 May 2020).

Macfarlane, N. (1980) *Education for 16–19 Year Olds: A review undertaken for the government and the local authority associations*. Stanmore: DES.

Ministry of Education (1945) *Youth's Opportunity: Further Education in county colleges*. London: HMSO.

Ministry of Education (1947) *Further Education: The scope and contents of its opportunities under the Education Act 1944*. London: HMSO.

Nash, I. and Jones, S. (2015) 'The politicians' tale'. In Hodgson, A. (ed.) *The Coming of Age for FE?* London: IOE Press, 24–45.

Peters, A.J. (1967) *British Further Education*. Oxford: Pergamon Press.

Richardson, W. (2007) 'In search of the further education of young people in post-war England'. *Journal of Vocational Education and Training*, 59 (3), 385–418. Online. https://doi.org/10.1080/13636820701551943 (accessed 11 May 2020).

Scott, J. (1990) *A Matter of Record: Documentary sources in social research*. Cambridge: Polity Press.

Simmons, R. (2009) 'Further education and the lost opportunity of the Macfarlane Report'. *Journal of Further and Higher Education* 33 (2), 159–69. Online. https://doi.org/10.1080/03098770902856686 (accessed 11 May 2020).

Social Exclusion Unit (2007) *Bridging the gap: New Opportunities for 16–18 year olds not in education, employment or training*. London: HMSO. Online. http://dera.ioe.ac.uk/15119/2/bridging-the-gap.pdf (accessed 11 May 2020).

Tomlinson, M. (2004) *14–19 Curriculum and Qualifications Reform: Final report of the working group on 14–19 reform*. Online. https://webarchive. nationalarchives.gov.uk/20070221120000/http://www.dfes.gov.uk/14-19/ documents/Final%20Report.pdf (accessed 24 September 2019).

UK Government. *Education Act 1944*. Online. www.legislation.gov.uk/ukpga/ Geo6/7-8/31/contents/enacted (accessed 24 September 2019).

Widdowson, J. (2018) *Mending the Gap: Are the needs of 16-18 year olds being met?* Online. www.campaign-for-learning.org.uk/mending-the-gap-are-the-needs-of-16-18-year-olds-being-met (accessed 24 September 2019).

Wolf, A. (2011) *Review of Vocational Education: The Wolf report*. Online. www.gov.uk/government/uploads/system/uploads/attachment_data/file/180504/ DFE-00031-2011.pdf (accessed 24 September 2019).

*On driest land*
*The rain falls down*
*Our shadows and hearts*
*The colour of us*
*Into the waves we drown*

(Peter Coyle)

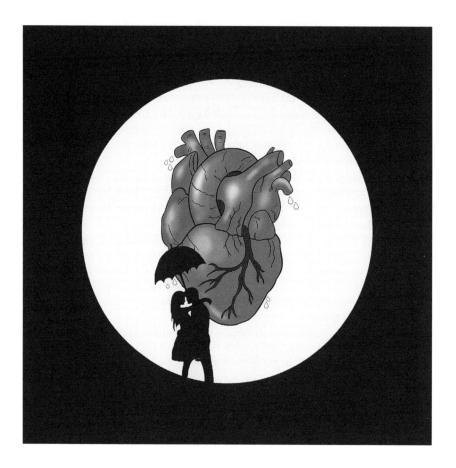

Eva Rati

opposite: Oliver Snell

*Chapter 18*

# Caliban, monstrosity and college-based Higher Education: College Scholarship Centres as islands of possibility

*Craig Hammond*

## Caliban the Monster: A 'CBHE' creature for potential

Asma (2009) locates and explains the etymology of the word 'Monster', noting that it derives from the Latin word *monstrum*, which is in turn associated with the term *monere* – that translates as 'to warn or to remind'. As powerful creatures of both narrative and imagination, monsters operate as portents, sometimes mediating warnings from the gods, or navigating cruelty in the form of an oppressed creature at the mercy of human vice and moral bankruptcy (Asma, 2009: 13). In both of these senses, culture-born monsters are beautiful creatures that lurk at the threshold or border of what is, and that, through their alien strangeness, enable us to glimpse beyond our familiar territories towards permutations of quite different possibilities.

In *The Tempest*, Caliban is an intriguing and beguiling representation of such a beautiful monster, his creature-like characteristics perform a narrative function that corroborates and embodies many of the principles identified above. As Vaughan and Vaughan (2014: 67) tell us, Caliban is 'constructed as monster, brute and savage', and throughout the unravelling of the play seems to shift between creature and human being. Lupton (2000) takes this further, suggesting that Caliban's monstrosity operates as a provocative 'creature metaphor' that serves to uncover and relay aspects of stifled human possibility. The notion of creature is an apt term to apply to the monstrosity of Caliban, as it derives from the Latin verb *creare* – 'to create'.

This definition of Caliban as a creature – as an entity *ripe* for creation – can be utilized as an allegory for College-based Higher Education (CBHE). To be clear, universities that validate or franchise HE courses provided in FE do not make Calibans out of their college-based partners. Rather, I would suggest that CBHE as a sector contains Calibanesque and creaturistic elements, harbouring a latency or at least the potential to be transformed from its current guise, when it could become a site of malleable and proactive activity. A number of factors operate to stymie and restrict not only the identity of CBHE, but also its ability to adapt and grow. Indeed, a range of daunting sectoral characteristics generate difficulties and obstacles for scholarship, teaching practice and academic leadership in CBHE. For example, systems built for the requirements of FE programmes, including achievement metrics, teaching quotas and teaching observation processes, commonly still dominate CBHE environments. Furthermore, many CBHE staff are expected to navigate teaching activities that extend across a challenging range of educational levels; it is not uncommon for CBHE colleagues to teach across the FE and HE-in-FE spectrum of courses within the same week.

The concise parameters of this chapter prevent a detailed dissection of such an extended remit of issues and constraints. That being so, the area I highlight for constructive reflection within the CBHE environment is academic leadership and associated structures of institutional recognition and support. Rather than engage in a critique that negatively unpicks and unravels the minutiae of these elements, I wish to put forward a more constructive scenario: a proposal to develop an intra-college entity that I will refer to as the College Scholarship Centre.

## Pearl diving – in search of College Scholarship Centres

Shakespeare's *The Tempest* inspired some of the key writing and ideas produced by the political philosopher Hannah Arendt (1906–1975). As Arendt notes in her book *The Life of the Mind* (Arendt, 1978), one particular segment from *The Tempest* effectively encapsulates and summarizes her philosophical method of interpreting – and seeking redemptive shards from – history. The key part of *The Tempest* identified by Arendt is Ariel's song in Act 1, Scene 2:

> Full fathom five thy father lies,
> Of his bones are coral made.
> Those are pearls that were his eyes.
> Nothing of him that doth fade

But doth suffer a sea-change
Into something rich and strange

(Hannah Arendt, 1978: 212)

From this, Arendt develops the notion of 'pearl diving' to refer to the seeking of new ways of discussing – and therefore conceiving and ultimately transcending – fixed or stagnant methods or *traditions* of thought and practice. By incorporating and conjoining the Arendtian sense of *pearl diving* along with the Calibanesque principles of creaturism, we can bring to the fore how CBHE harbours a potential to transform. Through this idea for a new form of distinctive academic leadership, CBHE as a Calibanic entity could become quite different if we develop – or at least conceptualize – the intra-organizational CBHE-based academic mechanism of the *College Scholarship Centre* as embryonic. As a formal grouping, the *College Scholarship Centre* (or CSC) could aim to support the recognition and development of academic and professional identities within CBHE. By promoting scholarship activities through a formalized, accredited and practitioner-led organizational structure, the CSC could create a foundation for a localized sense of professionalism and autonomy.

As a high profile and successful CBHE practitioner, Sam Jones (2019) has written passionately about scholarship; she explains that in recent years John Lea's AOC funded project The Scholarship Framework (2018) has given a valuable boost and increased visibility to the CBHE scholarship agenda. Jones explains that The Scholarship Framework utilized and continues to promote Ernest Boyers's four-pronged Scholarship model, which identifies the following key areas:

- the development of teaching and pedagogy
- the creation of new knowledge
- the application of knowledge across disciplines, and
- the application of knowledge in the service of the community.

Jones explains that these key areas of Boyersian scholarship are already evident and – albeit sporadically – practised within some CBHE environments. However, she notes that there is a need to continue to capitalize on and push forward with the progress made by this scholarship framework, in pursuit of more locally robust, sustainable and impactful models (Jones, 2019).

Before we progress further, it is important to establish a caveat: by drawing on the Arendtian notion of pearl diving and redemption with regard to the CSC, this chapter invites readers to engage in an idealized thought experiment. So we must avoid the pitfalls of platitude and whimsy, and acknowledge that historical and entrenched bureaucratic and managerial traditions within CBHE environments pose quite a challenge to our developing a practitioner-led CSC. As Coffield (1998) has noted, the tendency of college management systems is to implement and follow the centralized, executive-directed practice of command and control. This could prove to be a stubborn and resistant heritage to tackle and transgress. In this sense, the notion of the CSC is not necessarily a neat and tidy 'pearl', but rather one that poses a new way of thinking, based on a 'redemptive relation to the past and a constructive bearing on the present' (de Valk, 2010: 40).

## University research centres: A model to adapt

The generative idea for the CBHE-focused CSC is based on an already established framework of university research centres; these existing organizational structures make up the internal academic fabric of most universities and promote diverse areas of academic research and practice. Kumar (2017) notes that the university research centre makes visible and organizationally facilitates interactions and activities between academics, students, and industry. By doing so it promotes 'research opportunities, academic excellence, real-world problem solving, and knowledge creation and dissemination' (Kumar, 2017: 454). The research centre is designed to induce and engineer interactions between and 'across multiple departments and disciplines, universities, industry, government, and sometimes multiple countries' (Boardman and Corley, 2008: 900–1). By operating as a semi-autonomous structure within specific university environments, the centre is also able to network and interconnect across wider regional, national and in some cases international contacts. By combining groups of academics and associated external stakeholders the research centre operates synergistically as a collaborative unit, to achieve, 'the resolution of scientific and technical goals' (Boardman and Corley, 2008: 901). The research centre thus establishes a unit of expertise that far surpasses the individual knowledge and activities of its members.

Through this brief analysis of the principles and processes associated with the university research centre, we can identify and tease-out the academic and practitioner focus of its remit and activities. Of course, there are limitations, but it is important to note that research centres operate as mechanisms that afford (at least) some influence and autonomy to their respective academic and affiliated memberships. By recognizing and accrediting the organizational space of the research centre for academic and research activities, universities not only facilitate memberships to influence and impact upon disciplinary areas, but also generate the scholarship practice and research focus of the group. Importantly, within this semi-autonomous sphere of academic practice, members of research centres are expected to achieve and maintain a level of practice and output by the accrediting university, in order to maintain their institutionally accredited status.

## The College Scholarship Centre

In a practical sense, developing and implementing the CSC would require college governance and committee frameworks to formally recognize and organizationally accredit it as a structure. An application and selection process, inclusive of a staffing and membership model for the CSC, could be invited, along with a requirement for it to reflect college-specific strategic aims, expertise and expectations. Any proposed CSC structure would likely consist of a CSC Chair and Vice-Chair, a remit and focus for the membership, along with any wider scholarship requirements. Terms of reference would be important, along with student and employer engagement strategies. As part of the institutional guidance provided by the college, a variety of activities and outputs could be specified, such as the production of papers, think-pieces, case studies, and other collaborative projects along with information dissemination workshops, seminars and other modes of scholarship development. The CSC application could then be considered and approved (deferred or rejected) by an internal committee-based decision-making process.

The systematized development and implementation of a CSC could operate as a mechanism to harness, generate and disseminate knowledge and practice relevant to the sector. By generating and supporting a new model of sustainable scholarship and academic leadership, the growth and context-specificity of the CSC in the areas of learning, practice and research in pedagogy, and community engagement, could unleash a much-needed boost of creative vision and innovation. Assuming that the CSC could be developed and facilitated along more devolved, collaborative and democratic organizational principles (as opposed to the heritage of command and control that persists in many colleges) the CSC structure could develop academic support mechanisms that professionally recognize and mentor CBHE staff. By establishing a flexible but formalized space that recognizes and develops scholarship activities, the bespoke, homegrown and locally administered CSC could generate additional opportunities for incorporating a wider range of college staff, students and potential employers.

As an island of transformative possibility, the CSC could become the key vehicle to generate and lead innovative change within (and across) CBHE. As Sam Jones noted here, CBHE has a distinctive and unique character and is populated with passionate, highly skilled and experienced practitioners. Through the CSC model, CBHE leaders and practitioners could define and pursue new directions. By recognizing and nurturing expertise that is internal and practitioner generated, college-grown and administered, CSCs could ultimately generate an interlinking national network of informative and effective college scholarship centres. The notion of academic and scholarship leadership being developed by staff and students at college-specific levels means that, should it ever become manifest, the CSC model could move colleges and college networks towards dynamic and transformative step-changes. In doing so, CSCs could take CBHE institutions and their local communities towards new, transformed and alternative futures.

## References

Arendt, H. (1978) *The Life of the Mind,* 2 vols. Vol. 1: *Thinking.* New York: Harcourt Brace Jovanovich.

Asma, S.T. (2009) *On Monsters: An unnatural history of our worst fears.* Oxford: Oxford University Press.

Boardman, P.C. and Corley, E.A. (2008) 'University research centers and the composition of research collaborations'. *Research Policy,* 37 (5), 900–13. Online. https://doi.org/10.1016/j.respol.2008.01.012 (accessed 12 May 2020).

Coffield, F. (ed.) (1998) *Learning at Work.* Bristol: Policy Press.

de Valk, E. (2010) 'The Pearl Divers: Hannah Arendt, Walter Benjamin and the Demands of History'. *Krisis: Journal for Contemporary Philosophy,* 1, 36–47. Online. https://krisis.eu/wp-content/uploads/2017/04/krisis-2010-1-04-devalk.pdf (accessed 12 May 2020).

Jones, S. (2019) 'Why we shouldn't be afraid of "scholarship" in FE'. *TES,* 24 October. Online. www.tes.com/news/why-we-shouldnt-be-afraid-scholarship-fe (accessed 24 January 2020).

Kumar, V. (2017) 'The role of university research centers in promoting research'. *Journal of the Academy of Marketing Science,* 45 (4), 453–8. Online. https://doi.org/10.1007/s11747-016-0496-3 (accessed 12 May 2020).

Lupton, J.R. (2000) 'Creature Caliban'. *Shakespeare Quarterly,* 51 (1), 1–23. Online. https://doi.org/10.2307/2902320 (12 May 2020).

The Scholarship Framework (2018, June 15) 'What is the Scholarship Framework?' Online. www.thescholarshipframework.co.uk (accessed 24 January 2020).

Vaughan, A.T. and Vaughan, V.M. (2014) *The Tempest: A critical reader.* London: Bloomsbury.

*Sun is shining, the weather is sweet*
*Make you want to move your dancing feet*

(Bob Marley)

Charlie Ong

overleaf: Livi Colley

## Chapter 19

# Joyful encounters: Caliban reimagines FE

## Carol Azumah Dennis and Lou Mycroft

*There's really no such thing as the 'voiceless'.*
*There are either the deliberately silenced, or the preferably unheard.*

(Arundhati Roy)

## The nomad

The character of Caliban is complex, troubled and – ultimately – tentatively hopeful. Refugee, settler and slave on his beloved island, he is a lightning rod for ideas around belonging/unbelonging and provides a useful figuration with which to trouble the landscape of Further Education.

In this chapter we identify Caliban as a nomadic subject, defined by Braidotti's (2013) posthuman theory as one who is unfettered by dominant narratives about what it means to be human. The posthuman lens liberates Caliban from the Enlightenment era view, in which the standard human is idealized as white, affluent, able-bodied and male, rendering anyone who does not fit this standard other than human. Built into this idealization is a hierarchical separation based on Cartesian dualism between body and mind, nature and culture, noble and savage, leading to man or woman, white or black, master or slave. But there are alternative genealogies of thinking: notably Spinoza, reclaimed by Deleuze (1988) and later channelled into posthumanism. Spinoza rejects nature-or-culture and other associated binaries, embracing a monism in which body and soul are not separated. After all, 'what is action in the mind is necessarily an action in the body. What is a passion in the body is necessarily a passion in the mind. There is no primacy of one over the other' (Deleuze, 1988: 18). This philosophy of monism operationalizes all matter as one to embody (in Spinoza's term) God, desecularized to joy, the kind of joy that finds expression in connecting with 'other'.

180

Here we explore how the nomadic Caliban enables new cartographies of Further Education and envision how he might reimagine the sector. We accomplish this in three broad moves. We first explain the ways in which the nomadic Caliban may be understood, we then consider what happens to the FE college when it becomes a momentary space of enunciation. This is followed by a careful listening. Caliban, unable to speak the master's language, refuses to concede to the master's ideology. He speaks the language of non-humans: angels and monsters. His reimagining presents the FE college as an unsettling but necessary utopia.

As a nomad, Caliban is positioned within an in-between space, one that allows him to symbolize the experience of the colonized subject while exemplifying outdated attitudes towards indigenous cultures. The singular thread that runs through each of his shape-shifting transformations, anchored in interpretations of Shakespeare, is the notion of Caliban as other than human: his most frequent sobriquet in *The Tempest* is that of 'monster'. He is referenced as such no fewer than forty times, often accompanied by other pejoratives. He embodies an alternative space of becoming that fails to fully occupy the category of animal, but falls short of being human. The impossibility of slotting him neatly into a taxonomy is significant. He is a discomforting, ridiculous human-like figure who troubles the nature of humanity. To take Caliban as a defining figuration for FE is to do more than offer a beguiling metaphor. It further requires a mapping of embedded and embodied social positions. The category of the human, around which humanist education centres, idolizes a specific form of subjectivity: the self-motivated and self-directed. Humanist education is a process through which the child, novice or newcomer is brought to reason. The humanist education project involves the newcomer being brought into a common, pre-established and pre-existent space. In rejecting the terms of belonging he is offered, nomadic Caliban shifts us into a new realm.

We take as our starting point Caliban, 'waked after long sleep' (3.2:133), a deep slumber from which he emerges 'disoriented, stupored, caught between the dream logic of capitalism and the newly forming worlds' (Taussig, 2012: 10). Prospero and his entourage have left the island, taking their subject disciplines, siloes, stereotypes and binaries with them.

## Here be dragons

The value of the nomadic subject is not to revel in its marginal status, or to become incorporated. It is instead to find a location from which to speak. Locating Caliban within an FE college signifies it as a space of othering. It is a space outside other spaces (frequently defined by what it is not: not school, not university). In Moten and Harney's lexicon (2004), the FE College is like the refugee colony, a gypsy encampment, in, but not of, public education. A space associated with social reordering, self-organization developed by the despised, the discounted, the dispossessed and the unbelonging, all of whom are other people's children, both students who aren't good enough for university and staff: the new part-time, fractional or zero-hours precariat.

Before Caliban has even spoken, his very presence as a nomadic subject redefines mainstream positions that are brought into being through their response to his otherness. The subsequent reordering of the FE site, signified by Caliban's presence, is reminiscent of a cautionary note: having reached the edges of known landscapes, the medieval mapmaker drew on their maps an image of a dragon to indicate uncharted or unexplored territory. As we step out with Caliban beyond the edges of a familiar humanist FE to encounter what is the reimagined or the unknown, we bring a vision into being through the joyous leap of possibility thinking.

## Joyful encounters

Spinoza's joy does not commodify happiness. Rather, it's what happens when people get together and pool their energy by coalescing around a common cause. Spinoza's immanent relational energy finds echoes in FE's culture of transformation, though 'transformation' is often accidental and has been significantly overclaimed. From his nomadic location, Caliban imagines what classrooms, organizations, policies, practices and pedagogies might look like when FE is liberated from its own assumptions of what belongs where.

That there is immense love for FE among those who have benefited from it (as teachers and taught) is beyond doubt. Often, this is channelled into a culture of gratitude (Donovan, 2019), which can be infantilizing, playing out via the tragic life-story narrative that privileges a student's back story more than their achievement. Ecclestone and Hayes (2008) associate this trend with the 'dangerous rise of therapeutic education' in which students are constituted as inherently vulnerable with fractured lives and fragile learning identities. Their conceptualization of the diminished self argues that depicting students as experiencing barriers to learning that are primarily dispositional replicates the hierarchies it purports to challenge. It stands in stark opposition to the idea of equality as axiomatic and offers 'stultification rather than emancipation' (Biesta, 2010: 40). Caliban, too, was infantilized by a newly arrived Prospero, 'strokedst ... and made much of' (1.2:481) until the island's secrets were revealed and he was no longer useful.

An infantilizing encounter cannot be a joyful one, since it assumes inequality. Nesta UK (formerly the National Endowment for Science, Technology and the Arts) spent much of 2018 working towards an evidence-based definition of non-infantilizing 'Good Help', as enabling people to '... feel hopeful, identify their own goals and confidently take action' (Wilson *et al.*, 2018: 6). To risk offering a binary, Caliban's presence points us towards the 'Bad Help' nature of FE that: 'undermines people's confidence, creates dependency and inaction' (ibid.). Students are not the only people who fail to thrive in this disempowering environment. Staff may practise in workplace cultures that are compliance-driven and risk-averse, and where uncertain contracts signal precarity and fear. Leaders, too, chasing the dollar, become detached from the values that had taken them into education in the first place. No wonder Caliban, looking at FE from the undercommons, trying to make sense of the frenzied activity of ethically impoverished 'busy fools', is confused.

## Ethical impoverishment

> You taught me language; and my profit on't
> Is, I know how to curse. The red plague rid you
> For learning me your language! (1.2:517)

It is hard to disentangle FE's potential from a context grounded in neoliberalism, expressed through the prism of capitalism and market logics. While humanism is somewhat antagonistic to the neoliberal takeover of education, it remains wedded to its shape. This leads to a hierarchical structure that places humans and everything they do as of primary importance. The power and privilege afforded the human by humanism would seem to justify the human domination of all forms of life, leading to the near destruction of a world that may well survive beyond human existence. The ravages of human superiority, referred to as the anthropocene, might just as easily be referred to as the capitalocene (Haraway, 2016). The neoliberal adjudication of life renders all non-profitable or non-productive existence dispensable, allowing a logic that equates good teaching to good data collection (Howlett, 2018).

Even before Caliban's imagination has found expression, his half-human half non-human nomadic presence disrupts humanism and with it the capitalocene. The discomforting ease with which he revels at the intersection between human and non-human, between human and object, embodies a powerful argument: human is not nor has it ever been a stable, coherent, neutral category of identity. His fictional presence is made factual in Sojourner Truth's celebrated speech in which she asks if she is or is not a woman. It is as if the attempt to humanize the non-human has given Caliban a language with which to speak his reimagination; his first utterance is a cursing rejection of a status he can aspire to but never actually accomplish. A rejection of a form of domination that would 'allow others to turn [his] mucus membrane, [his] skin, [his] sensitive areas into occupied territory – controlled and regimented by others,' (Guattari, 1996: 30–1). Caliban reimagines an FE college in which: where there is body, there is mind; where there is individuality there is connection; where there is a connection there is another individuated life with its concomitant reality; where there is theory there is materiality.

This reimagination of curricular and organizational principles holds the humanist project in critical abeyance, in an act of reversal it is the posthuman rather than the human that is inherently liberating. The category of 'post-human' embraces the constituents of FE. In addition, it refuses the ethical impoverishment of humanist philosophy. Posthumanism has the capacity to acknowledge forms of subjectivity other than that of the self-directed autonomous individual on a journey toward self-actualization; by decentring human supremacy it delegitimizes the Capitalocene, reasserting the value of non-profitable or non-productive existence. The incalculable substance of the pedagogic encounter – potentially immanent, potentially joyful – is remade as visible and relevant.

## Digital crossroads

An FE college reimagined by Caliban is one that celebrates life itself with its oneness of mind and body, the oneness of humans and the more-than-human world. As Braidotti terms it, 'we are all in this together, but we are not one-and-the-same' (Braidotti, 2019: 52). Subjectivity is not reduced to the individual but is instead an ecological construct. The nomadic subject is embedded, embodied, embrained, extended and enacted. It is a subjectivity that is – finally! – reflective of indigenous thought-systems that predate and have somehow survived the ravages of colonization (Tuhiwai Smith, 2012). The subjectivity referred to here does not and cannot prescribe this or that way of being. It signifies a mutuality of movement between us and our worlds. Situated at the digital crossroads, Caliban signifies intersectional spaces where the space between I and others, between educators and managers, between students and educators is always of inevitable connections. Interlocking aspects of identity don't allow us to swerve the responsibilities of a collective. Instead they nurture a space of not merely 'becoming' but 'becoming with'.

Moving towards Caliban's vision for FE is not easy. As we have seen, inequalities are inscribed into education's core via traditional hegemonies of what it is to be human. It is necessary for (posthuman) theory to encounter activism in a praxis of freedom (to paraphrase hooks, 1994); something that is not going to happen within FE as it is currently constructed and imagined. Fortunate, then, that like-minded educators have been able to coalesce around other spaces, such as online communities in which they prefigure alternative educational futures, in powerful, co-creational, intersecting 'constellations of practice' during the past decade (Mycroft and Sidebottom, 2018). Social media, though ethically not unproblematic, has the potential to cut through existing permissions and means of communication, enabling educators to 'transgress' (hooks, 1994), pool energies and enact change from within. Educator organized events such as #BrewEd (educators gathering to share ideas in their own time), #ukfechat (weekly co-hosted online Twitterchat) and the increasing involvement of educators in locally organized TEDx events (see, for example, Patel, 2019) mean that ideas worth spreading can take root. Two critical caveats: a lot more could be done to ensure that both students and educators encounter one another meaningfully in these spaces (beyond paying lip-service to student voice) – and all concerned must resist producing yet another dominant hegemony.

## Conclusion: Isle of wonder

In our reading of *The Tempest* we recognized the joy Shakespeare inscribed in Caliban through the beauty of his language, and the tentative optimism of the play's close, when he is left alone on his beloved island. Caliban's isle of wonder formed the nucleus of Danny Boyle's Olympic opening ceremony in 2012, a joyously democratic performance that drew on the diversities of the British Isles, a moment of national belonging and in itself a means to explore exactly what it means to be British in the twenty-first century.

Employing the figuration of Caliban, we have challenged the dominance of the silo mentality of FE, from policy to organizational level as well as challenging those silos in the head that block the capacity to reimagine things. Through Caliban's eyes, we glimpsed the potential of digital networking to pool the Isles of Wonder into intersectional spaces that move beyond the structures and hierarchies of colonization. Finally, we began to reimagine an affirmative, co-created further education sector where Caliban's joyous voice pierces the silence, refusing to remain unheard.

# References

Biesta, G. (2010) 'A new logic of emancipation: The methodology of Jacques Rancière'. *Educational Theory*, 60 (1), 39–59. Online. https://doi.org/10.1111/j.1741-5446.2009.00345.x (accessed 12 May 2020).

Braidotti, R. (2013) *The Posthuman*. Cambridge: Polity Press.

Braidotti, R. (2019) *Posthuman Knowledge*. Cambridge: Polity Press.

Deleuze, G. (1988) *Spinoza: Practical Philosophy*. Trans. Hurley, R. San Francisco: City Lights.

Donovan, C. (2019) 'Distrust by Design: Conceptualising the role of trust and distrust in the development of further education policy and practice in England'. *Research in Post-Compulsory Education* 24 (2-3) 185–207. Online. https://doi.org/10.1080/13596748.2019.1596414 (accessed 12 May 2020).

Ecclestone, K. and Hayes, D. (2008) *The Dangerous Rise of Therapeutic Education*. London: Routledge.

Guattari, F. (1996) *The Guattari Reader*, ed. Genosko, G. Oxford: Blackwell.

Haraway, D.J. (2016) *Staying with the Trouble: Making kin in the Chthulucene*. Durham, NC: Duke University Press.

hooks, b. (1994) *Teaching to Transgress: Education as the practice of freedom*. New York: Routledge.

Howlett, C. (2018) 'Teacher Education and Posthumanism'. *Issues in Teacher Education*, 27 (1), 106–18. Online. https://eric.ed.gov/?id=EJ1174909 (accessed 12 May 2020).

Moten, F. and Harney, S. (2004). 'The university and the undercommons: Seven theses'. *Social Text*, 22 (2), 101–15. Online. https://muse.jhu.edu/article/55785 (accessed 24 June 2020).

Mycroft, L. and Sidebottom, K. (2018) 'Constellations of Practice'. In Bennett, P. and Smith, R. (eds) *Identity and Resistance in Further Education*. London. Routledge, 170–8.

Patel, P. (2019) 'Decolonise the Curriculum' (lecture video). *TEDxNorwichED*. www.youtube.com/watch?v=8JjRQTuzqTU&app=desktop (accessed 12 May 2020).

Roy, A. (2004) 'Peace and the New Corporate Liberation Theology'. Sydney Peace Prize Lecture, 8 November. Online http://realvoice.blogspot.com/2004/11/arundhati-roy-2004-sydney-peace-prize.html (accessed 10 February 2020).

Taussig, M. (2012) 'I'm so angry I made a sign'. *Critical Inquiry*, 39 (1), 56–88. Online. https://doi.org/10.1086/668050

Tuhiwai Smith, L. (2012) *Decolonizing Methodologies: Research and indigenous peoples*. London: Zed Books.

Wilson R., Cornwell, C., Flanagan, E., Nielsen, N. and Khan, H. (2018) *Good and Bad Help: How purpose and confidence transform lives*. Nesta/OSCA. Online: https://osca.co/publications/good-bad-help/ (accessed 24 June 2020).

*If it keeps on rainin', levee's goin' to break*
*If it keeps on rainin', levee's goin' to break ...*
*When the levee breaks mama you got to move*

(Led Zeppelin and Memphis Minnie)

Tony O'Connell

overleaf: *Map of Utopia* – Abraham Ortelius

# Conclusion

*Kevin Orr*

Caliban knew all about the power and the magic of books. In his instructions to the treacherous Stephano and Trinculo he was adamant that they first take the mighty Prospero's books 'for without them / He's but a sot' (3.2:87–8). Caliban understood that without his books Prospero was a magician without magic. We, too, know about the power and magic of books. Over a hundred editors, writers, illustrators, dancers and others have directly contributed to the trilogy of books that opened with *Further Education and the Twelve Dancing Princesses,* went on to *The Principal: Power and Professionalism in FE,* and ends here with *Caliban's Dance: FE after The Tempest.* In this conclusion, I consider the place and purpose of this, the final book in our trilogy and I ponder on how all three have melded metaphor and irony with joy and steely intent to defend, to praise and to provoke FE.

In the five years between the first book and the last, colleges in England, as elsewhere, have been subject to brutal cuts in funding and to forced mergers that have weakened the sector. Yet colleges remain as important to the lives of their students and to their wider communities as they always have been. Acting on that knowledge, the contributors to the trilogy have displayed their own passion and commitment for FE. So, as we warned at the very beginning with our Princesses, don't be misled by the playfulness of our metaphors. We selected them carefully because our intention in speaking up for FE was always deadly serious.

'Metaphors are wonderful things', Ewart Keep wrote in the preface, and he is right – as contributors to this volume have confirmed. Metaphors may be as common as dirt but they can still carry some clout. For Sfard:

> metaphors are the most primitive, most elusive, and yet amazingly informative objects of analysis. Their special power stems from the fact that they often cross the borders between the spontaneous and the scientific, between the intuitive and the formal. (1998: 4)

She goes on to explain that 'the choice of metaphor is a highly consequential matter. Different metaphors may lead to different ways of thinking and to different activities.' So, choose your metaphor with caution. *The Twelve Dancing Princesses* was a metaphorical response to the dreary and pervasive trope that fixed the FE sector as a passive Cinderella awaiting a prince who seemed to be taking a terribly long time to show up. The book was both a celebration of the possibilities of the FE sector and a stubborn assertion of democratic educational values. The special power of the dancing metaphor was to represent those values as well as to represent a mischievous resistance to what threatened them.

'It is time for the sector of the dancing princesses to have its due', wrote Petrie in his preface, 'and for FE's cinders to be reignited.' That first book did, indeed, reignite a few embers and it even started a few fires. Astonished and delighted by the reception our Princesses received, we proceeded to the second book. *The Principal* still relished metaphor but it was an altogether more bitter examination of leadership at all levels in the sector. Our metaphorical choice was *The Prince* by Machiavelli who, according to his biographer, Benner (2017: xxi), had a 'determination to change the corrupt world he lived in' and also the belief that anyone 'could do their bit to make things better.' The contributors agreed with all of that, though in their chapters they disagreed about whether Machiavelli was writing in the service of the Prince or as a warning against him. No matter, the Machiavellian metaphor still had a special power and it provided fresh visions of what leadership in the sector was and what it could be. Here in our last book, *Caliban's Dance*, we turned to Shakespeare's *The Tempest* for our metaphorical conceit, as our contributors have contemplated their utopias and speculated on what FE might be. Why choose Shakespeare?

'Shakespeare is hard, but so is life, and so long as you see that there's a lot of life in Shakespeare, then the effort begins to make sense,' O'Toole reminds us (2002: 2). Getting to know Shakespeare's characters is worth that effort, 'not because they teach us lessons ... but because they enact something that is dangerous, powerful and disturbing' (O'Toole, 2002: 33). Demonstrating the potent effect of our Shakespearian metaphor, Avis invokes that dangerous, powerful and disturbing spirit in his contribution to *Caliban's Dance*. In doing so he provides important counsel that a conclusion writer needs especially to heed. Avis read *The Tempest* as an allegory for the politics of hope, about which he is chary, where those politics relate to FE. Such politics of hope are too often extolled from a comfortable moral high ground by teachers and academics alike, who 'conclude by drawing out the radical possibilities that lie in the present and that presage the transformation of society'. Avis finds that these hopeful politics may also conclude by simply replicating the status quo.

We should, on the contrary, conclude that FE needs more than the comfort of final paragraph radicalism if it is to be properly understood and if it is to thrive. The FE sector reflects and reproduces the unequal society within which it sits, even while it offers an island of sanctuary or fulfilment to those tossed about in society's waves. More on that later, but for the moment, let's be wary. 'For the island may breathe upon the jetsam'd most sweetly but it is with rotten lungs intended to make vassals of all,' Page cautions in these pages, 'For these shores of devils and saviours are colonized lands, with nary a free soul.' And yet, Dennis and Mycroft found that same colonized island is 'where Caliban's joyous voice pierces the silence, refusing to remain unheard'. These divergent descriptions simultaneously, metaphorically and accurately capture the FE sector. While heeding Avis's warning, let's nevertheless celebrate FE as we have done in this collection: 'How many goodly creatures are there here!' (5.1:188).

On the noisy island portrayed in this volume we have heard Caliban's joyous voice but we have also heard the sounds of 'a thousand twangling instruments' (3.2:131) that represent the variety of what FE already offers. But what of FE utopia? What does Caliban's dance look like after he (or she) has regained the island? For Finnegan and O'Neill, FE might offer 'the possibility of a disruptive creativity in amongst the chaos of life and work'. For Bennett, Scott and Wilde, FE remains a beautiful risk that is worth taking. Yet while they praise FE teachers who offer hope, they argue that the sector needs those 'who are committed to the heart and the head'.

Daley's utopia included a similar confluence of aspiration with direction: 'Teachers will continue not only to offer their magic to individual students in the classroom but contribute to the content and focus of the curriculum, their colleges and the communities where their students live.' In this spirit, our contributors have dreamt up utopia but they have also identified action that might get us closer to our destination. Emotional attachment as well as cool insight are necessary for that excursion and there has been plenty of both in these pages. Even achieving the innovative delight of Shukie's gonzo education class required him to remember the paint.

The utopias described here are not, therefore, outlandish or bizarre. Some may be whimsical but they aren't unachievable. Hammond's suggestion for research collaboration is a structured development of existing arrangements; similarly, the solutions that Crowson, Fletcher-Saxon, Jones and Woodrow seek from practitioner research 'are as likely to germinate in smaller scale, low-stakes projects as in formal, highly articulated, well-funded initiatives'. The utopia conjured by Lavender and Reynold seeks to 'reveal ... students' complex motivations and outcomes, prefiguring ways to better serve their preferences and aspirations' – which seems a realizable aspiration.

Hafez advises that unlearning what we falsely hold to be true is the hardest part of learning: yes, but this is already a normal part of good education. Unlearning the 'materialistic and unethical assumption that individuals exist in order to serve an economic need' is crucial, as Brown indicates, but perceiving FE students instead as 'citizens within society' is hardly outrageous. Hafez's utopia of FE as 'a bastion for powerful knowledge ... where great canons are shared with students, with the firm belief that they are legitimate heirs to that knowledge' is entirely achievable. Why should FE not 'be a place of unfettered pedagogical dialogue' as she proposes? Certainly, this means recognizing, as Calder and Husband argue in an echo of Brown, 'that FE provides more than just a route to work'. Indeed, the kind of qualification that an access to Higher Education student might gain from an FE college 'holds ... benefits both in terms of developing academic skills but more broadly in relation to levels of self-efficacy' according to Beaumont and Wyn-Williams.

Butterby, Collins and Powell write about prison education, but their objective that prisoners 'may learn "to live well in a world worth living in"' should be universal for everyone with a stake in FE. Our contributors indicate ways in which this reasonable objective may be brought nearer our reach. The description of Caliban from Lavender and Reynolds could also describe our contributors. Their Caliban is 'often incurably restive' but he is also 'pragmatic'. Implicit throughout our chapters is Playfair's observation that the ingredients for FE utopia already exist in today's colleges, in:

> the moments when learning comes to life and suddenly makes sense, when students start to apply what they have learnt, to challenge their preconceptions, to shape their own activity and pursue their interests, when they initiate and engage in reading, research, social action or campaigning for a purpose.

These moments constitute what Amsler called the 'trashed and exiled possibilities that, while real, are unintelligible from within prevailing critical educational identities, paradigms, imaginaries and horizons of hope'. In order to 'sharpen our sensitivity' to these possibilities, Amsler recommended that we attune 'to the Sycoraxes in our needs and desires'. Good advice because, for Amsler, Sycorax teaches that 'the otherwise is already (often absently) present within disenchanted and colonized realities'.

Smith details other FE utopias imagined in now forgotten policies. In 1945 optimistic policymakers in England wished for young people to leave imagined County Colleges with what was 'necessary for good citizenship in a democratic community' and 'to have developed their character so that they will (a) be honourable, tolerant and kindly in dealing with their fellows; (b) have an independent and balanced outlook on life'. However laudable, the imagined County Colleges were never built and the imagination was wasted.

The Spanish painter Francisco Goya who, like Shakespeare, had an eye for the grotesque, understood the need to combine imagination and rationality. The full epigraph for his 1799 etching *The sleep of reason produces monsters* reads in translation: 'Imagination abandoned by reason produces impossible monsters; united with her, she is the mother of the arts and source of their wonders.' Both imagination and rationality are required now because there have already been too many 'impossible monsters' for FE, and far less benign than were dreamt of in 1945.

The FE sector is vulnerable to other kinds of utopian aspirations and since the 1980s there have been at least 28 pieces of legislation affecting English FE (Norris and Adam, 2017: 3). Policymakers who are ideologically unwilling to intervene in markets are prone to perceive the sector as an engine for both economic development and social justice (light engineering metaphors like this one attract cross-party support in England). FE, like Caliban, may be wretched but it is indispensable and it is required time and again to alleviate the impact of the same unequal structures of society that hold the sector in a position of weakness. At the same time, those same policymakers in England have overseen year-on-year cuts in the funding of FE and skills since 2010/11, leaving the whole sector with a smaller real terms income than in 2002/3 (DfE, 2020: 22). The very people who set the targets for FE ensure that FE cannot meet them.

In the Coda to *Further Education and The Twelve Dancing Princesses*, I noted how progressive change was 'initiated by individuals who dared to defy and then to organize'. Though referring to ESOL in particular, Peutrell and Cooke capture this idea well: 'how we respond to the issue of citizenship and ESOL is a matter of individual responsibility and that of the profession as a whole. This chapter is a contribution to realizing that responsibility in a participatory, democratic way.' Their chapter, this volume and the whole *Dancing Princesses* trilogy have had that intention.

Marx (Marx and Engels, 1968: 96) wrote in the Eighteenth Brumaire of Louis Bonaparte that people: 'make their own history. But they do not make it as they please; they do not make it under self-selected circumstances but under circumstances existing already, given and transmitted from the past.' People are certainly enabled or restricted by the circumstances in which they live but their actions are not entirely determined by them. Individuals have the agency to make a difference and we editors, Joel, Maire and I, have been fortunate to have encountered so many individuals whose response to our 'you dancin'?' was 'you askin'?'

We're grateful to all of our collaborators in what has been a joyful and refreshing endeavour in support of FE. Two individuals in particular deserve our special gratitude: Frank Coffield, always committed to FE and who from the beginning was 'proud to make common cause' with us and our Princesses; and Gillian Klein, our fearless publisher who, likewise, dared to take a punt on our Princesses and for whom this is the last Trentham publication.

Let's finish this final book by repeating the urgent call from the introduction that drew on contributions from many of our Princesses and that was coordinated by Joel Petrie, who has been first among equals in the realization of our trilogy: 'dreams are for those asleep. This is a wake-up call. We don't have the luxury of waiting for a tempest to sweep all before it so we can rebuild anew. The time is now.'

# References

Benner, E. (2017) *Be like the Fox: Machiavelli's lifelong quest for freedom.* London: Allen Lane.

Department for Education (DfE) (2020) *Costs and Cost Drivers in the Further Education Sector: Research into the cost and income when providing further education.* London: DfE. Online. www.gov.uk/government/publications/costs-and-cost-drivers-in-the-further-education-sector (accessed 12 May 2020).

Marx, K. and Engels, F. (1968) *Selected Works in One Volume.* London: Lawrence and Wishart.

Norris, E. and Adam, R. (2017) *All Change: Why Britain is so prone to policy reinvention, and what can be done about it.* London: Institute for Government. Online. www.instituteforgovernment.org.uk/sites/default/files/publications/IfG_All_change_report_FINAL.pdf (accessed 12 May 2020).

O'Toole, F. (2002) *Shakespeare is Hard but so is Life: A radical guide to Shakespearean tragedy.* London: Granta Books.

Sfard, A. (1998) 'On two metaphors for learning and the dangers of choosing just one'. *Educational Researcher,* 27 (2), 4–13. Online. https://doi.org/10.3102/0013189X027002004 (accessed 12 May 2020).

# Index